Identity and Language Learning

LANGUAGE IN SOCIAL LIFE SERIES

Series Editor: Professor Christopher N Candlin

Chair Professor of Applied Linguistics

Department of English

Centre for English Language Education & Communication Research

City University of Hong Kong, Hong Kong

For a complete list of books in this series see pages *v* and *vi*

Identity and Language Learning:

Gender, Ethnicity and Educational Change

Bonny Norton

An imprint of **Pearson Education**

Harlow, England · London · New York · Reading, Massachusetts · San Francisco · Toronto · Don Mills, Ontario · Sydney
Tokyo · Singapore · Hong Kong · Seoul · Taipei · Cape Town · Madrid · Mexico City · Amsterdam · Munich · Paris · Milan

Pearson Education Limited
Edinburgh Gate
Harlow
Essex CM20 2JE
England

and Associated Companies throughout the world

Visit us on the World Wide Web at:
www.pearsoneduc.com

First published 2000

© Pearson Education Limited 2000

The right of Bonny Norton to be identified as author of this work has been asserted
by her in accordance with the Copyright, Designs and Patents Act 1988.

ISBN 0-582-38225-4 CSD
ISBN 0-582-38224-6 PPR

British Library Cataloguing-in-Publication Data

A catalogue record for this book is available from the British Library

Library of Congress Cataloging-in-Publication Data

Norton, Bonny, 1956–
    Identity and language learning: social processes and educational practice / Bonny Norton.
        p.   cm. — (Language in social life series)
    Includes bibliographical references and index.
    ISBN 0–582–38225–4 (csd) — ISBN 0–582–38224–6 (ppr)
    1. Second language acquisition.   2. Ethnicity.   3. Language and languages—Study and
teaching.   I. Title.   II. Series.

P118.2.N67   2000
418′.0071—dc21   99–086879

Set in 10/12pt Janson by 35
Produced by Pearson Education Asia Pte Ltd.
Printed in Singapore

LANGUAGE IN SOCIAL LIFE SERIES

Series Editor: Professor Christopher N Candlin
Chair Professor of Applied Linguistics
Department of English
Centre for English Language Education & Communication Research
City University of Hong Kong, Hong Kong

For Anthony, Julia and Michael, who have filled my life with love, joy and purpose.

Language is the place where actual and possible forms of social organization and their likely social and political consequences are defined and contested. Yet it is also the place where our sense of ourselves, our subjectivity, is constructed.

WEEDON, 1997, p. 21

Just as, at the level of relations between groups, a language is worth what those who speak it are worth, so too, at the level of interactions between individuals, speech always owes a major part of its value to the value of the person who utters it.

BOURDIEU, 1977, p. 652

Contents

Acknowledgements

This book has had a long history, though in the context of a new millennium, it can be seen as evolving in a brief moment of time. Learners, teachers, authors, colleagues, and publishers have contributed in countless ways to the production of this work, and I would like to gratefully acknowledge the diverse support I have received.

The women who participated in my research study generously worked with me as a researcher, a teacher, and a friend. Despite their many commitments in their homes and workplaces, they made the time to write, to meet, and to talk. Their insights and their voices have made this work possible. I extent to them my warmest thanks.

This book has developed from my doctoral thesis, supervised by Roger Simon of the Ontario Institute for Studies in Education (OISE) of the University of Toronto. With rigorous and compassionate guidance, Roger taught me not to fear theory, but to harness it to inform and critique my research and teaching. Other colleagues and fellow students at OISE contributed to numerous debates on language learning and teaching. Such debates have survived The Duke and are alive and well on the internet. For their intellectual support, I am grateful to Monica Heller, Jim Cummins, Merrill Swain, David Corson, Barbara Burnaby, Alastair Pennycook, Tara Goldstein, Brian Morgan, Arlene Schenke, Helen Harper, Elizabeth Yeoman, and John Clegg.

New colleagues, research assistants, and secretaries in the Department of Language and Literacy Education of the University of British Columbia have, in diverse ways, helped me to bring this work to completion. Patsy Duff, Margaret Early, Diane Fouladi and Bernie Mohan have been generous and supportive colleagues; Tammy Slater and Jim Hu carefully proofread the manuscript and tracked down references; and Anne White's secretarial skills have been invaluable. Other colleagues on the west coast, including Kelly Toohey and Diane Dagenais of Simon Fraser University and Sandy Silberstein of the University of Washington, have been a constant source of encouragement. I am indebted to all of them.

I would like to acknowledge the significant contribution of Chris Candlin, the General Editor of this series. His careful and rigorous critique of an earlier draft of this book was invaluable. His contribution to my work – and to the field of language learning and teaching more generally – has been profound. I add my voice of thanks to those of numerous authors whose work has been enriched by his guidance. As well, editors, proofreaders, and designers at Pearson Education, of which Longman is an imprint, have worked diligently to expedite the publication of this book. I appreciate the efficiency of all these professionals. I am also very grateful to the Social Sciences and Humanities Research Council of Canada and the Spencer Foundation of the National Academy of Education, USA, who have given me financial support at different stages of this project.

Without the unconditional love of my family, I could not have completed this work. Anthony Peirce, Julia Norton Peirce, and Michael Norton Peirce have been unfailing in their support. I am deeply grateful to them for cheerfully accepting that family does not always come first.

General Editor's Preface

I suppose that if one had to identify one of the most telling factors in the relatively short-lived, if intense, history of studies in second language acquisition, it would have to be the consistent anonymising, if not the actual eclipsing, of the learner. There are a number of reasons why this is so: the overwhelming and legitimate desire of researchers to raise the study of second language acquisition to the experimental heights reached by other studies in cognitive psychology, and to follow its traditions of research reporting; the advent of rich new data from such studies for theoretical linguists to test out theories not of language learning but of language as a system *sui generis*; the desire to resist contamination of data about such cognitive and linguistic processes and systems by neutralising the messiness and variability of everyday communication and concentrating on the analysis of abstract processes; a consequent privileging of the positivistic and the quantifiable in the presentation and elucidation of data; and, one would have to say, the lack, in practice, of some consistent and ongoing engagement by many researchers with the actualities of language learning in contexts other than their privileged, and often fleeting, encounters with selected learners in educational institutions. How different, one might say, to the history of that other applied linguistic practice, literacy, where the opposite might be held to be true: a continuing and principled involvement of researchers in the literacy lives of individuals in their communities of practice, the grounding of their research in the social conditions of those with whom they work in partnership, a commitment to connection and re-connection with the functionality of literacy, not only with its formal representations, and, stemming from this, a reliance on the qualitative explanation of narratives of experience as a source of question and as a resource for explanation.

In juxtaposing these epistemological differences, I am not taking sides; indeed, this would be quite foolish, despite the propensity of some writers to do so sharply, mischievously, and on occasion self-servingly, since one goal of any worthwhile intellectual endeavour should be, I suppose, to find accommodation, to show how in both cases, the experimenter's goal of generalisability does not have to be bought at the cost of ignoring the particular, or entail the disappearance of the subject, or, how, the richness of the data emanating from ethnographic studies does not necessarily imply any lack of researcher commitment to establishing more general conditions governing and explaining acquisition and development.

It is against just such a backdrop that Bonny Norton's important contribution to the *Language in Social Life Series* needs to be read. It has, it must be said, a case that it wants to make, a case quite related to the intellectual landscape whose map I sketch above, one which *does* take issue with subject anonymity, with researcher stance, and, more generally, with some of the dominant intellectual traditions in the study of second language learning. It comes, therefore, with a caveat to the reader, but this does not imply that we are faced with some polemic, worsening the climate. What the book offers is a powerful statement of position, whose goal is not just to describe the performances of learners and by inference to presume their rehearsal and their gradual approximation and suggest some general applicability. Rather it sets out to explore the practices of learning themselves, and the social and personal conditions under which this learning is done by learners, however variably and partially. In this way, the book extends the intellectual canon, pointing us to new research directions, establishing new constructs of value and significance, and suggests new methodologies for their exploration.

Central to this innovation is the interplay of lived and localised experience and the construction of theory. By interplay I mean less some conventional correlation of experience with existing theory, as it were testing out the tenets of second language acquisition against the communicative practices of learners, though the author does this tellingly, for example, in her perceptive critique of acculturation models, more that she encourages theory to develop through close observation of these experiences, voiced through the narratives of her learners. In doing this, of course, she is in good company, though it has to be said more in that of sociologists and ethnographers than until very recently that of second language acquisition researchers. Nonetheless, the current sociocultural turn in some SLA research is helpful to her project, though here a critical observer would want to note that this newly rediscovered Vygotskyan call for a social perspective on learning has largely been echoed and taken up by researchers working in the warm and convenient location of the classroom rather than in the less structured, extra-institutional world of adult language learning. That there have been few pioneers before her in the siting of such research in that world, notably that of Bremer *et al.*, whose seminal (1996) work she richly acknowledges here, serves only to underscore the refreshing innovativeness of Bonny Norton's own research, and to provide further support and backing to those as yet relatively underpublished accounts of adult non-instructed language learning. One is tempted here to rephrase Suzanne Romaine's celebrated opening comment in her book *Bilingualism* when she averred that it was mono-lingualism rather than bilingualism that was unusual, and to say here that it is consistent, organized and instructed language learning that is unusual in the still largely ad hoc world of second language learning, especially in the context of increasing human migration and social change.

Given the above, what is then at play in this interplay? Let me identify two interconnected research worlds, each with its own internal connections and relationships, which I discern from Bonny Norton's book, though she does not draw these as explicitly as I do here. The first relates to research resources, the other to research targets.

In his very useful book (1993) on research strategies in social research, Derek Layder sets out what he refers to as a *resource map for research*, (p. 72 ff) in which he explicitly seeks to incorporate macro and micro-sociological features in a research program which is sited both historically and contex-tually, and one in which individual actors are identified both as selves and as social persons. It is also a resource map which, as he says, has '*helped in the planning and the ongoing formulation of field research which has theory generation as a primary aim*'. From this, the link to my analysis above of Bonny Norton's project and its goals should, I hope, be clear to the reader. The dimensions and perspectives of such a map, and indeed the cartographic metaphor in general, not only has value for social research as a whole, but, in modified and disciplinary specific form, has particular applicability to the research agendas of applied linguistics, among which is the development of socially grounded studies of second language acquisition.

In his cartography, Layder sets out what he terms four *research elements*, each of which is interconnected to the others and each of which has a particular, and equally interconnected, *research focus*. None of these elements and foci is prime, and research in his view may begin with any, providing all are severally and differentially addressed. It is significant also that the four research elements are all set within a historical frame, though we should note that in Layder's conception, all elements, as social processes, have their *own* timeframes. Interactions among persons, for example, operate within a different time-perspective than do changes in social institutions, though both may influence the conduct and practices of the other, and these differences are significant.

What are these research elements Layder identifies, and how are they relevant to a reading of Bonny Norton's book?

He first (though not necessarily as prime) identifies *context* as that ele-ment which implicates the macro social organization, the values, traditions, forms of social and economic organization and power relations within the social formation, and illustrates these as '*legally sanctioned forms of ownership, control and distribution: interlocking directorships, state intervention*'. In the context of this book we can identify the locating of the immigrant learner voices within just such a macro context, as here in Canada, of immigration, of settlement, of organized and institutionalized learning, of the constraints of the economy, of language policy. The point of this book is that such features of the element of *context* are not peripheral to language learning, as it were some neutral backdrop to the frontstage of interaction, but central to its effectiveness, to its variable success, to its design. Each of the voices of the authorial partners in this book, Eva, Mai, Katarina, Martina and Felicia, not only allude to such features in their stories, but directly implicate their significance. Such voices and such allusions are, moreover, not localised to some national site. In a world increasingly characterised by mobility and change, the relevance is universal.

Layder's second element, that of *setting*, focuses on the intermediate social organization, featured as *work-related* (state bureaucracies; labour markets; hospitals; social work agencies; domestic labour; penal and mental institutions) and *non-work related* (leisure activities, sports and social clubs; religious and spiritual organizations). Important to *setting* is what Layder calls '*its already established character*', that is the social and institutional structure and practices within which particular *situated activity* (see below) occurs. In Norton's world of immigrant second language learning in Canada, these settings are clearly drawn, and their importance to the language learning chances – let alone the life-sustaining chances – of her participants and those they represent, is made very plain in the narrative accounts and her authorial commentary. Chapter 7, with its focus on classroom resistance to language learning described by Katarina and Felicia, would be an excellent example of the relevance of this element for language learning. So too, in a different way, and here implicating the significance for language learning of both of Layder's work-related and non work-related settings, is Mia's story in Chapter 4 of her role as language broker in the setting of the immigrant family in a new land, and how changes in the language practices in the setting of her workplace impacted on her language learning and language using opportunities.

If *settings* are in Layder's terms *established* – though we should be cautious here not to equate establishment with stability, as such stability will be highly relative across and within social formations, and certainly relative in relation to sectors of the population – then Layder's third element of *situated activity* permits a focus on that face-to-face, or mediated, social activity involving what he calls '*symbolic communication by skilled, intentional participants implicated in the contexts and settings*'. Here the focus is, interestingly enough, explicitly directed at the disciplinary world of applied linguistics: '*at emergent meanings, understandings and definitions of the situation as these affect and are affected by contexts and settings, and the subjective dispositions of individuals.*' No reader of Bonny Norton's book can fail to recognise the significance of these situated activities for language learning. As she amply acknowledges, such a recognition lies at the heart of Bremer *et al.*'s (1996) accounts, and those of many others one might name, Elsa Auerbach in the United States, Angel

Lin in Hong Kong, Suresh Canagarajah in Sri Lanka, the work of the researchers in the Adult Migrant English Program in Australia, in particular at NCELTR in Sydney. The message is plain: the appraisal of language learning potential, aptitude, success, utility cannot sensibly be, and ought not to be undertaken without the underpinning of a clearly defined program of sociolinguistic and discourse analytical study of a range of differentiated encounters. But *description* is not enough. Description needs to be accompanied by interpretive, ethnomethodological accounts of the meaning-making and imperfect meaning-making, of individuals in interaction in particular situated activities, emphasising the members' resources that can be brought to bear, or are prevented from being brought to bear, on the communicative challenges of the moment. However, even such a focus on *interpretation*, characteristic of conversational analysis, will not adequately include and bring to bear Layder's elements of *context* and *setting*. To include these as significant is not something to be insisted upon as a consequence of some partisan adherence of the analyst to some particular social theoretical position, rather their significance emerges in the talk and the allusions of the participants themselves, and embedded in their narrative accounts, and in the implications for access by language learners to situated activities likely to be conducive to language learning that analysts can draw from policy documents, from studies of organizational change, from accounts of shifts in national demography, from analyses of service provision. Their inclusion moves the research agenda from description and interpretation to what one can call *explanation*.

This book is made up of just such significant social activities and their implications for success and failure in language learning. Chapter 3, with its rich comparative account of the five participants in Bonny Norton's study has a simple, but for those who have been involved in the study of immigrant language learning, a telling message: for language learning to develop you need supportive interaction, yet to access that interaction you need at least an entry level of communicative competence in the majority language. So much is simple: the mistake is to presume that the responsibility for such access lies individually with the learner, that he or she has ultimate control of that speculative chimera the affective filter, or to presume that access to facilitative interaction is to be granted just by knocking on the door, or that, once inside, the conditions of communicative interaction will necessarily be conducive to the development of that competence. Bremer *et al.* (1996) pointed out that fallacy from their detailed discourse analyses, and Norton's narratives complement their critique.

Finally, in Layder's resource map, what is the significance for the reader of his fourth element, the *self*? Given Norton's theorising of the socially constructed nature of second language learning as focusing on the multiple identities of the learner, one would have to respond that this final element is of the greatest significance. If we see *self*, with Layder, as invoking identity within the context of social experience, what he refers to as the *'unique psychobiography of the individual'* located within a life career, then the struggle between the individuality and collectivity of the self as at once body, psychological entity and social person is revealed. As Norton herself acknowledges in her intellectual sources, the topic of individual and collective identity is central to the debates of modern and post-modern thinkers, and in any multicultural and multi-ethnic society like hers in Canada, public debates around issues of social concern, including language education, cannot but be imbued by debates surrounding identity. Indeed, the arguments she raises throughout her book against traditional paradigms in second language acquisition research essentially revolve around how *selves* are to be defined, as entities independent of social context, possessed by attitudes, motivations, conducive or non-conducive attributes towards language learning, or as context-dependent *persons* whose social roles within their social networks crucially affect the opportunities of individuals for language learning, and their willingness to take up those that become available. Her analysis of the variable *investment* of learners in the processes and challenges of language learning is a classic case in point. Identity, as such, needs teasing out, and it is this process which Bonny Norton addresses in her commentaries on the narratives of her participants. For one telling example, one might read carefully the accounts of the communities of practice of Eva and Mai in Chapter 4 or the contrasting experiences of Felicia and Katarina in Chapter 5. What such accounts reinforce is more than the asserting of the diversity to be found within identity. They make clear that Layder's other elements, cited above, of *social activity*, *setting* and *context*, all impinge directly upon the experiences of these selves and these identities. No-one after reading this Chapter 5 could possibly characterise as merely personal, idiosyncratic and stylistic, the rich and variable communicative experiences of these learners and the social circumstances in which their learning has to be done and which circumstances in turn condition learners' relative success and failure.

At the outset of this Preface, I spoke of the relevance to Bonny Norton's book of two research worlds, that of research resources and that of research targets. What are the targets to which her study is directed? Most obviously, of course, it is that already alluded to above and explicitly canvassed and addressed in her book, namely second language acquisition theory. I do not wish to reiterate her points here, save perhaps to underscore them. What is worth emphasising, however, is the degree to which the constructs most familiar to her, and on which she consistently draws, of identity, of power, of economy and capital, have been so noticeable by their absence in the mainstream SLA literature. One measure of this is the extent to which that central construct in second language learning, *motivation*, has until quite recently been largely innocent of any social engagement of the kind she emphasises. It is not that researchers into motivation have been unaware of these social conditions, it is that their focus on the individual self and the personal belief structures of the individual, while perfectly understandable in terms of the paradigm in which they have been accustomed to work, leads to a disregard for the influence of *context* and *setting*, as well immediate as historically and structurally construed, as a central variable in their analyses. It is notable, then, that very much as a consequence of Bonny Norton's work, and that of other researchers with similar orientations like McGroarty and Lin, that leading researchers into motivation like Dornyei (forthcoming) have come to recognise Norton's construct of motivational investment as going beyond the social psychological studies into ethnolinguistic vitality of Giles and Byrne, or the situational character of social identification studied by Clement and Noels, and the acculturation theory of Schumann. What makes Norton's study innovatory is her emphasis on the dynamism and the variability inherent in motivation, and its definition as a struggle between the individual investment of capital and the constraining effects of Layder's macro elements of *context* and *setting*.

It is however in the contemporary context of social change and diversity that Norton's reconception of second language acquisition theory, like society's conception of identity, has to withstand its greatest critical test. Following Bourdieu, her reconception has to prove its explanatory power in terms of illuminating the dynamics of a communicative and language learning market place where both the effectiveness of communication and the very access to the conditions for achieving communicative competence depend on the individual's linguistic capital, itself understood as the power over the mechanisms of establishing linguistic value. Norton's discussion in Chapter 6 of Bourdieu's concept of the *legitimate speaker* addresses these inequities directly, as does her critique of acculturation theory in the same chapter. She achieves these targets, in my view, by a subtle interplay of voicing and commentary, exposing doubtful assumptions of existing theory to a critique borne of experience. It is in this sense that this book is much more than an ethnographic account. It is a deeply theoretical work in which the author skilfully weaves a convincing texture from personal experience and carefully chosen contributions from disciplines both from within applied linguistics and from outside its normal canon. The significant introduction of feminist theory in Chapter 6 as a means to explain the conception of identity as a site of struggle is just one such example. As one practical consequence, one comes away from the book with an acute sense that a major revision of the content and process of courses in second language acquisition is both necessary and able to be constructed from this convincing account.

I spoke earlier of targets. Two remain to be identified. The first is addressed in some detail in the final chapter where the author engages with the implications for pedagogy and curriculum, and for teacher development, of the results of her study. Here, once again, the narratives of the participants provide both the trigger for change and the means by which change can be constructed and realised in action. Much in the manner of Auerbach's and

Wallerstein's early work on classroom codes where the themes and topics for discussion arise from the lived experiences of the learners, or in Morgan's more recent parallel work in Canada to which Norton makes reference, there is a need for classroom renewal in adult language learning, a renewal in which the investments of learners are not taken for granted but become the subject matter of teaching and learning, as do the social conditions outside the classroom. Here the analysis in Chapter 7 of formal language instruction is particularly relevant, suggesting as it does that success for learners in those classroom conditions crucially depends on learners' extra-classroom access to what are in her context anglophone social networks. If this is as true as her analysis suggests, then the picture is bleaker than we thought. For if classrooms cannot compensate for social isolation and communicative inequity, then what is to be done? At least a radical reappraisal of content and methodology, modes of instruction, learner participation, and modes of delivery would seem necessary. The response to Norton's analysis may lie in discovering ways in which we differentiate much more carefully what is best presented in instructional settings, what is best delivered directly to learners, perhaps utilising computer-mediated forms, or more conventionally by enhancing the home and workplace delivery of relevant language programs, sensitive to the conditions of living and the variability of investment time and energy so succinctly and poignantly put by her participants. That this is possible is amply evidenced in her final chapter, but is also available to readers in published and documented form elsewhere, in particular in my own Australian context where the work of the teachers and researchers in the Adult Migrant English Program, mediated by the National Centre for English Language Teaching and Research, has had such curriculum renewal as its major agenda for decades.

The second target for the book is more oblique and not so well identified, though of considerable potential. I refer to the potential significance of this book and its research for those engaged in the formulation and execution of national policies on immigrant settlement, not just in typical countries of major migration like the USA, Canada, Australia and Israel, but much more generally where the temporary migration of workers becomes more long term, as in parts of Europe. The relationship between the acquisition of language competence and the effectiveness of settlement is of major concern to those states, like Norton's Canada and my Australia, where government invests huge sums in language and settlement.

Three questions stand out awaiting answers:

- How can the relationship between these constructs be identified?
- How can it be quantified?
- How can it be appraised?

These are not abstract and academic questions but ones which govern policy decisions which have immediate effect on individuals' livelihoods. They are questions which, quite appropriately, tax bureaucracies. The sad fact is that second language acquisition research from its ivory tower position has very largely ignored the questions, or considered them irrelevant. However, from the perspective of someone whose work has involved much interplay between research in the academy and the formulation of public policy, one would have to say that if the problem-posing and problem-addressing stance of applied linguistics is to be more than a paper tiger, then the time has come to make a change and reorganise our house. Two ways forward suggest themselves in the context of Bonny Norton's book. One is to recognise the immediate importance of the questions, in all their sub-differentiation across ethnic, gendered, racial, linguistic, workplace, and community groupings, and to foster that mix of scoping, documentary and empirical research characteristic of Linda Burnett's recent NCELTR study (1998) on issues surrounding the nature of immigrant settlement, and the role of language learning as a determining factor in settlement success, and secondly, in parallel, to encourage the micro studies based on narratives of experience as evidenced here in this remarkable book, or in the work of Bremer *et al.* If then, perhaps within that framework offered by Layder, to that we can add more discourse-based studies of actual encounters, both within and outside classrooms, characteristic of the work of a new generation of researchers into the social construction of language learning, then we shall have the means to turn the lessons learnable from Norton's participants into an agenda for action and for change. As they say where I come from, 'It's time!'

References

Bremer, K., Roberts, C., Vasseur, M.-T., Simonot, M., and Broeder, P. (1996) *Achieving understanding: discourse in intercultural encounters. Language in Social Life Series.* London. Longman

Burnett, L. (1998) *Issues in immigrant settlement.* Research Series #10. Sydney. NCELTR. Macquarie University

Dornyei, Z. (forthcoming) *Teaching and researching motivation. Applied Linguistics in Action Series.* London. Longman

Layder, D. (1993) *New strategies in social research.* Cambridge. Polity Press

Christopher N Candlin
General Editor
Centre for English Language Education & Communication Research
City University of Hong Kong

1

Fact and fiction in language learning

*As Saliha takes the envelope, she says, 'Merci beaucoup, Madame
Rivest.' Stepping out the door, she switches the plastic bag
containing her work clothes from her right hand to her left hand
and extends her right hand to Madame Rivest and says, 'Bonjour,
Madame Rivest' and smiles. These are the first real words she has
uttered since she woke up that morning.*

*In the elevator, going down, Saliha is alone. She checks the
contents of the envelope and smiles with satisfaction. Before the
elevator reaches the ground floor, Saliha has time to reflect on her
day. She has earned enough for the week's food and cigarettes. Last
week, she paid the last instalment for her tuition at Plato College.
She is tired but life is under control. Her only regret is that she
hasn't answered Madame Rivest in longer sentences. But she
chases away her regrets with a light shrug and admits the reality.*

*We come here to speak like them, she thinks; but it will be a
long time before they let us practise.*

(TERNAR, 1990, pp. 327–8)

Although Saliha is a fictional character, her story is real to many language
learners, whether in Canada, Colombia or Korea. Saliha is eager to learn the
language of her new community in Quebec and she understands the need
to practice the French that she is learning in the formal context of Plato
College. However, although 'immersed' in the francophone community, Saliha
has little opportunity to practice French because of the nature of the work
she does and the way relations of power are structured in her workplace. In
the course of a long day at work, the only words she has uttered are 'Merci
beaucoup, Madame Rivest' and 'Bonjour, Madame Rivest'. It is with regret
that she notes she has not answered Madame Rivest in longer sentences.

The reality that Saliha has to confront is that Madame Rivest has the power to influence when she can speak, how much she can speak and what she can speak about. Saliha acknowledges that it will be a long time before Madame Rivest will 'let' her practice speaking the target language.

In this chapter, I draw on Saliha's fictional story in Quebec, Canada to begin an exploration of the relationship between identity and language learning, between the individual language learner and the larger social world. I use her story to illustrate notions of power, identity and investment, and conceptions of ethnicity, gender and class. In the following chapters of the book, I move from Saliha's fictional world in Quebec to the lived experiences of five immigrant women learning English in the neighboring province of Ontario, Canada. I demonstrate that the opportunities these women had to practice English were structured by unequal relations of power in the home and workplace. I illustrate how the women responded to and acted upon these relations of power to create opportunities to practice speaking English, and the extent to which they succeeded in their efforts. I argue, however, that their efforts must be understood with reference to their investment in English and their changing identities across historical time and social space. Thus the ideas and themes introduced in this chapter will re-emerge in later chapters, demonstrating, I believe, that truth is indeed stranger than fiction, life more intriguing than art.

Saliha and the SLA canon

Saliha would struggle to recognize herself in current theories of second language acquisition (SLA). She could be overwhelmed by perspectives from psycholinguistics, sociolinguistics, neurolinguistics, classroom research, bilingual education and social psychology.[1] She would probably agree, however, as Spolsky (1989) notes, that the more she is exposed to and practices French, the more proficient she will become. Extensive exposure to French, in relevant kinds and amounts, and the opportunity to practice the target language will reap many rewards for her. She will learn to discriminate between the sounds of the language, have the opportunity to analyze the language into its constituent parts, learn how its constituent parts can be recombined grammatically into larger units, and develop control over the grammatical and pragmatic structures of French. Saliha would be mystified, however, by Spolsky's distinction between the natural or informal environment of the target language community and the formal environment of the classroom:

> The distinction between the two is usually stated as a set of contrasting conditions. In natural second language learning, the language is being used for communication, but in the formal situation it is used only to

teach. In natural language learning, the learner is surrounded by fluent speakers of the target language, but in the formal classroom, only the teacher (if anyone) is fluent. In natural learning, the context is the outside world, open and stimulating; in formal learning, it is the closed four walls of the classroom. In natural language learning, the language used is free and normal; in the formal classroom it is carefully controlled and simplified. Finally, in the natural learning situation, attention is on the meaning of the communication; in the formal situation, it is on meaningless drills.

(1989, p. 171)

'How much communicating did I do today?' Saliha may well ask, 'How meaningful are my conversations with Madame Rivest?' Because many SLA theorists have not addressed the experiences of language learners with reference to inequitable relations of power between language learners and target language speakers, they have struggled to theorize the relationship between the individual language learner and the larger social world. In general, artificial distinctions have been drawn between the learner and the language learning context. On the one hand, the individual is described with respect to a host of affective variables such as her or his motivation to learn a second language. The personality of the individual is described as introverted or extroverted, inhibited or uninhibited. It is assumed that the learner's attitudes towards the target language community determine how motivated the second language learner is, and that levels of anxiety determine how much comprehensible *input* becomes cognitive *intake*.[2] The social, on the other hand, generally refers to group differences between the language learner group and the target language group. Where there is congruence between the second language group and the target language group, the social distance between them is considered to be minimal, which in turn facilitates the acculturation of the second language group into the target language group and enhances language learning (Schumann, 1976a). Where there is great social distance between the groups, little acculturation is considered to take place, and as a result members of the second language group are deemed not to become proficient speakers of the target language.

In theories of SLA which focus on individual differences, Saliha would be held primarily responsible for progress in learning the target language. The 'good language learner'[3] is one who seeks out opportunities to learn the language, is highly motivated, has good attention to detail, can tolerate ambiguity and has low levels of anxiety. If Saliha made little progress in learning the second language, she might be considered unmotivated and inflexible. In contrast, theories of SLA which focus on group differences in second language learning would consider Saliha to have little human agency: social distance and degrees of acculturation would determine the extent to which she learnt the target language, and the role of instruction would be considered tangential to this process. Thus, in many SLA theories, Saliha would be conceived of as an individual with various attributes independent of her relationship to the social or as having a group identity that leaves little room for individual action. The disagreements in the literature on the way affective variables interact with the larger social context would be also be puzzling for Saliha. While Krashen (1981) regards motivation as a variable independent of social context, Spolsky (1989) regards the two as inextricably intertwined. While Krashen draws distinctions between self-confidence, motivation, and anxiety, Clement, Gardner and Smythe (quoted in Spolsky, 1989) consider motivation and anxiety as a subset of self-confidence. While Krashen considers self-confidence as an intrinsic characteristic of the language learner, Gardner (1985) argues that self-confidence *arises* from positive experiences in the context of the second language. Such disagreements in the SLA literature should not be dismissed, as Gardner (1989) dismisses them, as 'more superficial than real' (p. 137). This debate arises, I suggest, because artificial distinctions are drawn between the individual and the social, which lead to arbitrary mapping of particular factors on either the individual or the social, with little rigorous justification.

In sum, in the field of SLA, theorists have not adequately addressed why it is that learners like Saliha may sometimes be motivated, extroverted and confident, and sometimes unmotivated, introverted and anxious; why in one place there may be social distance between learners and the target language community, while in another place the social distance may be minimal; why learners can sometimes speak and at other times remain silent. Although muted, there is an uneasy recognition by some theorists that current theory of the relationship between the language learner and the social world is problematic. Scovel (1978), for example, has found that research on foreign language anxiety suffers from several ambiguities, and Gardner and MacIntyre (1993, p. 9) remain unconvinced of the relationship between 'personality variables' and language achievement.

Identity and language learning

The central argument of this book is that SLA theorists have struggled to conceptualize the relationship between the language learner and the social world because they have not developed a comprehensive theory of identity that integrates the language learner and the language learning context. Furthermore, they have not questioned how relations of power in the social world impact on social interaction between second language learners and target language speakers. While many SLA theorists such as Ellis (1985), Krashen (1981), Schumann (1978a) and Stern (1983) recognize that language learners do not live in idealized, homogeneous communities but in complex, heterogeneous ones, such heterogeneity has generally been framed uncritically. Theories of the good language learner have been developed on the premise that language learners can choose under what conditions they will interact with members of the target language community and that the language learner's access to the target language community is a function of the learner's motivation. Thus Gardner and MacIntyre (1992), for example, argue that 'the major characteristic of the informal context is that it is voluntary. Individuals can either participate or not in informal acquisition contexts' (p. 213). Second language theorists have not adequately explored how inequitable relations of power limit the opportunities second language learners have to practice the target language outside the classroom. In addition, many have assumed that learners can be defined unproblematically as motivated or unmotivated, introverted or extroverted, inhibited or uninhibited, without considering that such affective factors are frequently socially constructed in inequitable relations of power, changing over time and space, and possibly coexisting in contradictory ways in a single individual.

In this book I take the position that notions of the individual and the language learner's personality in SLA theory need to be reconceptualized in ways that will problematize dichotomous distinctions between the language learner and the language learning context. I use the term identity to reference how a person understands his or her relationship to the world, how that relationship is constructed across time and space, and how the person understands possibilities for the future. I argue that SLA theory needs to develop a conception of identity that is understood with reference to larger, and frequently inequitable, social structures which are reproduced in day-to-day social interaction. In taking this position, I foreground the role of language as constitutive of and constituted by a language learner's identity. As Heller (1987) demonstrates, it is through language that a person negotiates a sense of self within and across different sites at different points in time, and it is through language that a person gains access to – or is denied access to – powerful social networks that give learners the opportunity to speak. Thus language is not conceived of as a neutral medium of communication, but is understood with reference to its social meaning.

Interest in language and identity has been growing in momentum, a trend reflected in the number of doctoral theses that have recently appeared on this topic. Kanno (1996), for example, examined the changing identities of Japanese students returning to their home country after a period of time abroad, and Miller (1999) studied the relationship between speaking and social identity among migrant students in a number of Australian high schools. As the comprehensive reviews of McNamara (1997) and Hansen and Liu (1997) demonstrate, different researchers, drawing on different sources and using a variety of methodologies, have brought diverse perspectives to our understanding of language and identity. Social psychologists such as Henriques, Hollway, Urwin, Venn and Walkerdine (1984) and Edwards and

Potter (1992) offer different conceptions of identity than that associated with the work of scholars such as Tajfel (1982) and Giles and Coupland (1991), while the recent research of SLA scholars in different parts of the world has provided important insights into the relationship between identity and language learning.[4] In calling for a reorientation of SLA research, the work of Hall (1997), Lantolf (1996), Rampton (1995) and van Lier (1994) is particularly noteworthy. As Rampton (1995) argues,

> The very undifferentiated portrait of the second language learner that emerges in SLA no doubt partly results from its tendency to thematise the learner's internal psychological condition. Rather than looking at interaction as a socio–historically sensitive arena in which language learner identity is socially negotiated, SLA generally examines learners' behaviour for evidence of the determining influence of psycholinguistic states and processes . . . At present, SLA could probably benefit from an enhanced sense of the empirical world's complex socio–cultural diversity.

(293–4)

As if on cue, international language journals are giving greater attention to research on sociocultural diversity in general, and identity in particular. In 1996, for example, Martin-Jones and Heller (1996) edited two special issues of *Linguistics and Education* on discourse, identities and power, and Sarangi and Baynham (1996) edited a special double issue of *Language and Education* on the construction of educational identities. These were followed by a special issue of *TESOL Quarterly* on language and identity, which I edited in 1997 (Norton, 1997a).

Given the subject of this book, a few comments on the *TESOL Quarterly* special issue are relevant. The five studies that constitute the bulk of the special issue represent perspectives from Canada (Morgan, 1997), Japan (Duff and Uchida, 1997), the United States (Schecter and Bayley, 1997), South Africa (Thesen, 1997), and England (Leung, Harris and Rampton, 1997). What I found particularly interesting was the way in which each author framed and conceptualized identity, with the focus of Morgan's research on social identity, Duff and Uchida's on sociocultural identity, Thesen's on voice, Schecter and Bayley's on cultural identity and Leung, Harris and Rampton's on ethnic identity. The apparent differences between the authors' conceptualizations of identity, I argue, can be explained partly in terms of the disciplines and research traditions that inform their respective studies, as well as the different emphases of their research projects. Notwithstanding such differences, however, I note that distinctions – such as those between social and cultural identity – become less marked as the researchers ground their theory in specific sites of practice.[5] Furthermore, most of the researchers noted that identity construction must be understood with reference to relations of power between language learners and target language speakers. It is to this relationship that I now turn.

Power and identity

An investigation of the ways in which relations of power impact on language learning and teaching has been initiated by researchers who adopt a critical approach to the field of second language education.[6] These researchers have argued that the very heterogeneity of society must be understood with reference to an inequitably structured world in which the gender, race, class and ethnicity of second language learners may serve to marginalize them. Much of this research has been motivated by educational theory within a critical tradition, such as that of Freire (1970, 1985), Giroux (1988, 1992) and Simon (1987, 1992), and has highlighted the fact that language teaching is not a neutral practice but a highly political one. In this book I use the term 'power' to reference the socially constructed relations among individuals, institutions and communities through which symbolic and material resources in a society are produced, distributed and validated. By symbolic resources I refer to such resources as language, education and friendship, while I use the term material resources to include capital goods, real estate and money. Following Foucault (1980) and Simon (1992) I take the position that power is neither monolithic nor invariant; it is not simply something that can be physically possessed, but a relation which always implies social exchange on a particular set of terms. By extension, it is a relation that is constantly being renegotiated as symbolic and material resources in a society change their value. As well, like Foucault (1980), I take the position that power does not operate only at the macro level of powerful institutions such as the legal system, the education system and the social welfare system, but also at the micro level of everyday social encounters between people with differential access to symbolic and material resources – encounters that are inevitably produced within language.

To illustrate these notions, consider again the relationship between Madame Rivest and Saliha. In their relationship, Madame Rivest has control over valued symbolic resources (French) and valued material resources (Saliha's wages). Saliha desires access to both these resources, but it is Madame Rivest who controls how and when these resources are to be distributed and what form they will take. When Saliha bids farewell to Madame Rivest, she does not attempt to prolong the conversation with Madame Rivest and create the opportunity to speak – she simply smiles. If Saliha had sighed, shrugged her shoulders or carried on talking without Madame Rivest's active participation, her behavior might have been considered inappropriate and she could have jeopardized her access to the material resources that Madame Rivest provided. This vignette illustrates that control of symbolic and material resources are not distinct facets of power, but are intimately connected to each other, as well as to the process of social interaction.[7]

Insights from West (1992), Bourdieu (1977), Weedon (1997) and Cummins (1996) are particularly helpful in conceptualizing the relationship between power, identity and language learning. Following West (1992), I take the position that identity references desire – the desire for recognition, the desire for affiliation and the desire for security and safety. Such desires, West argues, cannot be separated from the distribution of material resources in society. People who have access to a wide range of resources in a society will have access to power and privilege, which will in turn influence how they understand their relationship to the world and their possibilities for the future. Thus the quesion 'Who am I?' cannot be understood apart from the question 'What am I allowed to do?' And the question 'What am I allowed to do?' cannot be understood apart from material conditions that structure opportunities for the realization of desires. According to West, it is a person's access to material resources that will define the terms on which desires will be articulated. In this view, a person's identity will shift in accordance with changing social and economic relations.

Bourdieu's (1977) work is complementary to that of West because it focuses on the relationship between identity and symbolic power. In arguing that 'speech always owes a major part of its value to the value of the person who utters it' (p. 652), Bourdieu suggests that the value ascribed to speech cannot be understood apart from the person who speaks, and the person who speaks cannot be understood apart from larger networks of social relationships. His position is that the linguist (and, I would argue, many applied linguists) take for granted the conditions for the establishment of communication: that those who speak regard those who listen as worthy to listen, and that those who listen regard those who speak as worthy to speak. I have argued, however, in Norton Peirce (1995), that it is precisely such assumptions that must be called into question. In the following chapters I draw on Bourdieu to suggest that an expanded definition of communicative competence should include the 'right to speech' (what I have translated as the right to speak) or the 'the power to impose reception' (1977, p. 75).

Unlike West and Bourdieu, Weedon (1997) has worked within a feminist poststructuralist tradition. While West's work has focused on the relationship between identity and material relations of power, and Bourdieu's on the relationship between identity and symbolic power, Weedon has sought to integrate language, individual experience and social power in a theory of subjectivity. In this theory, the individual is accorded greater human agency than in Bourdieu's theory, while the importance of language in constructing the relationship between the individual and the social is given greater prominence than in West's theory. Three defining characteristics of subjectivity are comprehensively investigated in Chapter 6 of this book: the multiple, nonunitary nature of the subject; subjectivity as a site of struggle; and subjectivity as changing over time. Furthermore, and of central importance, subjectivity and language are theorized as mutually constitutive. As Weedon (1997) says, 'Language is the place where actual and possible forms of social organization and their likely social and political consequences are defined and contested. Yet it is also the place where our sense of ourselves, our subjectivity, is constructed' (p. 21).

In drawing a distinction between coercive and collaborative relations of power, Cummins (1996) makes an important contribution to an understanding of the relationship between identity and power. He argues that coercive power relations refer to the exercise of power by a dominant individual, group or country that is detrimental to others and serves to maintain an inequitable division of resources in a society. Collaborative relations of power, on the other hand, can serve to empower rather than marginalize. In his view, it is possible for power to be coercive or productive; it is possible for both dominant and subordinate groups in a society to exercise power, but the realm of influence of the dominant group will be far greater than that of the subordinate group. Indeed, the dominant group may try to exercise absolute power by encouraging all members of a society to accept the status quo as normal and beyond critique. Thus power is not a fixed, predetermined quantity, but can be mutually generated in interpersonal and intergroup relations. As Cummins (1996) notes, 'The power relationship is additive rather than subtractive. Power is created with others rather than being imposed on or exercised over others' (p. 21). By extension, relations of power can serve to enable or constrain the range of identities that language learners can negotiate in their classrooms and communities.

To continue with my illustration, how might we understand Saliha's identity and the way in which her identity constructs and is constructed by her interaction with Madame Rivest? Notwithstanding the complex history Saliha has had before coming to Quebec, Saliha identifies herself as an immigrant language learner who has little power to control the progress of her interaction with Madame Rivest. She signals the unequal relations of power between language learners and target language speakers in Quebec by using we/they referents ('we come here to speak like them'). The 'we' to whom Saliha refers are the immigrants who have come to Quebec and seek to speak like francophone Quebecers ('them') who have access to desirable symbolic and material resources in Quebec society. Saliha's identity in this context must be understood with reference to her contradictory relationship to Madame Rivest. On the one hand, Saliha wants to have more interaction with Madame Rivest, greater control over the symbolic resources of her new society, and access to the power and privilege enjoyed by Madame Rivest and other francophone Quebecers. On the other hand, Saliha does not want to jeopardize her access to desperately needed material resources which help to sustain her from day to day. Significantly, it is these conflicts about who she is, what she needs, and how she desires that keep Saliha silent. But such conflict between her desire for symbolic resources and her desire for material resources are captured in her smiles. Saliha smiles obediently when she bids Madame Rivest farewell, resisting the impulse to respond in longer sentences. And she smiles again, in private, when she opens the

envelope which contains the material resources to sustain her for the following week.

Motivation and investment

It is intriguing to consider whether Saliha was motivated or unmotivated to
speak. In the field of second language learning, the concept of motivation is
drawn primarily from the field of social psychology, where attempts have
been made to quantify a learner's commitment to learning the target language. The work of Gardner and Lambert (1972) has been particularly
influential in introducing the notions of *instrumental* and *integrative* motivation into the field of SLA. In their work, instrumental motivation references
the desire that language learners have to learn a second language for utilitar-
ian purposes, such as employment, while integrative motivation references
the desire to learn a language to integrate successfully with the target language community. While researchers such as Crookes and Schmidt (1991),
Dornyei (1994, 1997), and Oxford and Shearin (1994) have sought to broaden
the theoretical framework proposed by Gardner and Lambert, such debates
on motivation in the field of SLA do not capture the complex relationship
between power, identity and language learning that I have observed in my
research. The concept of investment, which I introduced in Norton Peirce
(1995), signals the socially and historically constructed relationship of learners
to the target language, and their often ambivalent desire to learn and practice
it. It is best understood with reference to the economic metaphors that
Bourdieu uses in his work – in particular the notion of cultural capital.
Bourdieu and Passeron (1977) use the term 'cultural capital' to reference the
knowledge and modes of thought that characterize different classes and groups
in relation to specific sets of social forms. They argue that some forms of
cultural capital have a higher exchange value than others in relation to a set
of social forms which value some forms of knowledge and thought over
others. If learners invest in a second language, they do so with the understanding that they will acquire a wider range of symbolic and material resources, which will in turn increase the value of their cultural capital. Learners
expect or hope to have a good return on that investment – a return that will
give them access to hitherto unattainable resources.

   It is important to note that the notion of investment I am advocating is
not equivalent to instrumental motivation. The conception of instrumental
motivation presupposes a unitary, fixed, and ahistorical language learner who
desires access to material resources that are the privilege of target language
speakers. The notion of investment, on the other hand, conceives of the
language learner as having a complex social history and multiple desires.
The notion presupposes that when language learners speak, they are not

only exchanging information with target language speakers, but they are constantly organizing and reorganizing a sense of who they are and how they relate to the social world. Thus an investment in the target language is also an investment in a learner's own identity, an identity which is constantly changing across time and space. In this spirit, the questions 'Is Saliha motivated to learn the target language? What kind of personality does Saliha have?' may not be as helpful as the questions 'What is Saliha's investment in the target language? How is Saliha's relationship to the target language socially and historically constructed?' As I will demonstrate in this book, a learner's investment in the target language may be complex, contradictory and in a state of flux.

In a study of Chinese adolescent immigrant students in the United States, McKay and Wong (1996) extend the notion of investment developed by Norton Peirce (1995). Like Norton Peirce, they demonstrate how the specific needs, desires and negotiations of the learners were not distractions from the task of language learning, but 'must be regarded as constituting the very fabric of students' lives and as determining their investment in learning the target language' (1996, p. 603). McKay and Wong (1996) note, however, that while Norton Peirce (1995) focused on opportunities to speak, their research investigated students' investment in the four skills of listening, speaking, reading and writing. They argue that investment in each of these skills can be highly selective and that different skills can have different values in relation to learner identities. This latter theme is developed in greater detail by Angelil-Carter (1997), whose study addresses the development of academic literacy by English language learners in a South African university. She argues as follows:

> For [Norton] Peirce's (1995) concept of investment to take on meaning in the academic language learning context, I believe, it can usefully be broken down from its broad idea of investment in a target language such as English to investment in literacies, forms of writing or speaking – let us call them *discourses* – that are dislodged and reconstructed over time and space. Such investments may play a powerful facilitating or hindering role in the acquisition of new discourses.

> (p. 268)

There is evidence that the notion of investment is receiving some attention in the mainstream SLA literature. Ellis, in his 1997 book, *Second Language Acquisition*, contrasts the work of Norton Peirce (1995) with that of Schumann (1978a), defining investment as the 'learners' commitment to learning an L2, which is viewed as related to the social identities they construct for themselves as learners' (Ellis, 1997, p. 140). In McKay and Wong's study, as in Angelil-Carter's and Norton Peirce's, the relationship between ethnicity, identity and language learning is a central motif in the analysis. I turn next to a fuller investigation of ethnicity, gender and class in relation to identity and language learning.

Ethnicity, gender and class

Heller (1987) argues that people growing up in a homogeneous society would not define themselves as ethnic, and that ethnicity is a product of opposition. It is this kind of opposition that Saliha experiences in her relationship with Madame Rivest, and Saliha's sense of *otherness* is socially constructed within relationships such as this one. Saliha is excluded from Madame Rivest's powerful ethnic social network – a network which Heller would argue is defined by common language:

> Thus the first principle of ethnic identity formation is participation in ethnic social networks, and therefore in activities controlled by ethnic group members. Language is important here as a means by which access to networks is regulated: If you do not speak the right language, you do not have access to forming relationships with certain people, or to participating in certain activities.

(p. 181)

Drawing on her research with immigrant women in Canada, Ng (1981, 1987), like Heller, argues that ethnicity must be understood as a set of social relations that organize people in relation to larger social processes in society. She notes in particular that conventional research draws on observable features such as language and customs to determine criteria for ethnicity and pays little attention to the day-to-day experiences of immigrants. Yet, Ng stresses, it is only in the context of such interactions with members of the larger society that ethnicity becomes an issue for immigrants. Furthermore, Ng (1981) notes that immigrant women occupy a particular and different location in society to immigrant men, and that experiences of immigration must be understood as gendered ones.

In theorizing the gendered nature of the immigrant language learner's experience, I am concerned not only with the silencing that women experience within the context of larger patriarchal structures in society,[8] but also with the gendered access to the public world that immigrant women, in particular, experience. It is in the public world that language learners have the opportunity to interact with members of the target language community, but it is the public world that is not easily accessible to immigrant women. As will be discussed in the following chapters, even when such access is granted, the nature of the work available to immigrant women provides few opportunities for social interaction.

Like ethnic and gendered identities, a classed identity is one that is produced in specific sets of social, historical and economic relations of power which are reinforced and reproduced in everyday social encounters. In this regard, the concept of class articulated by Connell, Ashendon, Kessler and Dowsett (1982) is helpful. While in conventional sociological terms, a class is understood as sets of individuals who share the same attributes or possessions, such as level of income, type of occupation, level of education and ownership of capital, Connell *et al.* argue that 'it is not what people are, or even what they own, so much as what they do with their resources' that is central to an understanding of class (p. 33). In their view, it is problematic to consider the relationship between individuals and class as a 'location', in which people are passive markers of a 'geometrical spot'. Their research indicates that the relationship between individuals and class cannot be reduced to a system of categories; it is, rather, a system of relationships between people. In sum, like Rockhill (1987b), I take the position that ethnicity, gender and class are not experienced as a series of discrete background variables, but are all, in complex and interconnected ways, implicated in the construction of identity and the possibilities of speech.

Rethinking language and communicative competence

In arguing that language is constitutive of and constituted by a speaker's identity, I take the position that language is more than words and sentences. Saliha's words and sentences, her extended hand, her ambivalent smile and light shrug, cannot be understood apart from her unique relationship with Madame Rivest and the particular time/space configuration of this social relationship. The theory that helps me to understand the language of this relationship is associated with the work of critical discourse researchers who have framed their work with reference to poststructuralist theories of language.[9] Poststructuralist theories of language achieved much prominence in the late twentieth century, and are associated, among others, with the work of Bakhtin (1981), Bourdieu (1977), Fairclough (1992), Gee (1990) and Kress (1989). These theories build on, but are distinct from, structuralist theories of language, associated predominantly with the work of Saussure. Saussure's (1966) distinction between speech (*parole*) and language (*langue*) was an attempt to provide a way of recognizing that, despite geographical, interpersonal and social variations, languages have shared patterns and structure. For structuralists, the building blocks of language structure are signs that comprise the signifier (or sound-image) and the signified (the concept or meaning). Saussure asserts that neither the signifier nor the signified preexists the other and that the link between them is arbitrary. He notes that it is the linguistic system that guarantees the meaning of signs and that each linguistic community has its own set of signifying practices that give value to the signs in a language.

One of the criticisms poststructuralists have levelled at this notion of language is that structuralism cannot account for struggles over the social meanings that can be attributed to signs in a given language. The signs /feminist/, /research/ and /SLA/, for example, can have different meanings for different people within the same linguistic community. Witness, for example, debates over the meaning of SLA theory in the field of Applied Linguistics.[10] While structuralists conceive of signs as having idealized meanings and linguistic communities as being relatively homogeneous and consensual, poststructuralists take the position that the signifying practices of societies are sites of struggle, and that linguistic communities are heterogeneous arenas characterized by conflicting claims to truth and power.

Thus the theory of discourse that is central to this book represents a departure from notions of discourse (units of language larger than the sentence) associated with much of the traditional sociolinguistic research. In critical discourse research (Norton, 1997b), discourses are the complexes of signs and practices that organize social existence and social reproduction. The discourses of the family, the school, the church, the corporation are constituted in and by language and other sign systems. Discourses delimit the range of possible practices under their authority and organize how these practices are realized in time and space. As such, a discourse is a particular way of organizing meaning-making practices. Kress (1989, p. 7) offers a particularly cogent illustration of this concept:

> Discourses tend towards exhaustiveness and inclusiveness; that is they attempt to account not only for an area of immediate concern to an institution, but attempt to account for increasingly wider areas of concern. Take as an example one discourse which determines the matter in which the biological category of sex is taken into social life as gender, the discourse of sexism. It specifies what men and women may be, how they are to think of themselves, how they are to think of and to interrelate with the other gender. But beyond that the discourse of sexism specifies what families may be, and relations within the family: What it is to be a 'proper father' or a 'mother' and 'the eldest son', 'our little girl'. It reaches into all major areas of social life, specifying what work is suitable, possible even, for men and for women; how pleasure is to be seen by either gender; what artistic possibilities if any there are for either gender. A metaphor which I use to explain the effects of discourse to myself is that of a military power whose response to border skirmishes is to occupy the adjacent territory. As problems continue, more territory is occupied, then settled and colonised. A discourse colonises the social world imperialistically, from the point of view of one institution.

To extend Kress's military metaphor, it is important to note that while discourses are powerful, they are not completely determined. It is possible for people in border towns to resist the dominance of a colonising power, and to set up what Terdiman (1985) calls 'counter-discourses' to the dominant power. In this regard, as Foucault notes, power and resistance frequently coexist:

> It is true, it seems to me, that power is 'always already there', that one is never 'outside', that there are no 'margins' in which those in rupture with the system may gambol. But this does not mean that it is necessary to admit an unavoidable form of domination or an absolute privilege of the law. That one can never be 'outside of power' does not mean that one is in every way trapped . . . There are no relations of power without resistances.

> (Quoted in Morris and Patton, 1979, p. 55)

Given a theory of language as discourse, this book, particularly in Chapter 7, will reiterate and develop concerns I have raised in Norton Peirce (1989) about the normative views on communicative competence that have dominated the field of second language education in the 1980s and 1990s. In what has become a classic framework for conceptualizing communicative competence in the field of SLA, Canale and Swain (1980) and Canale (1983) identified four characteristics of a learner's communicative competence: grammatical competence (knowledge of the code itself); sociolinguistic competence (the ability to produce and understand utterances appropriately); discourse competence (the ability to combine grammatical forms into larger stretches of spoken or written discourse); and strategic competence (the mastery of communication strategies). I have argued (Norton Peirce, 1989, p. 406) that, while it is important for language learners to understand what Hymes (1979) calls the 'rules of use' of the target language, it is equally important for them to explore whose interests these rules serve. What is considered appropriate usage is not self-evident (Bourne, 1988), but must be understood with reference to inequitable relations of power between interlocutors.

Turning once again to Saliha and Madame Rivest, it is instructive to consider whether Saliha demonstrates communicative competence in their interaction. Clearly, Saliha has grammatical competence as her utterances are well formed. She is sociolinguistically competent in that she shows appropriate regard for the status of her interlocutor and recognizes her employer's desire not to engage in further interaction; she is strategically competent in that she is sensitive enough to step out of the door before bidding Madame Rivest farewell, thus reassuring Madame Rivest that she will not draw her into further interaction. While it is impossible to determine whether Saliha has discourse competence (because Madame Rivest does not allow her to respond in longer sentences), it is possible to conclude that Saliha has learnt the linguistic rules of use in this particular social interaction. However, as a language educator concerned with social justice, I am not satisfied that Saliha has learnt to produce grammatically acceptable and sociolinguistically appropriate utterances in the target language. It is disturbing that Saliha resigns herself to what she unproblematically calls 'reality', rather than investigating how that reality is socially constructed. I suggest in this book that theories of communicative competence should extend beyond an understanding of the appropriate rules of use in a particular society to include an understanding of the way rules of use are socially and historically constructed to support the interests of a dominant group within a given society.

In sum, this book draws on a different set of theoretical perspectives to those commonly associated with traditional SLA research and begins with a different set of assumptions. The questions I bring to this reader include the following: What opportunities are available to second language learners to interact with target language speakers? What happens when target language speakers avoid interaction with second language speakers? Is Krashen's (1981, 1982) notion of the affective filter adequately theorized? Are there alternative ways of theorizing motivation? Under what conditions is a language learner introverted, sensitive to rejection, inhibited? When will a language learner take risks, and why?

Structure of book

In Chapter 1, I have argued that, since practice in the target language is centrally important in the learning of a second language, both SLA theorists and second language teachers need to understand how opportunities to practice speaking are socially structured in both formal and informal sites of language learning. Furthermore, it is important for theorists and teachers to understand how language learners respond to and create opportunities to speak the target language, and how their actions intersect with their investment in the target language and their changing identities. Research which addresses these issues will be of benefit to language teachers who wish to meet the needs of learners like Saliha. If learners do not make progress in learning, teachers cannot assume that learners do not wish to learn the second language or that they are unmotivated or inflexible; perhaps the learners are struggling because they cannot speak under conditions of marginalization.

In Chapter 2, I address the complex relationship between the methodology and the theory of my study. I argue that any approach to methodology presupposes a set of assumptions that guides the questions that are asked in a research project and how these questions are addressed. Furthermore, I suggest that *how* data is collected will inevitably influence *what* data is collected and what conclusions are drawn on the basis of data analysis. I describe the theory that informed my approach to methodology, and then describe the methodology that I used in the light of this theory, focusing on the diary study as particularly important in the data collection process.

In Chapter 3, I locate my study in the context of other studies of immigrant language learners in both Canada and the international community. I then introduce the five participants in the study: Eva from Poland, Mai from Vietnam, Katarina from Poland, Martina from the former Czechoslovakia and Felicia from Peru.[11] I comment on their exposure to English and their practice of English, and describe the conditions under which they feel most comfortable speaking English. I draw attention to the contradictory position in which these women find themselves in relation to anglophone Canadians: They need access to anglophone social networks in order to practice English in the wider community, but knowledge of English is an *a priori* condition of entry into these social networks.

In Chapter 4, I describe the language learning experiences of the two younger women in the study, Eva and Mai. I argue that each woman's investment in English must be understood with reference to her reasons for coming to Canada, her plans for the future and her changing identity. I describe Eva as a multicultural citizen in that, over time, she gained access to the anglophone social networks at work and described herself as having the same possibilities as Canadians. With respect to Mai, I demonstrate that she took on the position of language broker in the home to enable her to resist the patriarchal structures in her extended family. I also examine how and why Mai's workplace offered opportunities for Mai to practice English, and how changes in the language practices in the workplace represented a threat to her investment in English, her opportunities to practice English and her identity as a language broker in the home.

In Chapter 5, I describe the language learning experiences of the three older women in the study, Katarina, Martina and Felicia, indicating how their investment in English intersects with their identities as mothers. Katarina's ambivalent relationship to English is described in depth: On the one hand, she feared that English would undermine her relationship to her only child; on the other hand, it would give her access to the fellow professionals with whom she would most like to interact. Martina, on the other hand, as the primary caregiver in the home, needed to speak English in order to relieve her children of the responsibility of defending the family's interests in the larger social world. Despite her sense that her immigrant status afforded her little social value, she was not silenced by marginalization. Felicia's investment in her identity as a wealthy Peruvian is intriguing, and her resistance to being positioned as an immigrant in Canada is addressed.

In Chapter 6, I address the implications of my findings for second language acquisition theory. With reference to data from my study, I critique current SLA theory on natural language learning, the acculturation model of SLA, and the affective filter hypothesis respectively. I argue that SLA theorists need to address the inequitable relations of power which structure opportunities for language learners to practice the target outside the classroom. I demonstrate that the acculturation model of SLA does not give sufficient recognition to situations of additive and subtractive bilingualism, and I suggest that a learner's affective filter needs to be theorized as a social construction which intersects in significant ways with a language learner's identity. I suggest that a poststructuralist conception of identity and Bourdieu's (1977) notion of *legitimate discourse* are theoretically useful in helping to explain the findings from my study, and are a valuable contribution to SLA theory. In the final section of the chapter, drawing on Lave and Wenger's (1991) conceptions of situated learning, I incorporate these ideas into an expanded notion of language learning as a social practice.

In Chapter 7, I consider the implications of my study for classroom practice. I examine the expectations the participants had of formal language classes and analyze these expectations in view of findings from the study on natural language learning and identity. I suggest that my study has a number of implications for classroom practice, defending my arguments with reference to two stories of classroom resistance described by Katarina and Felicia. However, with reference to Mai's story of a particularly problematic classroom experience, I raise questions about how student experience should be incorporated into the language curriculum. I then take the position that the diary study itself was a pedagogical practice that had the potential to expand and transform language learning possibilities both inside and outside the classroom. Finally, noting the limitations of the diary study, I suggest that classroom-based social research might help to bridge the gap between formal and natural sites of language learning for immigrant language learners, giving them the more powerful identity of ethnographer in relation to the larger world of target language speakers.

Notes

1. For a comprehensive overview of these topics, see Tucker and Corson (1997) and Cummins and Corson (1997).
2. See H. D. Brown (1994), Gardner and Lambert (1972), Krashen (1981) and Schumann (1978b) for more detailed analyses.
3. The work of Rubin (1975) and Naiman, Frohlich, Stern and Todesco (1978) has been central in defining 'the good language learner' in SLA theory. Drawing on social theory and their research with adults and children respectively, Norton and Toohey (1999) have documented changing notions of the good language learner.
4. As illustrative of the range of this work, see the work of Lin (1996) in Hong Kong, Rampton (1995) in England, Kramsch (1993) and Hall (1993,

1995) in the USA, Toohey (1998, 2000) in Canada and Thesen (1997) in South Africa.

5. In my previous work (Norton Peirce, 1993, 1995), I had been drawn to theories of social identity as distinct from cultural identity. As I understood it, social identity references the relationship between the individual and the larger social world as mediated through institutions such as families, schools, workplaces, social services and law courts. I asked to what extent this relationship must be understood with reference to a person's race, gender, class or ethnicity. Cultural identity I understood to reference the relationship between individuals and members of a group who share a common history, a common language and similar ways of understanding the world. I tended not to draw on theories of cultural identity because I debated whether such theories could do justice to the heterogeneity within the groups I had encountered over many years of research, and the dynamic and changing nature of identity I had observed. Over time, however, I have come to see the difference between social and cultural identity as more fluid, and the commonalities more marked than their differences.

6. For a comprehensive overview of such research, see Hornberger and Corson, (1997), focusing in particular on the chapters by Faltis (1997), Goldstein (1997), Martin-Jones, (1997), May (1997) and Norton (1997b).

7. See Heller's (1992) research on codeswitching and language choice in Ontario and Quebec which reveals the ways in which the regulation of access to symbolic resources is tied to the regulation of access to material resources. Furthermore, her research depicts how French is now set up, parallel to English, as a crucial linguistic resource in Quebec society to which relatively powerless groups, such as natives and immigrants, must aspire.

8. See for example hooks (1990), Lewis and Simon (1986), Smith (1987b), Spender, (1980).

9. See for example Corson (1993), Fairclough (1992), Gee (1990), Heller (1999), Kress (1989), Lemke (1995), Luke (1988), Norton Peirce and Stein (1995), Pennycook (1994, 1998), Simon (1992) and Wodak (1996).

10. See Beretta and Crookes (1993), Gregg (1993), Long (1993), van Lier (1994), Lantolf (1996) and Schumann (1993).

11. All the names of people and places used in the study have been changed.

2

Researching identity and language learning

All methods are ways of asking questions that presume an underlying set of assumptions, a structure of relevance, and a form of rationality.

(SIMON AND DIPPO, 1986, p. 195)

Since critical research has a relatively recent history in the field of SLA, I have found the work of researchers in related disciplines invaluable in helping me develop a methodological framework for the study described in this book. In this chapter, I first discuss how three groups of educational researchers have influenced my work, and then outline my central research questions. I turn next to an examination of the complex relationship between researcher and researched, followed by a detailed description of the study itself.

Methodological framework

In investigating the relationship between identity and language learning, the questions I have asked, the data I have considered relevant and the conclusions I have drawn have been informed by the work of educational researchers in cultural studies, feminist research and critical ethnography. The first group of educational researchers include Connell *et al.* (1982), Simon (1987, 1992), Walsh (1987, 1991) and Willis (1977); the second include Briskin and Coulter (1992), Luke and Gore (1992), Schenke (1991, 1996), Smith (1987a, 1987b) and Weiler (1988, 1991); and the third include Anderson (1989), Britzman (1990), Brodkey (1987) and Simon and Dippo (1986). While these educational theorists do not always ask the same questions or share the same assumptions, I have found that the ideas they share, six of which are outlined below, highly productive for research on identity and language learning.

(i)   The researchers aim to investigate the complex relationship between social structure on the one hand, and human agency on the other, without resorting to deterministic or reductionist analyses. For example, Anderson (1989) notes that critical ethnography has grown out of dissatisfaction with social research on structures like class, patriarchy and racism in which real people never appear, and cultural interpretations of human action in which broad structural constraints like class, patriarchy and racism never appear. Likewise, Weiler (1988) suggests that the specific mandate of feminist scholarship is to investigate the relationship between the individual and the social, with a particular focus on the everyday world of women.

(ii)   The researchers assume that in order to understand social structures we need to understand inequitable relations of power based on gender, race, class, ethnicity and sexual orientation. Walsh (1991, p. 139), for example, argues that in an unequal world, in which power relations are constantly at work, 'participation and dialogue never just happen'; students are differentially positioned in relation to one another, the subject matter, and the teacher. Further, Weiler (1988) notes that while women share a gendered history, women should not be treated as a single group with no differences; questions of race and class are as important as questions of gender.

(iii) The researchers are interested in the way individuals make sense of their own experience. Connell *et al.* (1982), drawing on their landmark research in Australia, note that they wanted to get close to the situations people found themselves in and to talk to them in depth about their personal experiences. Smith (1987b, p. 9) notes that what she calls an 'institutional ethnography' is a method of analysis that returns the researcher to the actualities of what people do on a day-to-day basis under particular conditions and in defined situations.

(iv)   The researchers are interested in locating their research within a historical context. In this regard, Simon and Dippo (1986, p. 198) note that 'history is not to be relegated to the collection of 'background data', but rather becomes an integral part of the explanation of the regularities explored in any specifics'. Walsh (1991) notes that the purpose of her study on the struggles of Puerto Rican students in the United States was to highlight how the past and present intersect in people's voices and transform pedagogical conditions. Luke and Gore (1992), in a similar spirit, note that the identities that feminist academics have forged for themselves have been influenced by feminists past and present and by the extensive feminist literature of the preceding two decades.

(v)   The researchers reject the view that any research can claim to be objective or unbiased. Weiler (1988) notes that feminist research begins with the assumption that the researcher plays a constitutive role in determining the progress of a research project and that the researcher has to understand her own subjective experience and knowledge as well as that of the women she studies. Likewise, Simon and Dippo (1986) make the point that the production of knowledge cannot be understood apart from the personal histories of the researchers and the larger institutional context in which researchers work. They suggest that critical ethnographic work should define data and analytic procedures in a way consistent with its pedagogical and political project.

(vi)   The researchers believe that the goal of educational research is social and educational change. Brodkey (1987) for example, makes the point that the goal of critical ethnography is to help create the possibility of transforming such institutions as schools. Briskin and Coulter (1992) note that feminist pedagogy is situated firmly within the discourse on progressive education and critical pedagogy, while Simon's work, and that of his colleagues, is centrally concerned with what schools can do to address inequities in educational and social institutions (Simon, Dippo and Schenke, 1992).

Central questions

In my own study with immigrant language learners in Canada, I sought to investigate the relationship of learners to the larger social world, without resorting to oversimplification. I frequently asked how questions of gender, race, class and ethnicity were central to the analysis. I sought to investigate how the learners made sense of their experiences and to what extent their particular historical memories intersected with their investment in language learning. Through these enquiries I recognized increasingly that my own history and experiences structured the study in diverse and complex ways. The questions addressed in this book can be collapsed into two broad sets of questions. (i) Since interaction with target language speakers is a desirable condition for adult SLA, what opportunities for interaction exist outside the classroom? How is this interaction socially structured? How do learners act upon these structures to create, use or resist opportunities to speak? To what extent should their actions be understood with reference to their investment in the target language and their changing identities across time and space? (ii) How can an enhanced understanding of identity and natural language learning inform both SLA theory and classroom practice?

The researcher and the researched

Having established a methodological framework for my research, I needed to consider the kind of relationship I wished to establish with the participants in my research, a topic of increasing interest and concern in the social sciences. In this regard, the work of Cameron, Frazer, Harvey, Rampton and Richardson (1992) is particularly helpful. Drawing on their research, primarily conducted in England, Cameron *et al.* distinguish three positions that researchers may take up in relation to their subjects, defined respectively as ethical, advocacy and empowerment research. In ethical research, they argue, there is an appropriate concern that subjects do not suffer damage or inconvenience while participating in the research, and that the contributions of subjects are adequately acknowledged. They characterize such research as research *on* social subjects. Advocacy research, in contrast, is characterised by a commitment on the part of the researcher to do research *for* subjects as well as *on* subjects. In this regard, researchers might be asked to use their skills to defend the interests of subjects and to advocate on their behalf.

While ethics and advocacy, Cameron *et al.* argue, are associated with positivist assumptions about research, empowerment presupposes a more radical research project. It is characterized by research that is *on*, *for* and *with* subjects, as Cameron *et al.* (1992, p. 22) explain:

> One of the things we take that additional 'with' to imply is the use of interactive or dialogic research methods, as opposed to the distancing or objectifying strategies positivists are constrained to use. It is the centrality of interaction 'with' the researched that enables research to be empowering in our sense; though we understand this is as a necessary rather than sufficient condition.

In making the case for empowering research, Cameron *et al.* (1992) argue that three tenets should be observed: (i) Persons are not objects and should not be treated as objects. The central point here is that the researcher's goals, assumptions and procedures should be made explicit, and that research methods should be open, interactive and dialogic. They argue further that interaction can enhance research, and that claims for non-intervention as a guarantee of objectivity and validity are 'philosophically naive' (p. 23). (ii) Subjects have their own agendas and research should try to address them. Cameron *et al.* make the point that, if a researcher is working *with* subjects, it follows that asking questions and introducing topics should not be the sole prerogative of the researcher. Indeed, helping subjects to address their own agendas may generate new insights and enhance the project as a whole. (iii) If knowledge is worth having, it is worth sharing. As Cameron *et al.* suggest, this is a particularly challenging tenet, since it begs the questions, 'what is knowledge?' and 'how do we share?' They conclude that each research project offers different opportunities for interaction with subjects on the findings of the research, acknowledging that divergent interpretations by researchers and subjects may arise. In research with adult immigrants, researchers need to be particularly cognizant of the unequal relationship between researcher and researched since such subjects, new to a society, have few institutional protections and are frequently vulnerable and isolated. I did not want to do what Rist (1980) calls *blitzkrieg ethnography* by taking a brief look at a few language learners, collecting a handful of anecdotes and writing up decontextualized stories. Such an approach to ethnography is one that is being increasingly questioned by scholars such as Watson Gegeo (1988). How I sought to develop both an ethical and empowering relationship with my participants is discussed in the next section.

The project

As I embarked on my study, I immediately faced three challenges. First, I wanted to work with participants over an extended period so that I could examine to what extent language learning experiences changed over time; second, I needed a methodology adequate to the task of exploring complex and intimate experiences in a language that had not yet been mastered by the participants; third, I hoped to work with participants who had only recently arrived in Canada and were in the initial stages of language learning. This stage places the greatest demands on the immigrant to learn the second language and cultural practices of the new society. Such cultural practices, as Willis (1977) notes, cannot be specified in mechanical or structural terms, but in terms of distinctive kinds of relationships that are often in flux. The way I approached my research project and addressed these challenges are best described in the form of a chronology that spans a period of two years. It will be evident in this overview that, in doing the study, which was qualitative in nature, I utilized what Wolcott (1994) describes as the three classic modes that qualitative researchers use to gather data: interviewing, the analysis of documentation and participant observation. From January to June 1990, I helped to teach a full-time ESL course to recent immigrants in Ontario, Canada, which gave me access to a highly diverse and interesting group of language learners. In the second six months of that year, I invited the learners in this course to be part of the research, developed a detailed questionnaire for them to complete, and began initial interviews with the five women who agreed to participate in the three parts of the study. From January to June 1991, I conducted a diary study with the women, and thereafter (July to December 1991) did follow-up interviews and a second questionnaire. The sections below describe the two-year process in greater detail, highlighting how I sought to capture the relationship between identity and language learning.

January to June 1990: The ESL course

My first challenge was to find participants who were willing and able to take part in a long-term project. In most immigrant language training programmes in Canada, a teacher has access to learners for only a short period of time after the immigrant learner's arrival in Canada. If an immigrant is fortunate to be placed in a subsidized Employment and Immigration Canada (EIC) language training program, the teacher has access to learners for a maximum of six months,[1] thereafter, access to learners becomes increasingly difficult. Even in this six-month period, communication with learners may be particularly difficult if the teacher has no common language with the learners and the learners have only a limited command of English. Nevertheless, a course of this nature was the best means of gaining access to recently arrived language learners who were all living in relatively close proximity to one another. In January 1990, I was given the opportunity to participate part-time in an EIC language training program run by a community college, called Ontario College, in the town of Newtown in Ontario. My job was to teach the course one full day a week, in conjunction with the full-time instructor who taught the course for the remaining four days a week.

The ESL course was highly structured, and the learners were given a thorough introduction to English grammar and pronunciation. The full-time teacher was energetic and meticulous. As a team teacher once a week, I was asked to complement and reinforce what the students had learnt during the remainder of the week, but I was also encouraged to be innovative and to introduce my own materials into the classroom. At the conclusion of the six-month course, I told the learners that I was about to embark on a long-term project on the second language learning of adult immigrants. I informed them that they would each be invited to participate in the project, and that details of the project would be sent to them before the end of the year. At this point in the study, I did not know who might be willing to participate in the study, although a number did express considerable interest. I interviewed and tape-recorded each student about his or her plans for the following six months and asked them all to write a short essay on the following topic: 'Some people think that Canada is "a good country for immigrants". Do you think that this is true? Please explain.' I had chosen this topic with care because I wanted to gain some insight into the experience that these learners had had as immigrants in Canada. I knew that, when I used the topic in the study, I could gain insight into the learners' changing perceptions of immigrant life in Canada. In addition, by using the same topic, I would have the opportunity to determine to what extent their writing ability had developed over time. The same essay was written by participants in January 1991 (before the diary study began) and in December 1991, when the research project was completed.

July to October 1990: First questionnaire

The development of a detailed questionnaire aimed to secure information from each participant about the following areas: biographical information, language background, immigration information, accommodation, work experience, the English language course, language contacts, the extent of English usage, self-assessment of English progress, comfort levels in using English, the learning process and the students' perception of the relationship between language and culture.[2] All this information I believed would be useful in helping me to understand the respective histories of the participants, their particular social circumstances in Canada, and their progress in language learning. In the questionnaire, I asked the participants how they had found out about the EIC course, how much English they had learnt in the course and which specific skills (listening, speaking, reading, writing) had been developed, which activities (from the list provided in the questionnaire) they found most helpful in learning English, and how the course might be changed to facilitate learning. When developing this questionnaire, I was aware that some of the language might present a problem to the participants. I therefore pretested the questionnaire on advanced ESL learners as well as recent immigrants with limited command of English. On the basis of their recommendations, I modified the questions to ensure they would be as unambiguous as possible. For example, I revised the expressions *strongly agree*, *agree*, *disagree* and *strongly disagree* to the terms YES!, yes, no, NO! I used a variety of question types, including multiple-choice questions, fill-in-the-blanks, lists and open-ended questions. In the section on language and culture, I invited the participants to use their mother tongue if they chose to.

In November 1990, I distributed an information package to each of the students at a reunion of the ESL course, inviting them to participate in the study. The reunion was held at the home of the teacher who had taught the students full time. The reunion was not linked formally to the research project, although the full-time teacher had indicated to the learners that I wished to take the opportunity to invite their participation in a research study. The information package contained a letter which included a consent form, the questionnaire described above and a stamped, self-addressed envelope in which the participants could place their completed questionnaires. In the letter I indicated that the three parts of the study included a questionnaire, a personal interview and a diary study. The diary study was described as follows:

I would like to understand exactly how, when and where you use English; who you speak English to; what happens when you speak English. The best way to examine this is to ask you to keep a diary (a notebook) in which you regularly make comments about your experiences in learning English. I know that keeping a diary can take a lot of time. For this reason, there will be no rules about what you should write in your diaries or how much you should write. This will depend on what you are interested in and how much time you have. I hope that the project will run for 8 weeks. In addition, I think it will be useful for the people in the project to get together once a week or once every two weeks while the project is in progress. This will give you time to discuss the comments you have made in your diaries. I hope it will also give you the chance to improve your writing and speaking skills. We can meet at my house, which is in a convenient place for many of you. In addition, if you would like to meet individually at another place, this can be arranged. This part of the project will begin in the middle of January 1991.

Fourteen (eight women and six men) of the sixteen students completed the questionnaire, twelve agreed to be interviewed (seven women and five men), and five women agreed to participate in the diary study. Because the diary study was to be a major source of data, I decided at that point to focus my data analysis on the five women who agreed to be part of the diary study: Eva and Katarina from Poland, Mai from Vietnam, Martina from Czechoslovakia and Felicia from Peru. This approach provided an important focus for my data analysis and gave me the opportunity to concentrate my attention on a subset of language learners whose experience, Ng (1981) argues, has been largely unaccounted for because of their silence.

It is difficult to determine with confidence how the five women who chose to take part in the diary study differed from the other students in the ESL course, both male and female. It is possible, however, that the self-selection process could be understood in gendered terms. What distinguished the diary study from the other two parts of the study was the intimacy of the project as well as the time commitment involved. It is possible that the women in the course were more attracted to the writing of a diary on personal experience than the men were, an observation that is supported by much feminist research.[3] bell hooks (1990, p. 338), for example, describes how writing is paradoxically both a form of resistance and a form of submission for women who have few means to make their voices heard:

> Writing was a way to capture speech, to hold onto it, to keep it close. And so I wrote down bits and pieces of conversations, confessing in cheap diaries that soon fell apart from too much handling, expressing the intensity of my sorrow, the anguish of speech – for I was always saying the wrong thing, asking the wrong questions. I could not confine my speech to the necessary corners and concerns of my life.

With reference to the time commitment involved in the diary study, the women who volunteered for the diary study had generally fewer demands on their time than the remainder of the women in the ESL course. The volunteers fell into two categories – they were either working or studying part-time and had school-age children (Katarina, Martina, Felicia) or they were working full-time outside the home but had no children (Eva, Mai). The remaining four women in the course were either mothers in full-time paid employment or mothers of pre-school children, working full-time in the home. In their interviews and telephone calls to me, they indicated that their 'double days' gave them little opportunity to participate in other recreational or educational activities. They took on the responsibility for most of the domestic work in the home, as well as undertaking full-time paid employment or full-time child care responsibilities respectively. Access to this diary study then, and the symbolic resources it provided, must itself be understood with reference to patriarchal relations which structure double days for many women. Further, although the women who took part in the study may have appeared privileged relative to other immigrant women, they were privileged only in so far as their desires were not in open conflict with larger patriarchal structures. If the circumstances of their gendered lives changed, so too did their opportunities to learn English. As a particularly telling example of this, I note the case of Mai, who changed her status from single to married within a few years of her arrival in Canada. As I indicate in Chapter 4, at the time of her wedding, Mai was already expressing concerns that her opportunities to learn English would be limited once she was married. She indicated that her opportunities depended on the wishes of her husband and the extent to which he would let her study and work in the public world.

December 1990 to January 1991: Initial interviews

The initial interviews took place in the homes of the women, in December 1990 and January 1991, and lasted between 45 minutes and 3 hours. The interviews were tape-recorded and transcribed. In these interviews, I asked the women to clarify comments they had made in their questionnaires, and to respond to questions they had left unanswered. I also discussed the diary study with them, and explained what I hoped to learn from the project. I indicated that I hoped to be able to use the diary study to gain greater insight into their language learning experiences on a day-to-day basis, and the extent to which such experiences change over time and place. I also indicated to them that I hoped the diary study would provide some opportunity for them to get more experience in writing English, and in speaking it in our diary study meetings. All five women wished to make use of the opportunities that the project offered. During the initial interviews I also had the opportunity to gain some familiarity with the domestic lives of the women, as well as their immediate neighborhoods, more details of which will be given in Chapters 3 through 5. I was introduced to their partners and their children, and had the opportunity to talk informally to members of the family during the course of the visits. In Mai and Katarina's homes I was taken through family photograph albums of past and recent events in their lives. In Felicia's home I was shown the beautiful furniture that the family had brought with them from Peru, and which had been damaged as a result of the change in climate. I was generously offered refreshments at the home of each of the women, from espresso and cake at Eva's home to Chinese tea and cookies at Mai's.

January to June 1991: Diary study

From January to June 1991, I had the opportunity to return the hospitality of the five women at my house for the duration of the diary study. As far as transportation was concerned, Felicia had access to a car; Eva, Katarina and Martina were driven to my house by Martina's husband, while I gave them a ride home; Mai was picked up and dropped off by me. The initial meetings were scheduled as a weekly event for a total of eight weeks. The sessions took place in the evening – Friday nights and Sunday nights were considered the most suitable – and lasted approximately three hours. While our first meeting was held in the kitchen around a large kitchen table, our subsequent meetings took place in the living room where the chairs were more comfortable and the setting more intimate. After eight weekly meetings were over, I faced a delicate situation. On the one hand, I wanted to continue with the study, but didn't want any of the women to feel obliged to continue with the meetings, particularly since my letter of invitation had indicated that we would be meeting for eight weeks. I wanted to be sure that any of the participants could comfortably leave the group without feeling that they had let the group down. On the other hand, I didn't want the women to interpret my tentative attempts at closure as a summary gesture on my part to bring our meetings to a premature end. I decided at the end of eight weeks to simply thank the women for participating in the study, and indicated that, if anybody was interested in continuing with the meetings, I would be happy to join them. There was general consensus that the meetings should continue, but that we should schedule the meetings on a monthly basis. We thus met once a month for the next three months, making a total of 12 group meetings between January and June 1991.

Establishing a venue, schedule and transportation for the diary study proved a great deal simpler than deciding on a format for the diaries themselves. In the field of SLA research, a number of researchers have made use of diary studies to explore the process of second language learning. However, with the exception of Yu (1990), such studies[4] were introspective accounts of the learning of a foreign language: None of the diarists in question was learning the language for the purposes of remaining in the target language country for an extended period of time. Furthermore, all of the accounts except that of Yu (1990) were written in the mother tongue, and all but Brown's (1984) research involved the use of diaries by the researchers themselves in the process of language learning. Brown's study required participants, who were studying Spanish in an intensive formal program in the United States, to spend 15 minutes a day writing entries in their journals about their language learning experiences. Most of the entries referenced by Brown dealt with student responses to formal aspects of grammar teaching and the scheduling of the classes, though there were some hints of resistance by some students at being required to perform this duty. My diary study had a very different purpose as it invited participants to reflect on their language learning experiences, not only in the classroom, but in the home, the workplace and the community. The emphasis of the diary study was on what participants thought, felt and did, in response to different language learning situations and different encounters with speakers of the target language. The participants were encouraged to write as much and as often as they chose to. In addition, there was consensus that the diaries should be written in English, the target language, rather than the mother tongue. Although I had asked the women if they would prefer to use their mother tongues for their diaries, which would then be translated, they were adamant that they wanted practice writing in English, as well as regular feedback on their writing progress. In addition, they indicated that a translation of their diaries would not accurately reflect what they were trying to say. Furthermore, the participants were encouraged to share extracts from their diaries at our diary study meetings, so that the audience for their writing included other participants as well as me. I hoped that the opportunity to write for an authentic and interested audience would be a desirable feature for the participants in the study. Zamel (1987, p. 707) has written at length about research on the social context of writing development:

> This research has revealed what can happen to students when they are acknowledged, given numerous opportunities to write, and become participants in a community of writers. In classrooms in which risk taking is encouraged, trust is established, choice and authority are shared, and writing is viewed as a meaning-making event, students change as writers, adopt positive attitudes toward written work and demonstrate real growth in writing performance.

Although all the women had asked me what was expected of them in the diaries, I did not want to prescribe a right or wrong way of approaching the task. However, given my own research questions, I did wish to provide some guidance as to how they might proceed. I did this by articulating my objectives in written form and by responding to the diary entries that the women made. First, at the initial diary study meeting, I gave the women an introductory letter which outlined my interest in the project, and provided each woman with a chart on which she could record day-to-day activities that were conducted in English. I indicated that the chart might provide a starting point for further reflections which could be recorded in the diaries. (A new chart was given to each woman at each meeting.) After we had discussed the contents of the letter, I asked the women to consider under what conditions they had used English in the course of that particular day. Martina volunteered to share her experiences, focusing on her experiences of attending Church, listening to the sermon and singing hymns in English. She discussed how strange it was to perform such intimate functions in a second language. I used her discussion as an example of how the diary entries might be made, and I elaborated on this discussion in my letters to the participants in the subsequent two weeks. Second, I gave the women regular feedback on their diary entries. Sometimes I asked them to clarify or expand on issues that had been raised. For example, one of my comments to Katarina was as follows: 'Very interesting, Katarina! It would be nice to know more about some of the conversations you mention. For example, how did you find out about the Community Services job? Could you give more details about the interview? Who did most of the talking? What precisely did you talk about?' Similarly, a comment to Eva read as follows: 'Very interesting Eva! Please explain why you feel better when you don't have to do the heavy jobs and why this makes you want to talk more.' However, my comments did not only request clarification or amplification. I would often give words of comfort and support such as those I gave Mai: 'You're doing a FANTASTIC job, Mai! Don't let your brother tell you otherwise!' I would also comment on the quality of the women's writing. For example, to Felicia I said 'Very nicely written' and to Martina, 'Very clear and easy to understand, Martina.' There were times when I would ask the women to give me feedback on my comments. For example, a note to Mai was as follows: 'Your comments are very interesting, Mai. Is it useful for me to correct your writing as much as I have? Let me know.'

Within two to three weeks, each woman had developed a method of communication with which she felt most comfortable. Mai and Martina were the most prolific writers in the group and wrote long, detailed entries on a broad range of topics. Eva said that she liked to respond to questions that I had asked, and did not like to sit down and write without having something specific to say. Felicia enjoyed writing, but did not attend the meetings as regularly as the other women did. Katarina didn't write very much, though we did talk on the phone a number of times during the course of the study. In some respects, defining my own relationship to the women was even more complex than helping the women develop a format for their diaries. I wanted to create a supportive and intimate environment in which the women would feel sufficiently comfortable to discuss their desires, fears, joys and frustrations. This was one of the main reasons why the meetings were held in my home. I hoped that my home, as a private sphere, would facilitate the expression and analysis of personal and private experiences. At one level, I wanted the women to relate to me as another woman, functioning as a mother, wife and homemaker. I did not want my role as researcher to dominate my relationship with the women as I thought this might create too much distance between us. It was for this reason that I did not use a tape recorder at our meetings; I already had sufficient experience with the use of a tape recorder to know that some of the women felt uncomfortable discussing personal issues in their lives in the presence of a tape recorder. However, I occasionally took notes at the meetings when I wanted to remember direct quotes from the women.

Although I wished to avoid relating to the women as a 'teacher' within the context of the diary study, it was a relationship that could not easily be displaced since our initial relationship had been structured in an educational setting. Furthermore, I understood that one of the reasons why the women took part in the study was to take the opportunity to improve their oral and written English in a supportive environment. For this reason, I encouraged the women to read some of their diary entries to the group each week. This gave them the opportunity to develop their oral skills, and it gave the group the opportunity to examine and discuss the issues that had been raised. Sometimes, during the course of our meetings, I would discuss vocabulary and grammar issues with the women when they asked me for comments or when they were struggling to express themselves. I also attempted to make suggestions as to how they might improve their written expression. Correcting the women's work also gave me the opportunity to comment on what had been said in the diaries and to ask for clarification. As indicated above, my comments played an important part in influencing the direction that the diary entries took.

I do not know how well I succeeded in maintaining a balance between my diverse positions as friend, teacher and researcher. I wanted to apologize on those rare occasions when I corrected the women's pronunciation – even though I knew that pronunciation training was what they had requested. Sometimes, when I picked up my notepad in a meeting to record a comment that a woman had made, I almost felt as though I was undermining a friendship, betraying a confidence. I sometimes felt that my comments on the women's writing of their intimate and often unsettling stories were hopelessly inadequate. I found myself trying to compensate for what Britzman (1990) calls guilty readings by helping the women to find employment, write résumés, provide references and deal with immigration officials. In retrospect it is highly ironic that I should try to reconcile my multiple relationships to the women or attempt to resolve the conflicting tensions of being friend, teacher and researcher in our diary study meetings. I was simultaneously exploring the complexity of identity while trying to maintain an unambivalent relationship to each woman. It was a misplaced endeavor. Not all the women attended all the meetings and, as indicated above, some diaries were more detailed than others. However, the discussions that arose from the extracts that the women chose to read to the group were a rich complement to the written diary entries. During the course of the study, I also kept a journal of my reflections. My analysis of the diary entries and the subsequent discussions are the most important source of data for the study.

July to December 1991: Final interviews and questionnaire

In December 1991, six months after the diary study was completed, I had follow-up interviews with each of the women. At this time, the women rewrote the essay on immigration that they had written twice before – once at the end of the six-month ESL course in June 1990, and once at the beginning of the diary study in January 1991. I wanted to see whether the women's perceptions of immigration had changed over the eighteen-month period. I also took the opportunity to demonstrate to the women how much progress they had made in writing English over the course of two years. Furthermore, in December 1991, I developed another brief questionnaire that explored a few of the questions that had been asked in the first questionnaire. The purpose of this questionnaire was to investigate whether the participants' views on certain crucial issues had changed in the intervening period. The questions I was most interested in concerned the women's perceptions of what had helped them the most to learn English, under what conditions they felt comfortable or uncomfortable speaking English, and to what extent they still felt like immigrants in Canada. All the women except Eva completed this questionnaire in December 1991, while Eva, who was undergoing much change in her personal life, completed it in April 1992.

Data organization

After working on the project for two years and actively collecting and recording data for twelve months, I had accumulated hundreds of pages of data. I had data from the women's diaries, data from my own journal, data from individual interviews (which had been transcribed), data from the two questionnaires and data from the written essays. My next task was to organize these data in a way that would help me to understand the relationship between identity and language learning. As Wolcott (1994) suggests, a major challenge for qualitative researchers is not how to get data, but how to decide what to do with the data they get. The three ways in which he suggests data can be presented are defined as descriptive, analytical and interpretive, respectively. My study, and the presentation of data in this book, draws to a greater or lesser extent on all three presentation formats. To a lesser extent, in the voices of the women, the data speak for themselves; to some extent, an analysis proceeds from systematic comparisons and contrasts among the data, and to a greater extent I have sought to reach for understanding and explanation that goes beyond a limited conception of analysis. Thus organizing data is a theoretical task. On what basis would I choose which data to use, which issues to focus on, which stories to tell?

The first approach I took was to organize each individual woman's data into one composite file. There was a separate file for Eva, for Mai, for Felicia, for Katarina and for Martina. Each woman's file included the questionnaires, the essays, the diary entries (which had all been typed) and transcripts of the interviews. In order to help me focus on different parts of the data, I began to cross-collate the data. The first cross-collation of data was made on the basis of the different sites in which the women had the opportunity to practice English. I focused on the home, the workplace and the school respectively. I went through each woman's file, categorizing data that pertained to her use of English in each of these sites. I then collated these in the form of chapters on the home, workplace and school, respectively focusing on changes in the women's experiences across time. This approach helped me to understand the way language practices are structured within a particular social site, and how institutional relations of power in the home, workplace and school, respectively, offer different kinds of opportunities for as well as constraints on the practice of the target language. However, in adopting this approach, I tended to lose sight of the composite language learning experiences of each of the women across the different domains of her life. For example, I was not able to address in a satisfying way how a particular woman's investment in English and practice of English in the workplace intersected with her investment in English and practice of English in her home. Thus, although I could capture aspects of identity and language learning across historical time, I could not capture it across social space.

I then decided to write up a comprehensive chapter on each woman, one which would allow me to make cross-references across both historical time and social space. While completing this exercise, I looked for data that would help me to understand how the position of these language learners as female immigrants influenced their access to and practice of English. This was a very valuable exercise in that it gave me a comprehensive picture of each of my participants, and insight into their experiences as immigrant women in Canada. However, the chapters began to read like anecdotal narratives in which all observations became idiosyncratic. Under these conditions, while I could capture the complexities of individual experience, it was difficult to link individual experience to larger social structures. My next strategy was to categorize all the data that pertained to everyday experiences implicated in the production of gender and ethnicity. I wrote up a chapter on each of these issues respectively, drawing comparisons across participants. This was a valuable exercise in that it gave me the opportunity to examine how gendered and ethnic identities are structured across time and space, and how opportunities to practice English must be understood within this context. What was particularly interesting is that I found myself making comparisons and contrasts between the two younger participants in the study, Eva and Mai, and the three older participants, Katarina, Martina and Felicia. It became clear that the older women had very different investments in English from Eva and Mai because they had been professionally and domestically well established in their native countries prior to immigration and had arrived in Canada with children and spouses. The accumulated memories of their private and public lives in their native countries and their positions within their respective families had an important influence on the way they understood their relationship to the public world in Canada. This in turn influenced how they created, responded to and resisted opportunities to speak English.

While the focus on the production of gendered and ethnic identities was valuable, the limitation of this approach was that many language learning issues centered on the production of both gender and ethnicity. I found that at times making distinctions between gender and ethnicity became an artificial activity that oversimplified the discussion at hand. Indeed, as Lorde (1990) notes, to deal with one without dealing with the other is a distortion. Furthermore, as Ng (1987) notes, questions of gender and ethnicity are integral constituents in the organization of class relations and should not be abstracted from the larger social relations in which they arise: 'The fact that we can think of ethnicity and gender as separate social phenomena is itself a product of our kind of society which introduces an artificial separation between economic and social life' (p. 14). It was at this stage in the preparation of my data that I decided to organize the analysis by comparing and contrasting the experiences of the two younger women, Eva and Mai, with those of the three older women, Katarina, Martina and Felicia. This approach gave me the opportunity to investigate how the language learning experiences of the younger, single women who had not yet established themselves professionally compared with those of the older, married women who arrived in Canada with well-established professional histories. As well, the approach enabled me to investigate how opportunities to practice English are socially structured across space (the home and workplace) and across time (a period of twelve months).[5] Furthermore, by comparing the experiences of only two or three participants at a time, I hoped to do justice to the individual histories and changing identities of each of the women, while still being able to make interesting comparisons within and across the sets of data. While the European Science Foundation Project undertaken in Europe in the 1980s (Perdue, 1984, 1993a, 1993b) will be discussed in greater detail in the next chapter, it is interesting to note that using age as a principle of organization in my data was, to some extent, consistent with one of their central findings. As Perdue (1993b) notes:

> In a comparison of the lexical richness scores, it was found that learners in a position to benefit from everyday contacts acquired faster and more successfully. Propensity to benefit from contact could be defined: the learner who is younger, more educated in the source country, not married to a compatriot and with no children is likely to benefit from contact, at least as measured by vocabulary richness scores.

> (p. 264)

Comment

It is important to note that, while this study was not focused on literacy as such, it is informed by and may lend insight to recent research on literacy as a social practice. Such research is associated with scholars such as Barton and Hamilton (1998), Mitchell and Weiler (1991), Solsken (1993) and the New London Group (1996). As Barton and Hamilton (1998) note:

> The notion of literacy practices offers a powerful way of conceptualising the link between the activities of reading and writing and the social structures in which they are embedded and which they help shape. When we talk about practices, then, this is not just the superficial choice of a word but the possibilities that this perspective offers for new theoretical understandings about literacy.

> (p. 6)

What is particularly important for my study is Barton and Hamilton's finding, based on their research in Lancaster, England, that literacy practices, among other purposes, were regularly used to assert or create identity. They note the case of Harry, who had begun to write his life history as a way of asserting a sense of time and place, and June, Terry and Mumtaz, who documented their lives through photographs. The lengthy diary entries of Mai and Martina are reminiscent of Harry's literacy practices, while June, Terry and Mumtaz's investment in photographs mirrored the many occasions I pored over volumes of photographs in Mai's and Katarina's homes. The following observation by Barton and Hamilton (1998) speaks eloquently to the literacy practices that were central to my study:

> People's interest in documenting their lives very often extended beyond their own life, and was part of a process of situating themselves within the

wider context of family, cultural group, nation and even world history. In the case of minority cultural groups, or those who have been displaced, this can create a sense of identity.

(p. 241)

In Chapter 3, I provide a preliminary introduction to each of the five women, locating their stories in the context of other research on immigrant language learners, in general, and immigrant women in particular. In Chapter 4, I focus in greater depth on the stories of the two younger women, and in Chapter 5 on the stories of the three older women.

Notes

1. This program, currently under review, is now referred to as LINC: Language Instruction for Newcomers to Canada.
2. The questionnaire has many similarities with the information elicited from participants in the European Science Foundation project (see Perdue, 1984, pp. 268–74).
3. See Van Daele (1990) for a comprehensive examination of this issue.
4. See for example Bailey (1980, 1983), Bell (1991), C. Brown (1984); Cooke (1986); F. Schumann (1980); Schumann and Schumann (1977).
5. Note that while Chapters 3, 4 and 5 address the home and the workplace as sites of language learning, Chapter 7 addresses the language learning experiences of the women in the formal context of the school. Note further that in investigating how opportunities to practice English are socially structured across time, I need to draw on the participants' memories of language learning *prior* to the timing of the research project.

3

The world of adult immigrant language learners

In the ESF project, most studies of understanding have been linked to an awareness of, and concern for, the paradoxical situation that these learners have to cope with, namely, that they have to learn in order to communicate, whilst communicating in order to learn – and this in a racist society.

(BREMER, BROEDER, ROBERTS, SIMONOT AND VASSEUR, 1993, p. 154)

The international context

In his research on the development of community languages in Australia, Clyne (1991) describes patterns of immigration to Australia, in which migrants have sought to escape unjust or unstable social orders in Europe, Asia and South America. The waves of immigration coincide with key events in world history in the twentieth century, in which migrants and refugees from the Russian revolution (1917), the Second World War (1939–45), Soviet intervention in Hungary (1956), anti-Allende (1970) and pro-Allende (1973) forces in Chile, and ethnic Chinese from Vietnam and Cambodia (1975) entered Australia. Such massive displacements of people, not only to Australia but to other parts of the world, were commonplace in the twentieth century. A recent fallout from political instability was highlighted in the *Vancouver Sun*, in Canada, on 6 May 1999, which declared in bold headlines: '900 refugees from Kosovo expected to come to B.C.' Increases in international migration have precipitated a major new study, the International Metropolis Project, begun in 1995 and including over twenty countries from different parts of the globe.[1] The purpose of the Metropolis project is to examine the effects of immigration, especially on cities, and the extent to which government and non-government intervention has helped to facilitate the integration of immigrants into their new countries.

Researchers and teachers in the field of SLA come face to face with adults migrating from one country to another, many of whom are struggling with the challenge of learning the language of their new country. As a result, there is a growing body of research that addresses the provision of formal second language instruction for adult immigrants, including perspectives from community-based programs, workplace training, postsecondary education and family literacy programs.[2] A recent special issue of *Prospect*, published in 1998, for example, documents the challenges and successes of the Australian Migrant English Program, while a comprehensive collection of articles, edited by Smoke (1998), examines the relationship between politics and pedagogy in the North American adult ESL context. Research on the natural language learning of adult immigrants is, however, less prolific than research on formal language learning. Johnson (1992) indicates that there has been surprisingly little research on the language learning of adults within a sociocultural context, an area of investigation which, she says, merits more attention than it has received. Indeed, most of the much-cited literature that addresses natural second language learning of adult immigrants, such as that of Acton and de Felix (1986) and Clarke (1976) is based on speculation. Klein (1986), argues thus:

> Until a few years ago, spontaneous language acquisition remained a side issue in research; even today the bulk of second language investigations are addressed to guided learning. Moreover, students of spontaneous learning are chiefly preoccupied with child second language acquisition; very few of them deal with spontaneous learning in adults, or at an age when the first language is fully established.

> (p. 18)

As Klein notes, an obvious reason for the paucity of research on the natural language learning of adults is the accessibility of data: It is easier to conduct SLA research in the formal language classroom than the informal world outside it. Notwithstanding this bleak picture, however, there are a number of research projects on the natural language learning of adult immigrants that have received greater or lesser attention in the mainstream SLA literature. One such study was conducted at Harvard University in the USA in the 1970s and another, the European Science Foundation project, was conducted in five European countries in the 1980s. At approximately the same time, there was also a large-scale community ESL literacy study of Hispanic immigrant women in the USA that has received little attention in mainstream SLA research. While the Harvard study will be discussed in greater detail in Chapter 6, I will draw on the latter two studies to highlight important aspects of my study with immigrant women.

The European Science Foundation study

One of the most ambitious longitudinal studies on the SLA process of adults under conditions of immigration was conducted by the European Science Foundation (ESF) in the mid-1980s. A description of the study first appeared in 1984 (Perdue, 1984), with more recent description and analysis available in two volumes (Perdue 1993a, 1993b). As well, a particularly interesting aspect of the study on achieving understanding in intercultural encounters is addressed in a book by Bremer, Roberts, Vasseur, Simonot and Broeder (1996). The design of the research was to conduct a five-country, five-year coordinated comparative study of the spontaneous acquisition of a second language by adult immigrant workers. The study included five target languages, six mother tongues and ten interlanguages. The primary purpose of the study was to investigate the widespread existence of fossilized interlanguages and the processes and determining factors of second language acquisition. Most of the data analysis was based on 26 informants learning English, German, Dutch, French or Swedish. Data was collected through a mix of experimental tasks and naturally occurring or role-played and simulated interactions over a two-and-a-half-year period.

One of the important characteristics of the ESF Project was its focus on the larger social and political context in which language learners and target language speakers interact. Among other issues, it noted that adult immigrants are frequently subject to discrimination, which has a significant impact on social interaction. In addition, it addressed the fact that misunderstandings between target language speakers and language learners can occur because of different culture-specific assumptions about the way social interaction should proceed at both a verbal and nonverbal level. Thus, while the ESF project had three major questions, the one of particular relevance to this book is as follows: What are the characteristics of communication between native and non-native speakers of a language? This question was the central focus of the report written by Bremer, Broeder, Roberts, Simonot and Vasseur (1993) at the conclusion of the ESF project, and formed the foundation of the book described above.

The insights and findings from Bremer *et al.* (1993, 1996) are extensive, but two are particularly noteworthy. First, Bremer *et al.* propose a different conception of understanding than that associated with traditional SLA research. In contrast to studies which conceive of understanding as the purview of research on listening and reading, they argue that understanding is an active rather than passive skill, co-constructed by both learners and target language speakers (Bremer *et al.*, 1993, p. 153). They demonstrate that, if both parties actively participate in the negotiation of meaning, language learning is enhanced. They note, however, that in most inter-ethnic encounters, it is the learner who is expected to work to understand the native speaker, rather than the native speaker ensuring that the learner understand. Further, they make a useful distinction between a *misunderstanding*, in which both parties may be unaware that a difficulty has occurred, and a *lack of understanding*, which becomes more immediately apparent in an interaction. Second, Bremer *et al.* are centrally concerned with the paradoxical situation that adult immigrant language learners face in that they have to learn in order to communicate, and to communicate in order to learn – frequently under difficult sociocultural conditions. By extension, they argue that learners face the paradox that learning to behave appropriately in interaction can only be learnt through participation, but that the learner is likely to be assessed according to the way she participates. While such a Catch-22 situation can be alleviated with sustained contact with the majority community, they make the argument that opportunities for learning are frequently limited to bureaucratic and gate-keeping encounters in which learners are doubly disadvantaged by their limited competence in the target language as well as the power imbalance between the learners and their interlocutors. The authors demonstrate that difficulties of understanding can be managed successfully when there is a reduction of the asymmetry of the interaction and the overt establishment of shared knowledge. This is accomplished not only by pre-emptive action on the part of the target language speaker, but by a willingness on the part of the learner to demonstrate a lack of understanding. In either case, both parties need to ensure that understanding is achieved without loss of face.

While the ESF project was remarkable in both its objectives and outcomes, it did not focus directly on the relationship between identity and language learning. The biographies of the learners, included in the appendices of the ESF reports, provide thumbnail sketches of the learners, and the histories, memories and desires of the 26 informants were not central to the analysis. In my study I hope to demonstrate that important insights about language learning can be gained through a comprehensive analysis of the multiple identities of language learners in the different domains of their lives.

Literacy and Hispanic immigrant women in the USA

Rockhill's (1987a, 1987b) influential literacy study with Hispanic immigrant women in Los Angeles in the USA is distinguished from the ESF Project in its attempt to link the acquisition of English literacy to the daily lives and experiences of informants. Because Rockhill worked with a relatively large number of women (approximately 50), while my study is a smaller case study of 5 women, Rockhill's research provides a lens through which I can interrogate my findings on identity and language learning. The conception of literacy in Rockhill's study, like that of the Barton and Hampton study discussed in Chapter 2, is more than simply knowing how to read and write. As Rockhill (1987a, pp. 327–8) notes, 'Literacy is a social practice, as well as a discursive and ideological practice, and it symbolizes becoming "educated".' The women that Rockhill interviewed did not talk directly about illiteracy, they talked about not knowing English. Despite the fact that learning English was extremely difficult, given the material and social conditions of the women in the study, the women nevertheless expressed shame and guilt at not being able to communicate in English and blamed themselves for making little progress in learning English. Rockhill notes that, while all the women expressed the desire to go to school, to learn English, to become literate, they did not think of literacy as a right for themselves, although they perceived it to be a right for their husbands and their children. Even those women who were talented and highly educated put their own needs last in the family: Success for these women was interpreted to be the extent to which their children and husbands were successful, and they concentrated their energies on providing a better life for their families.

Rockhill's study provides a larger framework for my study because it investigates literacy as both a social practice and a gendered one. I demonstrate in this book that the way the women learnt English, their exposure to English, and their opportunities to practice English, were structured to a large extent by their identities as women. For example, in contrast to the older women, the young women in my study, who had no children, had fewer domestic responsibilities and more time and energy to devote to learning English and finding work that would give them access to English speakers. The older women, on the other hand, were torn by the demands of their domestic duties and their desire to learn English. Like the women in Rockhill's study, their own needs were always considered secondary to the needs of their families. In making the argument that second language learning is a gendered activity, I explore how the use of the mother tongue, the language of the private sphere, and the use of English, the language of the public sphere, intersect in diverse ways with the identities of the women and their practice of English. Rockhill's study, however, also contrasts with findings from my study in that knowledge of English, for my participants, was not synonymous with being educated: All the women in my study were relatively well educated. However, the concern for these women was that their education and experience had little social value in Canada, and hence gave them little access to the material resources they desperately sought. This had an important impact on their access to desirable social networks, their classed identities and their opportunities to speak English. Such an analysis is absent in Rockhill's work. Because my study, unlike Rockhill's, is a longitudinal one, and because my participants are able to articulate and reflect on their experiences in written form, I have been able to gain some unique insights into the production of their identities as immigrant women and language learners.

The Canadian world of immigrant women

Immigration in Canada is experienced differently by newcomers from diverse parts of the world, settling in different regions in Canada, and at different points in Canadian history. The multiple meanings of immigrant must be also understood with reference to the reasons why people immigrate to Canada, the experiences they have had before coming to Canada and the conditions under which they live in Canada. While Canada's policy of multiculturalism invites immigrants of different backgrounds into a country in which acceptance and respect is fundamental to government policy, there is recognition that some immigrants have been marginalized and subjected to discrimination. Immigrant women may be particularly vulnerable in this regard. Boyd (1992) demonstrates how some foreign-born women are frequently triply disadvantaged by their status as female, as foreign-born and by their origins or race. As a result, certain groups of immigrant women are frequently at the bottom of the socio–economic scale, particularly if they are recent arrivals or from Asian or Southern European countries. Furthermore, Boyd notes that even after living in Canada for a number of years, immigrant women are more than twice as likely as their male counterparts not to know an official language well enough to carry on a conversation. Not knowing an official language results in fewer job opportunities for these women. Even when immigrant women do find work, it tends to be in ethnically segmented low-paying occupations in which extensive oral interaction is not a requirement of the job. Seven out of ten immigrant women without knowledge of English or French are employed in service, processing and fabrication occupations (Boyd, 1992). In order to appreciate the specific experiences of Eva, Mai, Katarina, Martina and Felicia, I turn to an examination of Canadian research that helps to locate the stories of these five women in a broader sociohistorical context.

Ng's study of immigrant women in Vancouver

In the summer of 1978, Ng (1981) conducted a study to determine how immigrant women's experience is located in the social and economic context of Canada. In particular, Ng focused her research on the social processes whereby a person comes to be labelled as an 'immigrant', or an 'ethnic' in Canada. Ng makes the point that some landed immigrants are not considered to be ethnic, while others who have been in Canada for 50 years are still regarded as immigrants. Of importance to my study is Ng's finding that it is in the social organization of immigrant women's lives – how they are organized in relation to the social service delivery system, the labor market, the educational system – that immigrant women's ethnicity becomes a significant feature. As she argues,

An immigrant woman's ethnicity becomes consequential when she interacts with the rest of society, e.g. the bus driver, the cashier at the supermarket, or the social worker. The attribution then . . . draws on the fact that she looks different; that she cannot function adequately or conduct herself properly on such occasions. Her ethnicity is posited as a reason for her incompetence. This is the point at which ethnicity arises for the immigrant.

(p. 103)

Ng stresses the fact that differences between the immigrant women's experience in Canada and their home countries are not merely cultural differences. In their home countries, immigrant women conduct themselves in a competent manner, and their physical difference does not have the same degree of consequence for their interactions in the larger society. In Canadian society – or any new society for that matter – the adequate functioning of an individual assumes a commonsense knowledge of the organizational forms which determine how the society works. Ethnicity is enacted and recreated for immigrant women whenever contact is made with members of the larger society, and Ng notes that an immigrant women's ethnicity is reinforced when there is a disjuncture between how the everyday world works and her knowledge and understanding of it.

Cumming and Gill's Indo-Canadian study

While Ng was interested in the construction of ethnicity among immigrant women in Canada, Cumming and Gill (Cumming, 1990; Cumming and Gill, 1991, 1992) focused their research on the extent to which language education might better serve one population of immigrant women. Bilingual ESL literacy classes and child care services were offered free of charge, two afternoons per week, to a small group of Punjabi-speaking women at a community service agency in Vancouver. The researchers sought to ascertain the women's decisions to study ESL literacy, as well as their uses of literacy, English and Punjabi in their daily lives. Of interest to my study is the finding that none of the women had any English-speaking friends or acquaintances, despite the fact that they had been in Canada for an average of six (one to 13) years. Only one woman occasionally spoke to her neighbor in English and the one woman who had worked regularly said that she only occasionally spoke to the security guard or representative of the contracting company at her janitorial job. Occasionally, anglophones would speak to the women on the street about their babies. Thus, prior to educational intervention, the women had few opportunities to practice the little English they had. This observation led Cumming and Gill to challenge the prevailing view in Canadian language planning circles that opportunities to practice the second language will occur through informal contact with the majority society. Further, Cumming and Gill note that 'gender is a fundamental consideration to be accounted for in conceptualizing adult's motivation or potential to learn a second language' (p. 248). For many of the women in their study, the most important priorities were to take care of the family and household. Only after domestic commitments had been met could they indulge in the luxury of an education. In addition, it was the husbands – most of whom were competent English speakers – who took on the major responsibility of interacting with the public world, buying major purchases, dealing with public institutions, thereby further restricting the extent and quality of interaction that the women had with the majority society.

Goldstein's bilingual workplace study

In another part of the country, with a different group of learners, Goldstein (1996) conducted a critical ethnographic study of bilingual life and language choice in a multicultural/multilingual factory in Toronto in which the majority of workers were Portuguese immigrant women. The study raised questions about the assumptions that are often made about the way immigrant workers need to communicate in the Ontario workplace in order to fulfil their responsibilities at work. Of particular relevance to my study is the finding that the use of English was associated with more social and economic costs than benefits. At the factory, most of the production workers were Portuguese, and the Portuguese language functioned as a symbol of solidarity and group membership in what was akin to an extended family of line workers, in which workers referred to one another as sister, brother daughter. The use of Portuguese was associated with the rights, obligations and expectations members of the family had of each other at work – for example, to help keep the line up, to substitute for those in need. In order for women (whether mother-tongue speakers of Portuguese, Italian or Spanish) to gain access to the friendship networks on the line, they had to speak Portuguese, a minority language, rather than English, the dominant language of the wider Canadian community. Portuguese speakers who used English at work ran the risk of being accused of insulting members of their community and of jeopardizing their access to symbolic and material resources in the workplace. Goldstein argues that the value of friendship and assistance at work is not to be underestimated because workers need the help of co-workers in order to meet efficiency standards. As I will indicate in Chapter 4, this finding speaks directly to Mai's experience in the workplace.

As well, Goldstein argues that access to English must be understood with reference to the gendered structure and dynamics of the Portuguese family and the class position the workers hold in the Canadian political economy. Most of the Portuguese workers who were able to secure higher-paying jobs off the line were people who had access to English-speaking contacts and English literacy skills prior to joining the factory. This latter group consisted primarily of Portuguese men or women who had immigrated to Canada before the age of 16, and had access to anglophone schooling. Like Katarina's and Felicia's husbands, the Portuguese men had access to English speakers through the nature of their work in their home countries and/or in Canada while others had attended federally sponsored formal language training in Canada. The reasons why the women had not accessed such formal language training include resistance from their fathers because of the presence of so many boys in the classroom, domestic responsibilities, fear of going out at night and a lack of self-confidence. Goldstein notes that working-class women with only four years of schooling in Portugal saw nothing better than the line work that they did, work that is associated with the use of Portuguese.

Burnaby, Harper and Norton Peirce's Levi Strauss study

Another study, commissioned by Levi Strauss & Co. (Canada), highlights the challenges that immigrant women face in learning English in some Canadian workplaces. In the early 1990s, Burnaby, Harper and Norton Peirce conducted an evaluation of the ESL programs in three Levi Strauss garment factories in Canada.[3] The objective of the study was to evaluate the social impact of the English workplace programs on stakeholders in the three plants, plants that were staffed predominantly by women. The researchers found that the opportunity for the learners to practice their English was minimal. There was little evidence of social conversation on the factory floor, a situation exacerbated by the stressful nature of the piecework system, in which workers were paid in proportion to the amount of work they did rather than by the hour, and by the noise level in the plants, which made the wearing of ear-plugs mandatory. Supervisors had the most individual contact with line-workers, but they tended to communicate in formulaic English, sometimes referred to as Levi-English. Friendship networks were generally based on common language and English speakers would seldom socialize with non-English speakers. In the canteen, employees tended to sit with people who spoke a common language.

Further, many of the non-English speakers felt marginalized within the factories by virtue of their lack of command of English and the fact that they perceived themselves to be non-Canadian. For example, some said they needed to speak English to defend themselves against exploitation by supervisors who favoured the Canadians by giving them the easy bundles of jeans to work on; others said they felt like invalids because they could not speak English. Many did not access the opportunity to participate in the ESL program in their plant because their experience of marginalization kept them silent. In addition, the domestic lives of the workers intersected in a number of interesting ways with the women's investment in the ESL program, para-doxically leading many women to avoid participating in the ESL program (Norton Peirce et al., 1993). For many women, the workplace represented a release from the tedium of their domestic lives, and they did not want to do anything to jeopardize their independence. Thus some women were afraid that they might lose their jobs – and access to the few friends they had in Canada – if they took the ESL course and became distracted from the demands of production. Others were the sole breadwinners in the family and lived a hand-to-mouth existence. They wished to focus all their energies on earning as much money as they could to support their families, and were afraid that taking English classes would hamper their productivity by reducing the momentum required for piecework. Others did not want to attend the ESL class because their husbands did not want their wives to become more educated than they were.

Morgan's action research study with immigrant women

On a more optimistic note, Morgan's (1997) action research with immigrant women in a community-based ESL classroom in Toronto offers a compelling example of how ESL teachers can help address social iniquities in their classrooms. In providing a detailed account of his teaching of intonation to a group of predominantly Chinese immigrant women, he notes as follows:

> What stands out most in this activity is how the foregrounding of social power and identity issues seemed to facilitate greater comprehension of sentence level stress and intonation as strategic resources for (re)defining social relationships based on gender and ethnicity.

Drawing on critical research, he investigates how a common subject area such as pronunciation can have what he calls emancipatory potential. His central conclusion – that language teachers need to conceive of their students as having social needs and aspirations which may be inseparable from linguistic needs – is integral to my own study.

Biography, identity and language learning

To varying degrees, the European, American and Canadian studies cited above provide insight into the paradoxical position of immigrant language learners in relation to communication with target language speakers. On the one hand, immigrant language learners need access to the social networks of target language speakers in order to practice and improve the target language; on the other hand, they have difficulty gaining access to these networks because common language is an *a priori* condition of entry into them. What is absent from all these studies, however, are the voices of particular learners, their distinctive histories, their unique desires for the future. Such biographical insights are important in understanding the relationship between identity and language learning. As Weiler (1991) argues, while the category *women* references women of different races, classes and sexual orientations, the category *woman* is multiple, shifting and subject to change. By extension, *immigrant women* must not be understood as an undifferentiated group, united in their experiences of language learning, whether in the classroom or community. By drawing on the voices, histories and desires of five distinct and unique women, at a particular time and place, I have sought to develop an enhanced understanding of the relationship between identity and language learning. In this spirit, I provide below a preliminary introduction to each of the five women, an introduction that will be given greater depth and texture in Chapters 4 and 5.

Eva

When I first met Eva, I was struck by her friendly demeanor and generous spirit. Born in Poland in 1967, she finished high school and worked as a bartender before she left Poland at the age of 20. Before arriving in Canada in 1989, in the refugee class, she spent two years in Italy where she became fluent in Italian. She had also learnt Russian at school, and could understand what she called Czechoslovakian and Yugoslavian.[4] She knew no English before arriving in Canada. Eva immigrated because she wanted 'economical advantage' and chose to come to Canada because it is one of the few industrialized countries that encourage immigration. She came alone, with no family or friends, but did know one person in Newtown before she arrived. Fairly soon after arriving in Canada, Eva moved into an apartment with Janusz, a Polish man, having resisted the attention of other men who were not Polish. Eva explained that her choice of a Polish partner was not coincidental. 'For me, I prefer somebody from Poland, because this person can understand you better, the same way as they, instead of someone who is Canadian.' The home seemed to be a place of refuge for Eva and she was comfortable with her domestic situation. Very little English was spoken in Eva's home, though she did occasionally watch TV and listen to music on English radio stations.

When Eva arrived in Newtown, she found employment at what she calls the Italian store, which is situated in the heart of an established Italian neighborhood in Newtown. Eva herself lived in this neighborhood, as do many recent immigrants to Newtown, and was given the job because she was a fluent speaker of Italian. She was well liked at the Italian store because many Canadians of Italian background patronized the store, and liked to be served in Italian. Eva was very happy at the store, but was concerned because she wanted to learn English, and had little opportunity to practice English at work. She was pleased therefore that, after only two months in Canada, she managed to get a place in a language training programme at Ontario

College in Newtown. Eva reduced her hours at the Italian store and worked only one day a week, on Saturdays. After Eva finished the language course, she began looking for another job in earnest, at a place where she could become a more proficient speaker of English. She found employment at a restaurant in Newtown, Munchies, where she was the only employee who could not speak English fluently. Munchies is an upmarket fast-food restaurant situated in a trendy part of town. Eva was a full-time employee who performed a variety of jobs, the most important of which was to clean the store and prepare the food for cooking. Her experiences at Munchies will be more fully documented in the following chapter.

Eva was happy that she came to Canada. In response to the essay topic 'Some people think that Canada is "a good country for immigrants". Do you think this is true? Please explain', Eva wrote:[5]

> I do agree with those people's statement. I don't know what particular issues they have on their minds, but I can come up with some examples supporting this point of view. Canadian government gives money to programmes that help the immigrants develop the basic skills needed in settling down in a foreign country. The most important thing for a newcomer is to be able to communicate in English. Everyone interested in learning it has a variety of day or night courses offered by local schools. At the same time, a qualified immigrant can be financially supported by government so it is possible for an individual to devote most of one's time to learning process. Government also assists in finding jobs related to immigrant's previous positions. Overall Canada is a good country for immigrants because the government as well as ordinary people try to help during the difficult process of assimilating in a new country.

Eva felt that she has made a good deal of progress in learning English: 'I can communicate with outside world, I can be confident while talking to Canadians. Finally I can work in the place where speaking English is a necessity,' she wrote. To explain her progress, Eva drew a distinction between formal and natural sites of language learning: 'The English as a Second Language course helped me to learn the basics of English. Later, practicing English in everyday conversations helped me to be more fluent.' Nevertheless, she was well aware that opportunities to practice English were not readily accessible because of the social organization of Canadian society:

> I think it is difficult to have friends who would be willing to help to learn English. It is caused by the fact that social life doesn't offer many chances of meeting different people. Often conversations that are not connected with the place of work would certainly be very helpful in the process of learning English.

After two years in Canada, Eva reached the stage in which she could feel confident talking to Canadians and finding work in mainstream anglophone jobs. However, despite the fact that she understood the importance of practicing her English in order to become more fluent, she did not have much opportunity to meet Canadians outside her work situation. There is a disjuncture between the anglophone world and her own. As she said: 'At home I live in the Polish community.' This disjuncture is not only one of difference however. Despite the fact that Eva was able to communicate with the outside world, she still felt marginalized by it: 'Because of my distinguishable pronunciation I am viewed as an immigrant by others and therefore I still feel like one,' she said.

Mai

Like Eva, Mai was young, courageous and spirited. She was born in 1968 in Vietnam and arrived in Canada in October 1989, when she was 21 years old. She immigrated with her elderly parents 'for my life in the future'. Mai's father is Chinese, her mother Vietnamese, and Mai is fluent in both Cantonese and Vietnamese. She had no knowledge of English before coming to Canada. Mai has eight brothers and sisters, two of whom live in Canada. One of her brothers who lives in Newtown helped to sponsor Mai's immigration to Canada in the Family class. Before coming to Canada, she had not lived in any other country. Mai remained in her brother's home in Newtown from the time she arrived in Canada until the time she married in May 1992. At this time she moved to a neighboring city where her husband's family lived. In her brother's home, she left behind her brother, sister, three nephews and her mother and father. As I will discuss in greater detail in Chapter 4, a good deal of English was spoken in Mai's home because her nephews were all monolingual anglophones. However, unlike the situation for Eva, I demonstrate that home was not a place of refuge from the outside world.

Mai completed her high school education before coming to Canada, and had been trained as a dressmaker in Vietnam. Before starting the ESL course in January 1990, Mai worked for a short period at a packing factory in the Newtown area. Soon after she finished the ESL course, she found a job at a small garment factory in Newtown and worked there until she got married. Although Mai worked full-time, she also continued to take nighttime ESL courses at Ontario College. Initially, Mai's work in the garment factory gave her many opportunities to hear English and speak English. Mai says that the Canadian way of life makes it easy to learn English because 'with the life in here I need go to work. So at job I meet people. They all speak English.' Nevertheless, as I will indicate in Chapter 4, this situation changed dramatically when workers were laid off. Mai said that she ultimately hopes to return to college and study for a professional degree.

Despite the challenges that Mai faced in her first two years in Canada, she was happy she immigrated, writing as follows:

Canadian people are very friendly and helpful. It is a big country, there are a lot of companies, factories and farms with many kind of jobs. Don't need too much the knowledge of the English language or experience. People just come to Canada can find the job without too much difficulty. Also the Government of Canada is very caring about life of immigrants. It helps people go to school for six months. If someone is out of work they can go to Employment and Immigration Canada. More or less they will have some help from there to go though their hard times.

Mai noted that Canadian people have been friendly and helpful to her. She has had no difficulty getting a job because of her sewing skills; however, unlike the case for Eva, this kind of job was not dependent on a good command of the English language. She was also impressed with the social services provided by the Canadian government. Nevertheless, despite her positive comments on Canadians and the Canadian government, Mai noted that she still feels like an immigrant in Canada. Apart from her accent, Mai said that she did not have the features of a white Canadian, and was immediately recognized as different by strangers. For these reasons, Mai wrote that she would never be considered part of mainstream Canadian society:

I'm an immigrant in Canada. Even I'll be living in Canada for whole my life. Because I have a lot of things that completely different. Like the accent. Custom. Even sometimes people ask when they don't know me too well Are you Chinese? It makes me have more feeling that I'm immigrant, or Chinese Canadian citizen.

With reference to her learning of English, Mai expressed confidence that her English had improved significantly since her arrival in Canada: 'I'm able to read, write and speak English. I'm able to understand a lot of things that people talk with me, and I can talk with them whatever I need.' She indicated that what had helped her to learn English the most was 'the community, at work, watch TV and read the book or newspaper'. Like Eva, Mai felt comfortable speaking English to her friends or anglophone members of her family and felt uncomfortable speaking English with people she didn't know and with people she considered her superiors, such as her boss at work. However, it is significant that Mai also indicated that when she had personal domestic problems, she felt uncomfortable using English:

I feel comfortable using English most of the time except when I have some problems because by that time the problem's always in my mind. It makes me feel uncomfortable to use English.

Katarina

Katarina was born in Poland in 1955 and arrived in Canada in April 1989, with her husband and child, a daughter Maria, aged six at the time. The family immigrated to Canada because they 'disliked communism' and the family's immigration, in the refugee class, was sponsored by the Catholic church. Before coming to Canada, the family spent a year in Austria. Apart from her mother tongue, Polish, Katarina had a limited command of German and Russian when she arrived in Canada. Although Katarina had no knowledge of English, her husband was reasonably fluent as he had worked in international trade in Poland and had used English in his job. When the family arrived in Newtown, they stayed at a sponsor's home for a temporary period before renting a two-bedroom apartment in the same building in which Eva lived. In Poland, Katarina was a teacher with a Master of Arts degree in biological sciences; her husband is similarly qualified. When she first arrived in Canada, she worked full time at a German restaurant as a kitchen help for a period of eight months and then, after the ESL course, found part-time work as a homemaker for an organization called Community Service. In this job she had the opportunity to speak English on a regular basis. In September 1990 she began an English upgrading course to give her further practice in learning English, but switched over to a Grade 12 ESL course in early 1991. After receiving her Grade 12 ESL credit, she began an 18-month computer course, graduating in December 1992. Her plans for the future are to find a good, well-paying job.

Katarina wrote that many people feel good in Canada, a place where there is much diversity in the population:

> Most people feel good in Canada. A great deal of people came here after the Second World War but many came here in last years. Most of them had spent one or two years in Austria, German, Greece or Italy. Austria is a beautiful country but only to visit but not to live in. Another nationality person doesn't feel good in that country because most of people there are people who were born there. Immigrants feel good in Canada because they are aware of various nationalities. In Canada life has a high standard. The Government gives possibility for people to study. The mothers with children but without husbands have help from the government. People who aren't able to work or can't find the job receive social welfare. I think that Canada is a 'good country for immigrants'.

Despite the high standard of living in Canada and the support given by the Canadian government to immigrants, Katarina was nevertheless ambivalent about her immigrant status and unsure whether or not she has been accepted into mainstream Canadian society. She felt at a great disadvantage in Canada because, although she is well-educated, she was not a fluent speaker of English, nor did she have the financial backing to devote all her time to learning English: 'In my native country I was a teacher. I studied 17 years. I am not able to be a very good speaker of English because I need five to seven years to study English and I am short of money.'[6] She noted that a good education and knowledge of English give people options in life – the choice, for example, of doing a variety of jobs: 'The life is easier when somebody can communicate with other people, can explain exactly what somebody is thinking, can do another job than have to do, because some-body has good education and is a good speaker of English.'

However, Katarina was happy that she had made much progress in learning English and was able to speak with Canadian people, read the newspaper, listen to the radio, watch and understand television. She initially placed great faith in formal language learning to help her become a good speaker of English. In December 1990 she indicated that teachers – and textbooks – had helped her the most to learn English: 'Very important is a teacher. The second place has a textbook.' A year later, however, Katarina had changed her position a little. While still acknowledging the value of ESL courses, she also stressed the value of speaking with people and taking courses that weren't devoted solely to language instruction. Like Eva and Mai, Katarina felt comfortable speaking English with friends, but was less comfortable when talking to professional people such as 'my teacher; the doctor' noting in addition, 'I feel comfortable using English when I speak with one person or in a small group of people. I feel uncomfortable when I speak in a large group of people.'

Martina

Martina was born in Czechoslovakia in 1952 and came to Canada in March 1989 when she was 37 years old. She was accompanied by her husband Petr and her three children (Jana 17, Elsbet 14 and Milos 11 at the time). She came to Canada for a 'better life for children'. Before arriving in Canada, Martina spent 19 months in Austria and one month in Yugoslavia. Although Martina's mother tongue is Czech, she also learnt Slovak and Russian at school. When she was in Austria waiting for a visa, she learnt to speak German. Neither she nor her husband knew any English before she came to Canada, but her children had received some English language training in Austria. Martina and her family, officially classified as refugees, were sponsored by the Catholic church. They came to Newtown because this is where the sponsor found an apartment for them. The apartment was in the basement of a house and was noisy and very expensive. After a year, Martina and her family found a two-bedroom apartment in the same building in which Eva and Katarina lived. They remained there for a year before they moved to Winchester in July 1991 where Petr had found a job.

In Czechoslovakia Martina had a professional degree as a surveyor. When Martina arrived in Newtown she worked at Fast Foods as a cook help but left this job when she started the ESL course. Since Martina left the ESL course she attended an English skills course for the duration of the 10-month course, after which time the family moved to Winchester. In Winchester, Martina found a job as a cashier at a local community college, and took a part-time course as a tax preparer. She graduated top of her class. In the future Martina said she would like to get a challenging job, but was unsure of her prospects.

In December Martina indicated that the difficulties she was experiencing in finding a good job could be explained by her limited English skills: 'I'm not afraid about a work, and if my English is now better, maybe I'll be lucky and find a good job.' A year later, however, Martina began to think that knowledge of English was not enough to secure her the kind of job she wanted, stressing the employer's desire for Canadian experience: 'I'd like work as a surveyor or some other job, where is a lot of math. I thought that for getting this job I need more English, but now I am not sure, because everybody asks for Canadian experiences and references.' Martina's husband Petr, who is a plumber, has also had great difficulty finding a job in his profession, and has been laid off work on a number of occasions. This has come as a great shock to Martina's family because they never had to face the prospect of unemployment in Czechoslovakia: 'It is very different, because everything has different rules. In my country, everything is owned by the government, and almost every application goes to the government. We never were dreading that we can lose a job if we worked hard.' Very little English was spoken in Martina's home, and her jobs gave her little opportunity to practice it in the workplace. Furthermore, in the community in which she lived, there were few English speakers: 'For me is very big problem speaking, and if there are a lot of immigrants in Newtown, then is a small chance talk and correct all sentences.' She indicated, however, that she had made progress in learning English and was able to perform numerous tasks in English.

Martina was ambivalent about the family's decision to come to Canada, writing that they have had both good and bad experiences in the country: 'Some people are very friendly and helpful, but on the other side, some people take advantage of us.' Nevertheless, despite unpleasant experiences in Canada and job insecurity, Martina still thinks that Canada is a good country for immigrants. With 'capability and courage' a hardworking person should be able to make a successful life for themselves in Canada:

> Even though the economic situation is not good at this time in the whole world, I think that Canada is a good country for immigrants, especially for hardworkers. Canada is a very big country and if you are young you can move from one place to another and find a place according to your own imagination. First of all you must learn English to understand and to speak with the people, then if you cannot find a job in your profession you might take some courses and later on get a better job depending on your capability and courage.

Martina said that she still feels like an immigrant in Canada, someone less worthy than other Canadians: 'Because of my accent some people treat me as less worthy than they are (especially when I was looking for a job)' she wrote. Martina thought that people would treat her differently when she became a good speaker of English because 'some Canadians are fed up with people who are not able to communicate well in English'. She said that she never felt comfortable speaking English because she could not explain things as competently as she could in her mother tongue, noting, in addition, 'I feel uncomfortable using English in the group of people whose English language is their mother tongue because they speak fluently without any problems and I feel inferior.'

Felicia

The eldest of the five women, Felicia was born in 1945 in Lima, Peru. She arrived in Canada as a landed immigrant in March 1989 with her husband, who had a professional visa, and her three children, two elder boys aged 16 and 14, and a little girl aged six at time of arrival. They came to Canada because 'The terrorism was increasing in Peru'. Of the five women in the study, Felicia had lived the most opulent lifestyle before coming to Canada, was the only woman who knew some English before coming to Canada and had travelled to North America before immigrating. Her family had lived in an exclusive neighborhood in Lima and owned a beach cottage where they regularly went for weekend getaways. When the family arrived in Canada they came to Newtown because 'Newtown is like the place we used to live'. They lived in a three-bedroom apartment in a middle-class neighborhood where most of the people – predominantly elderly people – speak English as a first language. In 1992 they bought a house of their own in Newtown.

Felicia's mother tongue is Spanish, but she can understand some Italian and Portuguese. Her husband and two sons were good speakers of English before coming to Canada because they had attended private English-medium schools in Peru, and her husband had used English in his job. Her little girl Maria soon learnt English in the public elementary school she attended, but Spanish is still the language used in the home. Felicia had been trained as an elementary school teacher in Peru, although she had given up this job when she had children. Here in Canada she has had only part-time positions, delivering newspapers and babysitting at the Fair Lawns Recreational Center. In the future she hopes 'to study some career'.

Felicia and her family were under a great deal of emotional and financial stress in Canada because Felicia's husband was unable to find a job in his profession in Canada. Although he applied for countless positions and was interviewed many times, he struggled to find suitable employment. Felicia attributed their difficult position to the fact that Canadians discriminate against immigrants. Felicia was the only one of the five women who stated unequivocally that she was unhappy the family had come to Canada, writing as follows in June 1990:

> At the moment, I think the life is very quiet her, and very organized. But we haven't found yet our way in this country. Sometimes, I perceive that some Canadians look down at the immigrants. I don't know why, if ALL Canadians came from other countries too. Canada is formed from immigrants. I think that the authorities of the Canadian consulate should tell the truth about the difficulties to get a job for a person who has a very good preparation and experience in his profession. Canadians think that here there isn't discrimination, but I don't think so. I hope that, in the future, I could change my mind.

A year-and-a-half later, Felicia had not changed her mind. She stated in December 1991 that professional people who immigrate have a much more difficult time in Canada than immigrants who have lived under communism or lived in poverty. These people can 'work in any kind of work', said Felicia, arguing that it is difficult for wealthy people to have the kind of lifestyle they lived in their home countries, and it is difficult for them to return to the home country once the children have settled down. For Felicia, the only strength that Canada has is that it is a relatively peaceful, law-abiding country:

> Canada can be a good country for some kinds of immigrants; people who lived in countries under communism are happy here or people who never had anything in their countries. Here, they can work in any kind of work and get things. But professional people and wealthy people lose a lot coming to Canada. They are not welcome here as the Canadian Consul told them in their countries. They spend a lot of their money here and is not easy to come back when they have children looking for their way in life. Opportunities are very difficult to find for them, and life goes without emotion. The only thing I find is good, is that there is no terrorism and many thiefs here.

Felicia's disappointment over their immigrant experience led her to resist any identification with Canada. She strongly resisted being labeled an immigrant and sought refuge in her Peruvian identity. Wealthy Peruvians living in Canada were her reference group and she considered herself a 'foreigner person who lives here by accident':

> I've never felt an immigrant in Canada, just as a foreigner person who lives here by accident and I'll never feel Canadian, because I don't think that Canada is a friendly country. Canada only brings people because it needs them, not because it wants to help them.

Nevertheless, Felicia indicated that her English had improved since her arrival in Canada and, recognizing the need for what she called 'practice, practice, practice', she organized regular meetings in her home with a Canadian woman who wanted to learn Spanish. She noted that listening and speaking at her work helped her to improve her English, writing that 'it has been good for me to listen every day to the ladies who work with me'. Like Mai, however, she said that it is sometimes hard for her to learn English 'because I live here with many tensions. I have to do too many things too and I don't have enough time to study'. Like Eva, Mai and Katarina, Felicia felt comfortable speaking English to anglophone friends, but was uncomfortable speaking to strangers: 'I feel comfortable or almost comfortable with people that I know very well. I feel uncomfortable with people that I don't know'. She indicated, in addition, the importance of feeling confident in order to speak English. Such confidence, however, was absent when she was in the presence of Peruvian people who could speak English well:

> I feel comfortable using English with people I know and have confidence with them, especially with the lady who I meet each week to practice English and Spanish conversation. I feel uncomfortable with new people and never can speak English in front of Peruvian people who speak English correctly.

Comment

It is important to note that all five women in the study were good language learners. The very fact that they all took the opportunity to participate in the diary study is indicative of their desire to gain regular exposure to English and practice in English. While all the women had a strong drive to communicate, the data indicate, however, that all of the women had difficulty speaking under conditions of marginalization. If they felt inferior, they felt uncomfortable speaking. This is not to say that the learners had inhibited personalities, or were not willing to make mistakes (Rubin, 1975). Most often, the women felt marginalized because they felt positioned as immigrants and not because of invariant personality traits. They did not feel different but equal to their Canadian peers; they often felt, in Martina's words, 'less worthy' than Canadians. The women were thus sensitive to the social relations of power in their daily interactions and only felt comfortable speaking in the company of friends who knew them well.

A common theme running through these stories (apart from those presented by Felicia) is that all the women think that the Canadian government is generous towards immigrants and provides adequate social security in times of hardship. Eva, Mai, Katarina and Martina made distinctions between formal government policy and their day-to-day experiences of interaction with Canadians. As noted by Martina, 'Even though the economic situation is not good at this time in the whole world, I think that Canada is a good country for immigrants especially for hardworkers.' They all recognized that the Canadian government has a generous health and social welfare system and puts substantial resources into providing language training for certain classes of immigrants. Further, many of the negative experiences the women had in Canada related to economic conditions: Eva had difficulty finding a job, there were cutbacks at Mai's workplace, Katarina and her husband could not find jobs in their professions, Martina could not find a job in her profession and her husband was laid off work, and neither Felicia nor her husband could find jobs in their professions. For this reason, the symbolic resources that the women had brought with them to Canada were not validated in the places where they did find work. If they had managed to find work in their professions (and this is particularly true for the older women), they might have had easier access to anglophone social networks, and hence greater opportunity to speak and practice English.

In Chapter 4 and Chapter 5, respectively, I turn to an in-depth analysis of the stories of the two younger participants, Eva and Mai, and the three older participants, Katarina, Martina and Felicia. Although I recognize the multiplicity of each woman's identity, I have sought to capture what for me were particularly salient identities with respect to each woman's investment in English. It is important to note, further, that the stories these women have told are *their* stories. I have taken seriously their interpretations of events and their understanding of cultural practices in Canadian society. I have sought to understand the world as they have understood it, and have not questioned whether their interpretation of events was the correct or true interpretation. Since I have sought to understand identity and language learning, it has been necessary for me to understand the world as the language learner understands it.

Notes

1. See the website: www.international.metropolis.globalx.net
2. See Auerbach (1997), Benesch (1996), Burnaby (1997), Morgan (1997), Roberts, Davies and Jupp (1992), Wallerstein (1983).
3. See Burnaby, Harper and Norton Peirce (1992); Harper, Norton Peirce and Burnaby (1996); Norton Peirce, Harper and Burnaby (1993). It is important to note that, while these publications documented practices current at the time, a number of changes were taking place in these workplaces, particularly with regard to the use of the piecework system.

4. Eva made no distinction between Czech and Slovak, or between Serbian, Croatian, Slovenian and Macedonian.
5. Minor corrections, particularly those which impede comprehension, have been made to the writing of the participants.
6. Although Katarina and her husband did not have much disposable income, they nevertheless used the resources they had to upgrade her qualifications, with a view to securing skilled work in the future. (See Chapter 5.)

4

Eva and Mai: Old heads on young shoulders

We children, not rooted to white stolen land, must find our rest in small spaces, our home in small secure places of our own making.

(YEE, 1993, p. 19)

Both Eva and Mai made great progress in learning English, but in different ways and for different reasons. In this chapter I draw on my understanding of the lives and experiences of these two young women to examine the relationship between investment, identity and language learning, showing in particular how the construction of identity in one site, the home, intersects with the construction of identity in another site, the workplace. With respect to Eva's experience at Munchies, I demonstrate how she was initially marginalized and silenced because her symbolic and material resources were not valued in the workplace. This marginalization is explained with reference to the job Eva did, her limited command of English and ethnocentric relations of power. It was only after a period of months that Eva gradually gained acceptance and respect from her co-workers, and with it access to the anglophone social networks that gave her increased opportunities to speak. How and why these changes occurred is discussed in detail. With respect to Mai, I describe the language patterns in her home environment, demonstrating how they are best understood in the context of larger patriarchal, material and racist social structures. I suggest that her investment in English must be understood with reference to her desire to resist the patriarchal structures in the home and to redefine her identity in the private domain of her life. I examine how and why Mai's workplace offered opportunities for Mai to practice English, and how changes in the language practices in the workplace accompanied changes in the language of power, together with Mai's opportunities to practice English. How these changes in turn represented a threat to Mai's identity in the home and workplace, and to her investment in English, is addressed.

Eva

'I have the same possibilities as Canadians.'

Eva's investment in English must be understood with reference to her reasons for coming to Canada, her plans for the future and her changing identity. She had come to Canada for economic advantage and hoped ultimately to go to university to study for a degree in business. She knew that she needed to be a good speaker of English in order to work where she wanted to work, to go to the university of her choice and to rid herself of an immigrant identity. In other words, she valued English for the access it gave her to the public world – or what she called the outside world. Because she had no children and few domestic responsibilities, Eva could devote her time to pursuing her career goals in Canada.

Eva's home: A place of refuge

While Eva had a great deal of investment in learning English, she wanted the private domain of her life to be Polish. As indicated in Chapter 3, Eva had chosen to live with a Polish partner because she felt he would understand her better than an anglophone Canadian would. Most of her friends were Polish, and she describes herself as living her private life 'in the Polish community'. Although she did watch English TV and read English newspapers in the home, she always spoke Polish to her partner. As she said, 'You cannot speak with a Polish person in English. It doesn't – it's not – if you try, you always change because it's too difficult and it's easier for you to say it in Polish.' Her home within the Polish community was a place of refuge for Eva, where she was respected and well liked, and where she could lead a relatively independent lifestyle.

Eva's workplace: From immigrant to valued co-worker

The workplace – Munchies – was the only place where Eva had regular exposure to English and practice in English, as she was the only non-English speaker and the only recent immigrant to Canada. All the other employees, worker and management, were anglophone Canadians. Because the workplace was a fast food restaurant, the primary activities were the following: Workers had to take orders from customers, pass these orders on to other workers, take cash from customers, prepare food, clean the restaurant (tables and floors), keep supplies current and communicate with management. The only activity that was not dependent on spoken interaction was cleaning the restaurant and preparing food and drinks. All the other activities required a reasonably good command of English.

Eva left the comfort and security of the Italian store because she wanted to practice speaking English. However, when Eva started working at Munchies, she was given 'the hard jobs' to do, such as cleaning the floors and tables, clearing out the garbage and preparing the drinks. Not only was this solitary work in which she had little contact with anglophones ('I'm just alone and everybody doing something else – who can I talk to?'), but it was considered a job for 'stupid' people. Although Eva was in an anglophone environment, in contact with anglophones, she neither had access to the social networks within the workplace nor access to customers who spoke English. The process by which Eva finally gained access to social networks in the workplace and access to customers was a long and arduous process, intricately bound up with issues of social power. I will discuss, in turn, Eva's exclusion from the anglophone social network among her co-workers and access to customers who patronized the store, the process whereby she gained acceptance into the social network, and the privileges that accrued to her as a result of her acceptance in the workplace. I will link the analysis to Eva's opportunities to practice English.

Exclusion from anglophones in the workplace

Eva understood that, in order to practice English, she had to become part of the social network within the workplace: she had to form social relationships and affiliative links with her co-workers. However, the social network was structured in such a way as to privilege those workers whose material and symbolic resources were valued in the workplace. These were the workers who had the 'better' jobs in the store and fluency in English. Eva felt inadequate with respect to each of these resources. Eva had 'the heavy job', a job that nobody wanted to do, a job that carried little status in the workplace. As a result, she felt her co-workers had little respect for her and did not interact with her.

> E.[1]   I think because when I didn't talk to them, and they didn't ask me, maybe they think I'm just like – because I had to do the worst type of work there. It's normal.
> B.   Why is that, Eva?
> E.   When I started to work there I was on ice-cream and I had to clear out the garbage and nobody wants to do that.

Eva had a perceptive understanding of the relationship between the work she did and the standing she had in her workplace community. As a person who had 'the worst type of work' clearing out the garbage, she felt she could not claim the right to speak to her co-workers. She explained that a person who had the worst type of job was assumed to be a 'stupid' person with little contribution to make to her community.

B. I think I asked you in one letter why their [the co-workers'] respect is important to you. Why were you even worried about whether or not they respect you?

E. I don't want like somebody takes me for a stupid person. Who just came and doesn't know nothing and cleans the floor –

The relevance of such relationships for language learning is clearly articulated by Eva in the following words:

When I see that I have to do everything and nobody cares about me because – then how can I talk to them? I hear they don't care about me and I don't feel to go and smile and talk to them.

Eva takes it for granted that, since she is the person with the most undesirable job, her fellow workers would have little wish to speak to her. They would assume that she is 'stupid', and 'knows nothing'. As Eva says, because her co-workers do not appear to care about her, she herself does not have the confidence to 'smile and talk' to them. The lack of opportunity to practice her English is thus partly structured by social relations of power which exclude unskilled workers, supposedly uneducated workers, from language practices in this particular workplace. However, the picture is even more complex than this. At a later stage in the data collection process, Eva made the point that one worker at Munchies had said: 'I don't like working with people who aren't Canadian.' The fact that Eva was an immigrant with the 'worst type of job' exacerbated the marginalization she initially experienced at Munchies. It is important to note, in addition, that Eva's marginalization had a marked impact on her identity, which in turn limited her opportunities to practice English. Because she did not feel positive about her job, herself and her relationship with others, she could not enter into conversations with fellow workers – indeed, she was not welcome in the social network. Significantly, Eva's high 'affective filter' (Krashen, 1981, 1982) was not an invariant personality trait, but one that was produced within the context of inequitable relations of power in the workplace. Furthermore, Eva had only limited fluency in the English language and could not make herself understood with ease. As she wrote,

[Munchies] was the first place that I had to be able to communicate in English. I was having a hard time with understanding, speaking and making conversation with somebody. Many times we were having a break together and they were talking about something. Sometimes I didn't understand the topic and many times if I did understand, I didn't know enough correct words to take part in conversation. Having trouble while speaking in English, I meant the time when I said something and the other person couldn't understand me. Having trouble making conversation – the reason it's the same, my vocabulary was too poor to talk to somebody or to start a conversation.

Eva was in the Catch-22 position discussed in Chapter 3. She needed to have command of English in order to gain access to the social networks in the restaurant, but she couldn't develop fluency without access to these social networks. Thus her limited opportunity to practice English was, paradoxically, also structured by her limited ability to speak it. It is important to note, in addition, that Eva's exclusion from the social network in the workplace created the conditions for her exploitation.

> During my day at work we have half an hour break. We are talking about the things which we have to do, and the plans for the day. If we have time left we talk about other things. But usually I don't talk very much, because the subject is unknown to me, or it's very stupid, that I wouldn't talk about it. I think that I should explain it. Another girl which works with me is nineteen years old, and she is little crazy. She talks all the time, and as I wrote the things which she talks about are very stupid. All the workers are listening to her, and laughing with her. But even if she has to do something, she goes and repeats everything to everybody. Instead of her, I have to do everything. They take advantage, because they know that I wouldn't say anything. . . . After a while, when I started to feel more comfortable in English, they didn't notice it. I think they didn't want to notice it. They needed somebody to work while they were talking. They were keeping me busy all the time.

Part of the reason why Eva's exclusion from the social network was tantamount to exploitation was her inability to use English to defend her rights. She was acutely conscious of the fact that 'they takes advantage of me, because they know that I wouldn't say anything'. Even when Eva became more proficient in English, Eva felt that her co-workers did not think it was in their best interests to recognize it. The social network represents power. Through a process of marginalization, the social network can ensure that undesirable forms of work are done by those who do not have access to the dominant social network in the workplace or the language of power. Under such conditions, Eva's rights were not respected. Eva was particularly frustrated by the fact that her co-worker Gail, who was a contemporary (if a few years younger than her), colludes in this oppression. They both had similar job descriptions, but there was no solidarity between them. It was very disturbing for Eva that the other workers added insult to injury by respecting Gail more than they respected her. Like the women in Rockhill's (1987a, 1987b) study, despite her best efforts, Eva felt bad that she had the worst job in the store and was ashamed of her English.

Initially, Eva's access to anglophone customers was as limited as her access to her co-workers. The managers at Munchies had little confidence that Eva could deal with the customers, and would only give her access to the customers if they had no choice. When Eva was given the occasional opportunity to work on cash, her manager would hover around and make Eva anxious. This in turn would lead to errors in her work. Once again, Eva's high affective filter was not an invariant personality trait but one that was constructed within inequitable relations of power that limited her ability to speak.

> E. When I'm at the cash – when somebody goes for the summer – I take the order but the manager she comes and she listens and then I feel like – she's watching for my mistakes and I already do some mistakes when I say something.
> B. You mean that makes it worse? You think that makes you nervous?
> E. Mm – hmm.

Eva's anxiety, however, also arises from her inability to perform both an oral and a literate task simultaneously, that is, to speak to the customers and to write down their orders at the same time. Workers at Munchies are expected to perform both tasks successfully, a real-time task which, Norton Peirce, Swain and Hart (1993) have demonstrated, is a particularly threatening one.

> They [management] – are worried that I might – that my job is not good enough. I wouldn't speak to the customers because I wouldn't feel confident to speak to the customers, because I do not have enough time to speak to them. And when for example Gail, she's like 'oh hello, how are you?' she's a little like this way – and she says something to everybody. But I don't have time to talk about –

Significantly, however, Eva's lack of confidence and high anxiety does not detract from her investment in learning English. She is not unmotivated to learn English. Despite her beleaguered identity, she has no desire to return to the Italian store, where people respected her work and where she felt comfortable and confident.

> It's – I feel at the [Italian] store – I do not worry about it – how I feel there. I have my job and I, they gave me the important job. They made me that I do this job well. But there [Munchies], when it's busy I have to do drinks. I have no company. They don't want to put me with the people, just sometimes when they have to, when they had no choice.

Gaining access to anglophones in the workplace

After a period of months, Eva had managed to penetrate the boundaries of the social network at work, and also developed confidence dealing with the customers. This success can be partly explained with reference to the kind of activities that the workers engaged in both outside and inside the context of the workplace and how Eva herself acted upon the social structures of the workplace, resisting marginalization. Like the students in Walsh's (1991) study, the boys in Willis's (1977) study and the women in Morgan's (1997) study, Eva was not content to submit without struggle to her marginalization. She would not accept being positioned as an uneducated immigrant in the workplace with nothing to offer her co-workers.

With reference to activities *outside* the workplace, it was company policy at Munchies that about once a month the management would help to sponsor an outing for the workers at the restaurant. It was at these times that Eva was taken outside the workplace where she had been positioned as a 'stupid' person, only worthy of the 'worst kind of job' to a context in which her youth and charm were valued symbolic resources. It was also on these occasions that Eva's boyfriend would help provide transportation for her fellow co-workers. Outside the institutional constraints of the workplace, where the nature of the work undertaken by Munchies employees structured to a large extent the social relations of power in the workplace, a different set of relationships began to develop. Eva's identity in the eyes of her co-workers became more complex and their relationship to her began to change. This in turn opened up greater possibilities for social interaction.

> B.   I know you said here that sometimes the people respect Gail more than you. You think that's still true?
>
> E.   Now I don't feel that much. It might be sometimes. But before it was I felt it more.
>
> B.   Why? Why do you think they did, Eva?
>
> E.   Why? I don't know why. It's just I feel this.
>
> B.   Is it because of the work you were doing? You were doing the cleaning of the floors, and things like that?
>
> E.   For example yesterday when we went out, the manager she said to me, because I am just one year younger than she, 'You look really different when you are not at work.' Because when I am at the work I, when I do the hard job, I don't know, I'm different than like here.

Toohey (2000) discusses how one of the subjects in her study with elementary school language learners, a young girl by the name of Julie, recruited both child and adult allies in her attempt to appropriate a more powerful identity in the kindergarten classroom. Toohey notes in particular that Julie's outside school identity might have influenced her interaction with her anglophone peers. In the afternoons, and on the playground, Julie played a great deal with her cousin Agatha, who was proficient in English. Although Agatha was not enrolled in Julie's morning kindergarten, Toohey argues that this powerful part-time ally, with whom Julie had strong and long-standing ties outside the classroom, may have been important in how other students, as well as her teacher, perceived her. In a similar spirit, it is possible that Eva's co-workers began to perceive Eva differently once they recognized that she had useful and desirable allies outside the workplace. They recognized, in effect, that her identity was more complex than they had assumed, and they responded more favourably towards her.

With reference to activities that took place *inside* the restaurant, Eva was gradually given more responsibility at work. As she was given more status and respect in the workplace she felt more comfortable speaking:

> Situation at work is surprising me, especially today. Usually the manager at the morning tells us what we have to do. Then the girl (which I wrote about her) pretends that she is busy all the time. This way I have to do everything. Today the manager gave us the list what we have to do (each of us separately). I was surprised, but the girl was more than me. After that, when I had done everthing, she (the manager) asked me to do the order of vegetables, which we needed. Always I had to do the heavy job, this time was different. It made me feel better. When I feel well, than I can talk to the others. Today I was talking more than usually.

Eva explained that it was not that she wanted a job that was better than that of her co-workers, but one in which she would be on an equal footing with them. This in turn would open up possibilities for shared conversation.

B. So are you saying that when you are doing a better job you feel you can talk to people?

E. Not the better job. It's not just me who does this job. I don't want to just stay at the cash. I know it's not possible. But I want to, to me and Gail we do the same job because we are at the same position there.

B. I see. And so in other words when you are both working together you feel better and you can talk, but if you are working on your own and doing something nobody else is doing then obviously you're finding it difficult to talk –

E. Mm – hmm.

I pressed Eva on the issue of the relationship between the nature of work undertaken and the opportunities to practice English. She was unequivocal about their interrelationship.

B. So Eva, do you think that – really I'm trying to make sense of all this – so really the nature of the work you do has a very important impact on whether or not you speak English or how you feel about speaking English? In other words, the more responsibility you have and the more people respect you, the more comfortable you are speaking English to them?

E. I think it's true. Because for example she [the manager] knows that I can do everything – for example prepare, that I have the responsibility to prepare everything that has to be prepared. She like talks to me and I feel like more comfortable than with her, and sometimes when for example, during the break time, she says we have to do this, for example the onions, I already know but she might not know because she cannot notice everything.

B. So she respects that you can contribute.

E. I can help her, and she knows that.

However, Eva did not simply wait for structural relations in the workplace to change, thus facilitating her opportunity to practice English. She herself acted upon the workplace, taking the opportunity to listen to the way her co-workers spoke to the customers, participating in social conversation (to the surprise of her co-workers) and contributing in unexpected ways to the general running of the restaurant. The following extract depicts how Eva would pay attention to the way her co-workers would use English with the customers:

E. I started to take orders from them. For example, because for bacon sandwich we have this BLT –

B. That's right, 'Bacon, lettuce and tomato'.

E. Ya, and they don't understand sometimes what it is, and then I have to explain everything. And it's hard for me, because for another person who can speak English fluently, it's not as hard, and I cannot do this all the time – write and speak. During the lunchtime it's a little bit harder because I know I have to take the orders as fast as I can. But it's still OK. I learn how the other people explain this and then I learn how to – because I overhear it and I do the same thing. I know it's correct because it's from Canadian people.

Eva would also claim spaces in conversations with co-workers. Her purpose was to introduce her own history and experiences into the workplace in the hope that her symbolic resources would be validated. This surprised her co-workers.

B. You were saying, Eva, that you are starting to speak to other people? The other people who work there?

E. Ya. Because before –

B. Is everybody there Canadian?

E. Ya. Because there everybody is Canadian and they would speak to each other, not to me – because – I always was like – they sent me off to do something else. I felt bad. Now it's still the same but I have to do something. I try to speak.

B. How are you doing that?

E. For example, we have a half-hour break. Sometimes – I try to speak. For example, they talk about Canada, what they like here, the places which they like –

B.   Like to visit? Vacations?

E.   Ya. Then I started to talk to them about how life is in Europe. Then they started to ask me some questions. But it's still hard because I cannot explain to them how things, like –

B.   How do you actually find an opportunity in the conversation to say something. Like, if they're talking to each other, do you stop them?

E.   No.

B.   You wait for a quiet – Then what do you say?

E.   No. I don't wait for when they are completely quiet, but when it's the moment I can say something about what they are talking about.

B.   When you started doing that were they surprised?

E.   A little bit.

What is in evidence here is Eva's attempt to be seen, in Bourdieu's (1977) terms, as a 'legitimate speaker' of English. Bourdieu argues that, if an utterance is to be an example of legitimate discourse, four conditions need to be met. First, it must be uttered by an appropriate speaker, as opposed to an 'imposter': Only a priest, for example, would be authorized to use religious language. Second, it must be uttered in a legitimate situation: Wedding vows, for example, would only be appropriate in a marriage ceremony. Third, it must be addressed to legitimate receivers: A young child, for example, would not be a legitimate receiver of an academic lecture. Fourth, it must be formulated in legitimate phonological and syntactic forms. In this interaction, Eva is making astute judgements about the contribution she can make to a conversation on vacations. Since she cannot talk to her co-workers about vacations in Canada, she chooses to talk about vacations in Europe, a desirable destination for many Canadian travellers. She has judged that her co-workers are legitimate receivers of such an utterance. The situation is a legitimate one and she carefully chooses 'the moment [she] can say something about what they are talking about'. Though she still finds it hard to express herself in legitimate phonological and syntactic forms, she succeeds in making herself understood. Whether she is considered a legitimate speaker is somewhat unclear: her co-workers were somewhat surprised by her contribution. Nevertheless, they did invite her into the conversation by asking her questions about life in Europe.

Eva also tried to gain access to the social network by showing that she was able to make a positive contribution to the lives of her co-workers, to help in a variety of ways. Eva describes how she was able to help a manager learn some Italian so that the manager could surprise her husband:

B.   So when you told them a little bit about Europe or whatever, do they then ask you other questions or, how do they respond?

E.   They ask me a few more other questions and then we were talking about languages. They asked me, because my manager she has got married with an Italian – and I help her with a few words in Italian –

B. Just make sure you don't start speaking Italian at Munchies. Please!

E. (laughter) No. She is English, and her husband speaks English. Just she wanted to surprise him.

B. Were people impressed that you could also speak Italian?

E. mmmm. They already knew before. Maybe they were because they asked me if I can speak another languages and I told them I can understand Russian and I said that I can understand Czech and I learnt for example German and I know almost well the Italian. They were surprised I think.

As discussed in Chapter 3, Bremer *et al.* (1993, 1996) have argued that interaction between target language speakers and language learners is most productive when both parties work actively to achieve understanding. What these data seem to suggest is that, if the target language speaker is as invested in the conversation as the language learner is, she or he may work harder to achieve such understanding. Once Eva had identified which of her resources (e.g. knowledge of Europe or knowledge of multiple languages) was valuable in this context, she was able to reduce the power imbalance between herself and her interlocutors, and speak with greater confidence. Eva also tried to help her co-worker Gail when Gail had fallen behind in her duties. As discussed with reference to Kress's (1989) work, described in Chapter 1, the power of institutional discourses is such that people learn quickly what it means to be a good colleague, a helpful worker, a model employee. Such helpfulness can be understood as another resource that was valued in the workplace, serving to offset limitations in Eva's competence in English.

When I don't have a lot of things to clean on the table, and I'm really like, I don't have nothing to do, when the lunchtime is over and we don't have to prepare anything we just have to clean – she does, she has for example to clean the dishes and stuff like this, during the time when I'm at tables, when she has a lot of those dishes – then when I get back and I am finished I sometimes help her. And she saw it.

The privileges of access to anglophones in the workplace

In time, Eva gradually gained access to the social network at work. After a few months at Munchies, she described the following conversation that she had overheard. One worker, turning to another, said in passing, 'I don't like working with people who aren't Canadian.' When his companion replied 'Except Eva', he repeated, 'Except Eva'. Such data provide unequivocal evidence that, notwithstanding Eva's initial marginalization at Munchies, she had, over time, succeeded in achieving legitimacy in her workplace.[2] As Eva said in one interview, 'Now I think that they understand that I started to work there because I have no job because there was no possibility for the job because of the economic, because I didn't know that much English.' Eva feels that her co-workers no longer think of her as stupid, but as someone who is a victim of circumstance. Her level of competence in English no longer marginalizes her; it is no longer equated with ignorance. On the contrary, it now becomes an explanation for the type of work she has been compelled to do. In other words, while previously the type of work she did was understood to be a result of an intrinsic incompetence, it was then perceived as a result of an unfortunate set of circumstances.

As Eva became more comfortable and confident with her co-workers, she spoke more English and, as she spoke more English, she became more comfortable and confident. The relationship between comfort/confidence levels and use of English is an intricate one:

B.   I'm just trying to kind of imagine. So are you finding at Munchies now that you are speaking more English?

E.   Ya.

B.   Why is that?

E.   Firstly, I have more practice. I feel more comfortable there when I speak. And I'm not that scared anymore to say something. Because before I wasn't sure if I say something the right way or they like understand me or not – because sometimes I say something but they don't understand me.

B.   Do you think it's because your English has got better that you've got more confident or do you think that you've got more confident and so you're speaking more English?

E.   Mmmm. Both. Both.

It is significant that Eva is concerned, not only that she understand her co-workers, but that they understand her. One of the central findings of the ESF project, as discussed in Chapter 3 (Bremer *et al.*, 1993, 1996), is that in most inter-ethnic encounters, it is the learner who bears most of the responsibility for ensuring that mutual understanding has been achieved. This can be partly explained by the unequal investments that such interlocutors have in an interaction. Eva is highly invested in the interactions with her co-workers because she is seeking entry into their social networks; without such entry, she will have difficulty improving her English and finding better working conditions: it is the classic Catch-22 situation. Notwithstanding the counter-example given above, in which Eva helped a co-worker to learn some Italian, her co-workers, initially at least, appeared to have little investment in interaction with her.

Having gained entrance into the social network, Eva was able to participate in a variety of social interactions that she had not taken part in before: she was no longer powerless in the workplace. In the following extract, Eva indicates that she is now able to inform her co-worker Gail when work had to be done, rather than simply do it all herself. As a result, she is able to resist exploitation. It is interesting that one of the ways in which Eva asserts her rights is through the use of humour. She does not insist that Gail do her fair share of the work; she jokes with Gail and uses a lighthearted tone when speaking to her. Heller and Barker (1988) and Rampton (1995) describe how students use puns and code-switching to break down social boundaries; Eva, likewise, uses humour as conversational strategies to help her communicate her intentions.

> Now she [Gail] is little bit changing. She's like aa she – for example today she was doing something and I said to her 'Gail, we have a lot of things to prepare for the weekend.' 'Really, why didn't you tell me before?' I said 'It's logical, it's the end of the week!' And she helped to do everything with me – Because now that I feel she's more close to me, I feel like I can say 'Gail, we have to do something!' But when I don't know somebody, I think that she doesn't – like before she was – I couldn't go to her and say 'Gail, we've got to do something.'

The solidarity between Gail and Eva is such that they are able to discuss the possibility of asking for an increase in wages. In this regard, as Goldstein's (1996) work, described in Chapter 3 has shown, access to social networks does not have only symbolic value, but material consequences as well.

> B. Do you ever talk about your salary? Do you know what Gail earns?
> E. Ya. What Gail earns is the same as like me. Just, I cannot ask the manager how much she is paid!
> B. But you and Gail get about the same?
> E. Because Gail asked me – we have to ask about the rise together –
> B. Really?
> E. We asked and she [the manager] said 'not yet'. She can't ask the owner yet because it is too slow and we cannot ask before summer.
> B. Really? Did Gail suggest that you ask for a raise?
> E. Mm – hmm.

Comment

With reference to SLA theory, it is clear from these data that opportunities to practice English cannot be understood apart from social relations of power in natural or informal settings. Although Eva had access to anglophones in the workplace, she did not initially have access to the workers' social network or to customers who patronized the store. In this regard, it is not only sustained contact with the dominant community that is important, as advocated by Bremer et al. (1996), but access to social networks within this community. When Eva started working at Munchies, her material and symbolic resources were not valued in the workplace. She had a job with low status and she could not express herself adequately in English. Furthermore, she entered a workplace in which there was resistance to immigrants – 'people who aren't Canadian' – and unequal investments in social interaction. Because Eva was marginalized, she could not take part in the language practices in the workplace and was subject to exploitation. Her lack of confidence and anxiety were not invariant personality traits but socially constructed in inequitable relations of power. It was only after a number of months that Eva gained access to the social network in the workplace, and with it the right and opportunity to speak. Such access was gained because Eva acted upon the workplace, refusing to be marginalized, and because the organization of activities for workers outside the workplace gave her the opportunity to distance herself from the identity of an unskilled immigrant.

At one diary study meeting, I asked Eva if she felt she was part of Canadian society. Her response was that she felt comfortable in Canada because the people at work liked her and accepted her. The central point here is that it is only in the work environment that Eva had access to Canadians. In many ways, the workplace *was* Canada for Eva. Because Eva had gained access to the social network at work, she was able to practice English on a regular basis and become a proficient speaker of English. Indeed, she became sufficiently proficient to change her job to that of a waitress at another restaurant in Newtown where she was required to speak English fluently. In this workplace, not only did she earn more money, but she had a different relationship to her customers and increased opportunities to speak English. Eva may not be 'Canadian' but, as Eva is no longer marginalized, she is no longer powerless. As she herself said: 'I feel I have the same possibilities as Canadians.'

Arguably, Eva is a classic multicultural citizen. She says that she feels comfortable about being Polish in Canada. Polish is the language of the private sphere; English is the language of the public sphere. Further, if people look at her strangely on occasion, she thinks that is their problem and not hers. When she first arrived in Canada, she would have assumed that, if people treated her with disrespect, it was because of her own limitations. Eva said that the English course had helped her make a head start on the adaptation process. 'It would have taken a lot longer' if there had been no course. But the most important English teacher for her was 'real life'. Furthermore, work helped her, not only because of the increased exposure to English and practice in English, but also because she was able to observe how Canadians talk to one another and behave towards one another – how things 'get done' in Canadian society. At Munchies, Eva's identity was that of someone who was 'different but equal' to her co-workers. Because she was no longer marginalized by her co-workers, because she had their acceptance and respect, she could talk to them, practice her English, and become a good speaker of English. As well, it is significant that Eva not only wanted to be accepted, she wanted her 'difference' to be respected: 'When I started to work there, they couldn't understand that it might be difficult for me to understand everything and know about everthing what it's normal for them', she wrote. This sentiment was echoed another time when she said that the people working with her 'weren't able to understand why it's difficult to come to the other country and not know the language'. Eva wants her co-workers to try to understand her, to accept that she doesn't know everything that they take for granted. However, she doesn't want recognition of difference at the price of marginalization.

It was disturbing, therefore, that when I saw Eva after the diary study was complete, I learnt that she was still fighting the same battles for respect in the workplace, and that her competence in English still constituted a barrier to her acceptance by some Canadians. She told me a story of a male customer who had said to her 'Are you putting on this accent so that you can get more tips?' Eva had been angry, but had said to him: 'I wish I did not have this accent because then I would not have to listen to such comments'. Eva was no longer silenced by ethnocentric comments, she was angered by them. Her identity had changed and, with it, her inclination to speak in the public world.

Mai

'I feel so sorry for my parents and my nephews because they can not talk with each other . . . I am always in the middle.'

Mai, who had come to Canada for a better future, had great investment in English, not only for the access it gave her to the public world, as was the case with Eva, but also for the power it gave her within the private sphere of the home, where, as a language broker she sought to resist her brother's patriarchal authority. The opportunities that Mai had to practice English in the home and workplace were structured by highly complex sets of social relationships that underwent significant change over time. Where appropriate, I will contrast Mai's experiences with those of Eva because there are interesting similarities and differences in their experiences. Both Mai and Eva are approximately the same age, landed in Canada at the same time, arrived in Canada without a partner, did not speak any English on arrival in Canada and were the only two of the five women who obtained full-time employment shortly after arrival in Canada. There are important differences between them, however. Mai is a visible minority in Canada, she lived with an extended family from the time of her arrival in Canada till the time she married, she heard English spoken in her home on a daily basis, and her skills as a seamstress were economically desirable in Canada.

Mai's home: The Tower of Babel

Ming, the brother with whom Mai lived, had been in Canada for over ten years before Mai arrived. He is at least ten years older than Mai, is married to a Vietnamese woman called Tan and has three sons. Fourteen-year-old Trong was born in Vietnam, while the other two, Mark (aged twelve) and Kevin (aged eight), were born in Canada. The family lives in an opulent neighborhood in Newtown, with large new houses arranged on small, neat lots. Mai's brother works in a government department and has been financially successful in Canada. Her sister-in-law, Tan, has her own sewing business that she runs from home. Mai and her elderly parents all initially stayed at her brother's home. The occupants of the house included the two grandparents, the parents, the three children and Mai. At the time of Mai's arrival, a younger brother also lived in the same house, although he moved into another house soon after Mai arrived. Thus, unlike Eva, Mai had a complex set of domestic relationships in her place of residence: She was daughter to her two parents, sister (and sister-in-law) to her brother and his wife, and aunt to her brother's three sons.

Significantly, unlike the case for Eva, three languages were spoken in the home on a continual basis: Vietnamese, Cantonese and English. Mai's parents spoke Vietnamese and Cantonese, but no English. Her brother and sister-in-law spoke Vietnamese and Cantonese; her brother had good command of English, but her sister-in-law spoke only limited English. Her nephews spoke English only. This meant that Mai's parents and nephews were unable to communicate with one another, and that there was limited communication between Mai's nephews and their mother. As Mai wrote:

> It is funny when I think about my family, it's not too big but always had spoken by three languages. My parents can't speak English, I had to speak with them in Vietnamese or Chinese. I always spoke Chinese when my family's friends who are from Toronto came to visit us. They are all Chinese. With my brother and his wife, I spoke Vietnamese because they used to speak with each other by that language. And my nephews, they didn't know any other language except English. So I spoke English with them although it is the language I spoke more than the other. For me it doesn't matter when people speak with me in Vietnamese, Chinese or English. The only thing that I feel so sorry for my parents and my nephews because they cannot talk with each other. It is very worst in the family. I think I won't let it happen to my children if I have in my future.

The patterns of language use in Mai's home are linked inextricably to social relations of power within the home and Canadian society at large. These relations of power – which have patriarchal, racist and material histories – have contributed in complex ways to the breakdown of the extended family structure in Mai's home. This breakdown, in turn, has had a marked impact on Mai's identity, the status of English in the home and the opportunities for Mai to practice English. The first set of relationships I will examine is that between Mai's nephews and their parents. The following conversation describes the limited communication between Tan and her three sons:

B.   You hear a lot of English here at home?

M.   Ya I do. For my nephews, they all speaking English, so I'm have to speak with them.

B.   Now do they speak any Chinese[3] or Vietnamese?

M.   No they don't.

B.   Nothing? Nothing at all?

M.   No.

B.   Why not? Does your sister-in-law not speak to them in Chinese or Vietnamese?

M.   No. Because, um, for my sister-in-law she got this business, so she has to speak English, so she didn't want if she speaks Chinese with her kids, so she will lose her English. So she just try to speak English. My nephews speak better than her because they were born here and they go to school –

B.   But does she not speak Vietnamese to them?

M.   No. No. Not at all.

I asked Mai how Tan speaks to the boys if the boys do not speak Vietnamese and Tan's English is so limited. Mai said she hardly does speak to the boys. When she does, it takes a long time to make herself understood and the boys make fun of her efforts. Mai suggested that her brother and his wife are obsessed with making money, so much so that their children call the mother 'Money' instead of 'Mummy'. Mai says that her nephews treat their mother with disrespect because she doesn't know English, saying to their mother 'Shut up, Money.'

It appears that Tan avoided speaking Vietnamese to her children because she thought her command of English would improve if she spoke English to the boys. Part of her desire to learn English was driven by economic interest. Her children, however, who attended anglophone schools, very soon became more competent in English than she was, and she began to lose her authority over them. The boys, in fact, seemed to exert power over their mother, and used their English as a weapon against her. The disrespect with which they treated their mother seems partly explained by the fact that they observed their own father treating his mother and his sister with disrespect. When Mai's brother once chastised the boys for treating their mother badly, Mark, the middle son, said, 'But then why do you treat Grandmom and Aunt so badly?' Thus the patriarchal relations of power in the home have influenced the language patterns in the home and exacerbated the intergenerational breakdown.

There is another important point to note, however. On the way home from one diary study meeting, Mai discussed how the breakdown of the family structure and the use of English in the home were related to her brother's perception of Vietnamese and Chinese people in Canada. She said that her brother thinks that Vietnamese and Chinese people are 'low' while Canadian people are 'high'. Even though he himself is Vietnamese/Chinese and his wife is Vietnamese, he doesn't like the Vietnamese and Chinese people and thinks they are 'bad people'. Mai said that her nephews have been brought up as Canadians, and have never been encouraged to learn Vietnamese – only the eldest has any understanding of Vietnamese. They have no interest in finding out about Vietnam or Vietnamese people, and have said on occasion that they hate their appearance. Mai says that her brother tries to think he is Canadian but that other people don't see him that way. He tries to have Canadian rather than Vietnamese friends, treating the two groups very differently. It appears that racist practices in Canadian society – either covert or overt – have had a deleterious effect on the identities of the members of Mai's extended family. Such phenomena have been comprehensively studied in other contexts in North America by such scholars as Wong Fillmore (1991) and McKay and Wong (1996) and will receive further attention in Chapter 6.

When Mai and her parents arrived in Canada, it was in this set of relationships that she found herself. English was the language of power in the home, males had authority and Canadians were considered to be superior to Chinese and Vietnamese people. Mai, however, rejected her brother's patriarchal and racist views. When she arrived in Canada at 21 years of age, she was very comfortable with her Vietnamese and Chinese heritage. She was distressed that her brother wished to obliterate his Vietnamese past and that her nephews cared so little for their heritage. She was struck by the fact that her brother had changed so much and had little respect for his own parents: 'You can't just throw away what has been passed down from generation to generation.' At the same time, however, Mai said that her parents have no voice in Canada. It was for this reason that Mai became subject to her brother's authority. Although she could speak to Tan, Tan seemed to support her husband's patriarchal authority over Mai. As I will indicate, it was with the nephews that Mai developed a special relationship that was to create opportunities for her to speak English, resist her brother's patriarchal authority, and redefine her gendered identity.

Mai had come to Canada for her 'life in the future' but the future that her brother and sister-in-law had in mind for Mai did not coincide with Mai's desires. Because Mai wanted to be independent, learn English, drive a car and take an accounting course, she came into conflict with the patriarchal structures in her home. There were many ways in which her brother and sister-in-law attempted to curb her independent spirit. There was verbal pressure: Her brother and sister-in-law said that she was 'license crazy', and ridiculed her desire for a 'driver's license, an English license an accountant's license'. Further, they limited her economic independence as she was required to give her brother her regular salary check. As well, they tried to control her personal time. When Mai got home from work every day, she was required to join Tan in the basement and help her with sewing contracts. Finally, they belittled her status as a single woman, saying she was a girl who didn't need school. 'Just find a rich young man', they told her. Indeed, from the moment of Mai's arrival in Canada, Ming and Tan attempted to find a husband for her. The first person they introduced to her was a relation of Tan, who in fact came to pick Mai up at the airport when she first arrived in Canada. Mai described this meeting in the following interview:

> At the night I came here, the first time I came to Canada, he went to airport to pick me up. And after that the second time he came and brought something for me. He want to be my boyfriend. Ya. But, after I knew him, I didn't want to be that. I don't want to be. I don't that he's stupid but, it is not good way for me. Ya. And I just tell him, 'If you want me to be your friend, your sister, I'll be glad to be that, but for the – you want to be my boyfriend – no.' No, I don't think so. And for now he says 'OK, I'll be your brother.'

Mai's response to this pressure was complex. Sometimes she tried to reason with her brother, saying that she needed to be independent for her future; other times she defended her actions by saying 'At least I didn't do any bad thing to anybody.' Sometimes, Mai said, it was easier to be quiet and say nothing. While Eva often found herself silenced in the workplace, Mai often struggled for respect in the home. It is significant that Mai never challenged her brother directly. She never seemed to question his right to try to control her life, even though she opposed what he was doing; she never challenged the patriarchal structures, but tried to accommodate them while finding alternative routes to independence. Eva, on the other hand, was frustrated by what she understood to be discrimination and abuse of her rights in the workplace. Thus their relationship to the oppression they both experienced was very different. Like many of the women in Rockhill's study, Mai did not assume that she had the right to independence, she assumed that it was a privilege granted under sufferance.

Because of the breakdown of the extended family, and the emotional and material network that had hitherto supported Mai, Mai had to redefine her relationships within the family. Mai's parents offered her little support. Her non-English speaking father was no longer the patriarch; Mai said he had no power in Canada. Mai's mother cleaned the house, did the cooking and spent the rest of her time in her bedroom, alone and alienated from her extended family. Her sister-in-law had no authority in the home, little relationship with her sons and spent her days and evenings in the basement making garments and drapes for clients. In a sense, unless Mai redefined her status in the home, her options were extremely bleak. She could become an economic prisoner in the home, like Tan, with little identity or authority as a member of the family, she could accept a marginalized status as her mother had done or she could claim an alternative status that would provide her with an expanded set of possibilities. Mai chose the last option, despite her brother's desire to relegate her to Tan's status or marry her off as quickly as possible.

Mai's strategy was two-fold. First, she found employment outside the home. This enabled her to contribute to the economic welfare of the family and gave her increased opportunities to practice English. Second, as her English improved, particularly after the six-month ESL course, she took on the role of language broker in the home, a status that gave her a measure of power and authority that no other person, apart from her brother, had succeeded in achieving. At a diary study meeting, she described herself as always in the middle, interpreting between her parents and her nephews and occasionally between her nephews and their mother. This gave Mai respect and authority in the eyes of her nephews, who were important allies in Mai's struggle against her brother's patriarchal authority. As noted above, it was her nephews who came out in defence of her by asking their father why he treated Mai so badly. They were also impressed because she could speak English better than their mother who had been in Canada for more than ten years. As Mai wrote: 'One time Trong told me "I hope you won't be like someone they just care about money then they forget about English. It's no good in the future." I understood what he means'. What Mai understood was that her nephews resented their mother's preoccupation with the acquisition of material resources rather than symbolic resources. They were concerned that Mai should not follow in their mother's footsteps. It was Mai's friendly relationship with her nephews and her role as a language broker in the home that gave her numerous opportunities to practice English on a regular basis.

Thus, although Mai's brother grew wary of the developing relationship between Mai and his sons, Mai remained an asset in the home. She was more than 'a girl': she brought money into the home, she was a language broker in the home, she was able to take care of her nephews and give the parents the freedom to travel. Despite her brother's ambivalence towards Mai, it was Mai and not the grandparents who took care of the boys when Mai's brother went to Vietnam for a month. By this time, there was a mutually beneficial relationship between the boys and Mai. As Mai noted, they helped her practice English, and she took care of them:

My brother and his wife went to Vietnam 4 weeks go. Since they went I have to take care of my three nephews. I think they must be sad when their parents all gone, that's why I tried to keep the activity in the house always like they used to be with their parents. All the time I have to make up my mind to think about something that they like to eat. At night, before I went to sleep I went to check two of the younger to make sure that if they okay. And the happy thing I got from them is they all have been very good and listen to me everything that I tell them. They used to ask me when they wanted to go out or do something. The one very helpful to me and my study is Kevin. He is eight and a half years old and he is the third of my nephews. Whenever I asked him to help me for dictation and something else, he is very pleased to help me. He helps me more than the other one. He reads for me to write my dictation. Trong the older one is taking high school, he didn't have much time to help me. Neither does the second one Mark. I know they all busy. So I didn't want to bother them. But when I had some problems that Kevin couldn't explain to me, I had to ask Trong or Mark They all happy to help me and explained to me very clearly.

There was an interesting relationship between Mai's position of language broker and her investment in English. English represented both a weapon against her brother's patriarchal authority and a symbol of her value in the private and public world. Mai was an extremely diligent language learner – she took every opportunity she could to speak and use the language. She took course after course, despite the extreme inconvenience of attending courses at night, after a long day at work. She practiced at home with her nephews, she regularly attended the diary study meetings, she wrote reams in her diary. When Mai's brother evicted his parents from his house a year after they had arrived in Canada, Mai's strategies were rewarded when she was given the option to remain in her brother's home. Mai captured these traumatic events in the following words:

I am feeling so sad and very lonely now. Tonight will be the last night I am close to my mother. Then tomorrow she'll move to someone's house and stay there all the time. She's going to take care of one child who is six months old. Since I was born until I came here I used to stay with my parents. I couldn't miss them even ten days. But now, I can't help when something happen. It hurts me a lot come to think of it. Before we were living in Vietnam we always hoped that we could come here soon to see someone in family that we haven't seen for long time. Then we'll stay together and enjoy the time we have. But now so many bad things happened to us. It made my parents feel bad, because they never think about something like that happened to them. My parents didn't feel like to stay in my brother's house any more . . . Even me, I don't know where to go now. I am confused about what is going to happen with my parents and I in the future. Around me now all storm and big windy, I am not sure if I am strong enough to standup in this situation.

Having examined the language practices in Mai's home, and how her opportunities to practice English were socially structured, I now examine the kinds of opportunities Mai had to practice English in the workplace, how these opportunities were socially structured and their mutual relationship to Mai's investment in English.

Mai's workplace: Insider to outsider

When the ESL course was complete, Mai worked as a seamstress at a place called The Fabric Factory in Newtown. She was the youngest worker there and the only one from a Vietnamese/Chinese background. There were seven additional workers, all women ('just only seven girls') and no native-born Canadian workers. 'No any one Canadian people', said Mai. When Mai arrived at the workplace, everyone spoke English communally, although the women were from Italian (four), Portuguese (two) and Indian (one) backgrounds. Only occasionally did one woman speak to another in her mother tongue. 'Maybe they don't want us to know something. They cannot help it so, speak really fast.' As noted in Chapter 3, Goldstein (1996) describes in detail how the immigrant women and men in her study formed an intimate social network in the workplace, where workers referred to one another as sister, brother, daughter. Goldstein argues that in this context, work relationships were represented as family and community relationships. For example, a problem concerning a worker who is unhappy with the supervisor was referred to as a family problem. These sets of relationships had a significant influence on the language patterns on the production floor: Portuguese functioned as a symbol of solidarity and group membership. The language was associated with the rights, obligations and expectations that members of the community had of one another, including the obligation to help one another keep the line up and cover for slower workers.

It was into a set of relationships like this that Mai entered at The Fabric Factory, although the language of solidarity was English. Unlike Eva, Mai did not have difficulty gaining access to the social network in the workplace and had many opportunities to practice English. Unlike Eva, Mai did not have the worst job in the factory. On the contrary, Mai was a highly competent worker and soon gained the respect of both the management and workforce. Unlike the case with Eva, the better jobs were not reserved for those proficient in English; all the workers had the same type of job, and none of them needed to be good speakers of English to be competent workers. Furthermore, all Mai's co-workers were immigrants to Canada. Unlike the case at Eva's work, Mai was part of the camaraderie among the women. As well, Mai was younger than the other workers in the factory and was affectionately called a young chicken, a little girl by the other workers. In a sense, she was like a daughter to the older, more experienced workers there. Mai in fact referred to the most experienced worker in the factory as 'the mother of us all'. As in Eva's case, Mai's workplace was symbolic of the outside world for Mai; however, it was more than a place where she could have increased exposure to English and practice in English, it was a place that offered her refuge from the tensions of her family life and provided her with the emotional and material support of a surrogate family.

The first time I interviewed Mai in December 1990, she expressed great satisfaction with her work situation. She spoke a lot of English there, had great support from her supervisor, and was loved by the women she worked with.

B: So do you speak a lot when you work or do you just sit and work, work, work.

M: No, I speak a lot. [laughter] Some days they have to stop me! Because the jobs make me sleepy if we don't speak. We just listen to the sound of the machine. Something is –

B: It makes you sleepy?

M: For me not but for someone else. So I just want to make them wake up or something. If I was not very – I was very quiet, and then later on – I get used to everything, those people, and I try to speak more and – Ya. Because I actually want to practice speaking English. And even with my supervisor, I told her before – I'm not very good in speaking English. I hope when I be there so you can teach me some more for reading and writing or speaking. She said 'yes' so –

B: Is she Canadian? The supervisor?

M: She's Italian. But she come here since she was very young.

B: So she speaks good English?

M: Ya, she speaks good English.

B: Does she speak a lot to you? When you're working?

M: She speaks with me a lot.

B: And is she friendly? Is she nice?

M: She's friendly. And other day I got accident she was so worried about me –

B: Oh really.

M: Ya. I, I'm happy for my factory. Because – they love me.

This extract is highly significant. It indicates that the workplace is a very important source of self-esteem for Mai. She is happy when people care about her and, when she is happy, she can talk a great deal. Unlike the older women in the study, who find solace in their families, and Eva, who has a partner, Mai finds little solace in her extended family; it is in the workplace where she feels competent, has friends who love her and has the opportunity to speak a lot of English. Her own mother no longer has any voice, but Rita, 'the mother of us all', has a great deal of power in the factory.

When there was enough work for everybody, there was a positive atmosphere in the workplace and Mai had no difficulty practicing her English.

Things started to go wrong for Mai, however, when the company started feeling the effects of recession and women were laid off work. Because Mai was particularly competent, she was not one of those laid off. But the layoffs had a marked impact on the social interaction and language patterns on the factory floor and Mai's opportunities to speak English. As Mai wrote:

> Something's happened at work. It made me feel sad and uncomfortable. Today, after we had lunch, Emelia asked two ladies to stay home tomorrow because there isn't enough job for everybody. Now my boss decides that he can keep only people who know how to make everything from top to bottom. It doesn't matter how long have they been working here. Everyone in that factory all have been working there at least 8 months. I'm the only one here not so long. Then my supervisor tells me to stay. I know someone else doesn't like that way. But I can not say anything, it is not my fault, even though those ladies are very upset. They spoke in front of me with each other. One said 'that's not fair, how come I stay here longer, now she lays me off?' The other one says, 'someone else can't do everything. Why don't they lay them off too?' Then they started to speak their own language, Italian or Portuguese. By the way they look at someone who is still working it was very strange looking. They said a lot of things I couldn't understand. I don't know what do they think about me. I just have to do according to my supervisor.

The solidarity among the women was lost after the layoff, and the language patterns in the workplace altered dramatically. Except for Mai, the women remaining in the factory were all Italian: Emelia (the supervisor), Rita (the most experienced person) and Ilsa. The others no longer spoke English, they all spoke Italian. Because none of the workers had to speak to clients or customers, there were no constraints on the use of Italian and the other workers tried to convince Mai to learn Italian. Mai tried to resist this, saying she must learn English, but her co-workers tried to convince her that it would be good for her to understand another language. It is important to note that in this context Mai felt marginalized, not because of her limited command of one of the official languages in Canada, but because of her lack of command of a minority language:

> Since last Tuesday, I've been working at my factory in a very quiet condition. There were only three people at work. Rita, me and Ilsa with the supervisor. We didn't like to turn on the radio like we used to. Because they all Italian, that's why they speak Italian language all the time. Sometimes I feel so lonely like I was working by myself. Then all of them wanted me to learn Italian language. I liked that too at the beginning. Rita taught me how to say thank-you, good morning, understand and how to count from one to ten. It was harder than when I learned English even the

pronunciation. One time I told Rita 'I'm not going to learn anymore, the thing I need now is English language.' Over there I'm the youngest, so everyone like to tease me and call me by all different names. Rita told me 'Come on young chicken, it's good for you to understand some different language.' She started to speak with me by Italian like when she asked me to do or to get something. At those moments I couldn't understand what she said. I just stood there with a funny face. When Emelia saw me like that she asked me 'What happened with the little girl here.' Then Ilsa explained to her and she burst out laughing. I think Rita was a Fatsy Lady. She can just be happy or get mad at someone at anytime. But in these few days she has been very nice to me. Sometimes she teach me how to make something by her way. It was easier and faster than the way I did before.

After the layoffs, English was no longer the language of power in the workplace, but Italian. This put Mai in an invidious position. If Mai neglected her English, she might lose the little bargaining power she had in the home through her identity as a language broker; yet, if she insisted on speaking English, she might lose the friendship of the people at work. Indeed, not only might she lose their friendship, but she might lose access to their experience and skills, the symbolic resources that would help her to be a more competent worker. As Mai said, Rita helped her to do things easier and faster than the way she had done things before. Such support might be compromised if Mai did not respect the language of power in the workplace. It is significant that when two of the women who had been laid off came back to the workplace to get some paperwork done, they refused to greet Mai. Mai described how one of the women had reluctantly turned to Mai and said to her, in an unfriendly way, that she [Mai] had been allowed to stay because she didn't have a man. The laid-off workers refused to acknowledge that Mai had been kept on because of her competence and diligence. Their words suggested that, because Mai did not have a husband to provide security for her, she had been saved from dismissal.

The social meaning of these words must be understood with reference to the construction of Mai's gendered identity. In the home, she had struggled to resist the patriarchal oppression of a brother who insisted she was a 'girl' who didn't need school, but a rich young man; in the workplace, she was positioned as a young chicken, a little girl, but ultimately a person whose single status was used to explain the preferential treatment she had received from the management of The Fabric Factory. Like Eva, Mai did not want to have a better job than the others; she did not want preferential treatment; she simply wanted to be treated fairly. However, she became positioned as someone who had received preferential treatment on the grounds of her gendered identity. Within a year, Mai got married. Her husband 'saved' her from her brother's patriarchal authority and from the derision of workmates who used her single status as grounds for marginalization. Her husband has given Mai a status in Canada as a wife. How this affects Mai's exposure to and practice in English has yet to be determined. Her husband does not want her to work outside the home; at best, Mai says, he may 'let' her study.

Comment

While for both Eva and for Mai, the workplace represented Canada, their experiences and opportunities to learn in the workplace were radically different. In Eva's case, her identity shifted from that of an uneducated immigrant woman to that of a valued co-worker. In Mai's case, her identity shifted from that of a competent, energetic co-worker, to that of a marginalized, unattached female. The work of Lave and Wenger (1991) on situated learning provides some insight into the way Eva and Mai were initially positioned in their workplaces and why their identities and learning opportunities shifted over time. Lave and Wenger (1991), working within an anthropological framework, are centrally concerned with the relationship between learning and the social situation in which it occurs. Through a process of what they call *legitimate peripheral participation* newcomers interact with old-timers in a given community setting and become increasingly experienced in the practices that characterize that community. This perspective is useful in the field of SLA (see for example Toohey, 1998, 2000) because it focuses on the local analysis of communities and insists that learners should be conceptualized as members of social and historical collectivities, and not as isolated individuals. Further, Lave and Wenger (1991) call for closer examination of the conditions for learning and for the appropriation of practices in any given community, recognizing that particular social arrangements in any community may constrain or facilitate movement toward fuller participation.

In Eva's workplace community, the constraints initially placed on her movement towards fuller participation were particularly problematic because they violated the expectations that newcomers have when entering a community of practice; that is, the expectations that newcomers will have access to the central practices of that community, in all its forms. As Lave and Wenger (1991, p. 100) note:

> The key to legitimate peripheral participation is access by newcomers to the community of practice and all that membership entails. But though this is essential to the reproduction of the community, it is always problematic at the same time. To become a full member of a community of practice requires access to a wide range of ongoing activity, old-timers, and other members of the community; and to information, resources and opportunities for participation.

What is noteworthy in Eva's data is the struggle she had to undergo to achieve such access, and how her identity within the community changed as she was given information, resources and opportunities for participation.

With regard to Mai, however, she was, in many respects, an old-timer in a new community of practice. She was an experienced seamstress who was immediately identified as someone who could contribute actively to the practices of the community. To the extent that the community met with her expectations, she felt confident and competent, regularly engaging in conversation with her co-workers. After the lay-offs, however, it was Mai's competence that was seen as threatening to her co-workers, and some gradually withdrew from interaction with her. The isolation that she felt had both symbolic and material consequences, as her access to both friendship and expertise was compromised. Such reversals in the relationships between old-timers and newtimers receive little attention in Lave and Wenger (1991) and merit further research. Nevertheless, as I argue in Norton (in press), the community of practice perspective and Wenger's (1998) recent work on identity, offer much promise for theorizing about second language learning in classrooms and communities. In the next chapter, we gain greater insight into the practices that characterize the places in which Katarina, Martina and Felicia worked.

Notes

1. In all interviews, names are abbreviated: B for Bonny, E for Eva, M for Mai or Martina (depending on context), K for Katarina, and F for Felicia. A dash (–) indicates a pause and square brackets are used for clarificatory comments.
2. It is important to note, however, that she had not succeeded in changing the ethnocentric views held by some of her co-workers towards immigrants in general.
3. I did not at this point in the study acknowledge the differences between the variety of languages spoken in China.

5

Mothers, migration and language learning

'I want you to speak English. Pa hallar buen trabajo tienes que saber hablar el inglés bien. Qué vale toda tu educatión si todavía hablas inglés con un "accent",' my mother would say, mortified that I speak English like a Mexican.

(ANZALDÚA, 1990, p. 203)

Theorizing and researching gender and language learning is fraught with complexity. In a comprehensive article on researching gender in language use, Freedman (1997) distinguishes two traditions in research on gender and language use. The first tradition, associated with the sociolinguistic work of such researchers as Lakoff (1975) and Tannen (1990), focuses on how women and men use speech in social interaction. Lakoff, for example, demonstrates that women are more tentative than men, using tag questions and hedges more frequently than men do. While Tannen would agree with this observation, her analysis of *why* such differences occur would differ from that of Lakoff in that she would place less emphasis on power differentials between women and men than Lakoff does. The second tradition that Freedman identifies is that associated with the anthropological work of researchers in language socialization, such as that of Ochs (1992). Ochs argues that linguists should study how gender is constituted through acts, stances and activities associated with culturally preferred gender roles which have context-specific linguistic realizations. She demonstrates, more specifically, how differences in communicative practices across cultures socialize infants and small children into different local images of women in general and mothers in particular.

While both research traditions offer rich possibilities for research on gender and language learning, this chapter proposes an alternative framework for thinking about the significance of gender within language learning research. Instead of asking, 'How do women speak?' or, 'What communicative practices are associated with culture-specific gender roles?' I ask 'Under

what *conditions* do women speak?' More specifically, I address how an immigrant woman's gendered identity as mother is implicated in her investment
in the target language and her interaction with target language speakers. In
the previous chapter, there was some evidence that Eva and Mai's gendered
identities as young attached woman and unmarried young woman respectively may have had an important impact on the nature of their relationships
with target language speakers in their workplaces. The fact that Eva had a
boyfriend who could help drive co-workers to parties may have given Eva
greater esteem in the eyes of her co-workers and increase the possibility for
social interaction. With regard to Mai, her young, single status was treated
with ambivalence in the workplace. On the one hand, some of her co-
workers adopted a protective attitude towards her, calling her a young chicken
and a little girl, and invited her into their conversations. Others, however,
who had been laid off, positioned her as a person who was inadequate because she did not have a partner. 'You don't have a man', they said, as they
turned their backs. In neither case, however, was Mai fully acknowledged as
an independent woman in her own right.

I now wish to focus on the three older women in the study: Katarina,
aged 34 when she arrived in Canada, Martina, aged 37, and Felicia aged 44.
Katarina, the youngest of the three older women, had one child who was
still in elementary school; both Martina and Felicia had three children: two
teenagers and a preadolescent. All three women had received tertiary education in their home countries, they had all been married in their home countries and had children in their home countries, they had all worked for
extended periods of time in their home countries, but none had found jobs
in their professions in Canada. The differences between the women are also
significant, beginning with their reasons for immigrating to Canada. Katarina
and her family, from Poland, came to Canada because they 'disliked communism', preferring instead a capitalistic system, as well as a state with a Christian
orientation. Martina on the other hand, from Czechoslovakia, came because
she wanted a better life for her children and Felicia came because 'the
terrorism was increasing in Peru'. The women also had very different lifestyles in their home countries. Katarina stressed the fact that she was an
educated person who had taught for 17 years. Martina was a surveyor who
had worked for the same organization from the time she had finished her
post-secondary training. Felicia had been a primary school teacher who had
lived a life of luxury in exclusive neighborhoods in Peru, with weekends at
the beach cottage. In this chapter I demonstrate that the women's investment in English and their opportunities to practice English were influenced
by their gendered identities as mothers and wives, the disjuncture between
the symbolic resources that they had acquired in their home countries and
those valued in Canada, and ethnocentric social practices in their new country.
I analyze each woman's experience in turn, drawing comparisons and contrasts across the data.

Katarina

'I choose computer course, not because I have to speak, but because I have to think.'

Katarina and her husband have one child, a daughter Maria. When the family arrived in Canada, the daughter was only six years old. From the time of their arrival in Canada, Katarina was concerned that her daughter might lose command of her mother tongue, Polish. Katarina said that when she arrived in Canada she cried every day because she realized that her daughter would grow up speaking English. When asked to explain, she said that she was afraid Maria would grow up speaking another language that Katarina couldn't speak well. Katarina was afraid that she would lose contact with her daughter. The Polish priest at Katarina's church confirmed her fears. Katarina said that the priest had strongly urged all his parishioners to speak the mother tongue at home 'not for patriotic reason, not for love of the language, but for the parents'. He told them that, when the children grow up, and the parents want to talk about things that mean a lot to them, the parents would not be as comfortable in English as they would be in their native tongue. In order to keep contact with the children, he strongly encouraged his parishioners to speak their native language in the home. He also said that the children would always be fluent speakers of English, so the parents did not have to be concerned about their integration into Canadian society.

Thus the Polish language meant more to Katarina than a link to the past. It was an essential link to her future: her ongoing relationship with her daughter and her identity as a mother. At one of our first diary study meetings, Katarina talked at length about her daughter who was about to have her first communion. Katarina said that she wanted her daughter to have her first communion in Polish because 'That's the way I did it. I remember it so well in the long white dress.' She also said that, if the major communion texts Our Father and The Ten Commandments were in Polish, she could help Maria learn them, but if they were in English, she would have difficulty. Now Maria knows all these texts in Polish. In her diary, Katarina indicated the importance of motherhood to her when she expressed disapproval of women who had gone to the Gulf War, leaving children with fathers: 'Mothers have been to the war and children at home with fathers. I don't understand. What is more important, "war" or "children".'

Katarina was in strong support of the heritage language classes run by the local school board and sent her daughter to learn Polish every Saturday morning. She was the only one of the three mothers in the study who indicated that she was in strong support of her daughter learning the mother tongue in the regular classroom. There were times, however, when she expressed some concern that Maria seemed to be forgetting her Polish, saying, 'I started to read Polish to her. She had forgotten the Polish words. After a while, she could read better . . .' Because of Katarina's concern about her relationship with her daughter, the dominant language in Katarina's home was Polish. She never spoke English to her daughter or husband, something, echoing Eva, which was a hard thing to do.

It is interesting to note the comparisons between the language patterns in Mai's household with those in Katarina's. From the outset, Katarina was aware that the use of English in the home may not be in the best interests of the family unit and might drive a wedge between her daughter and herself. When I interviewed Katarina in her home on a number of occasions, it was clear that Katarina felt uncomfortable speaking English in front of her daughter. On one occasion, when Katarina was reading an English text onto the tape recorder, her daughter walked by and said her mother sounded like a child. This was very unsettling for Katarina. The social meaning of this comment for Katarina must be understood with reference to her investment in her identity as a mother and her ongoing relationship with her daughter. She was happy to watch English TV with her daughter, read English newspapers and listen to English news programs, but she was adamant that the spoken language in the home should be Polish.

In view of the forthcoming discussions on Martina and Felicia, it is important to note that Katarina's husband had developed good English skills before arriving in Canada. Katarina's husband had learnt English because the work that he had done in international trade had brought him in contact with anglophones. Katarina said that, when they first arrived in Canada, it was her husband who took on all the responsibility of dealing with the public world, answering telephone calls, speaking to teachers and so forth. Although Katarina's English improved at a rapid rate, she still has what she calls the poorest English skills in the family. Her daughter is fluent in English and her husband is highly competent. Unlike the experience of many women in Rockhill's study, Katarina's husband was supportive of her efforts to learn English. Because he provided enough income for the family's immediate needs, Katarina could attend school to learn English, and then later to do a computer course. She worked part-time to supplement the family's income, noting as follows:

> I have attended the school for the skills course from September 1990. It is possible because my husband works, then I don't have worry about money for apartment and food. My daughter attends the school from 9 am to 3.30 pm. In this time I have my English course – exactly 9 am–12 am. I only work nine hours a week in the Community Service as a homemaker. For the time being it is a good job for me.

Nevertheless, because of her age and domestic responsibilities, Katarina often found it difficult to study. As she wrote, 'It isn't easy to study when somebody has finished 30 years and has family. There is a lot of hardships on our way to learn English.'

Although Katarina was reluctant to use English in the home, she nevertheless had a great investment in learning the language. She believed that knowledge of English would help her regain the professional status that she had lost when she left Poland. 'I want life to be normal again, like in Poland', she said. When asked what her plans for the future were, Katarina referred to her past in Poland, in particular her educational status: 'In my native country I was a teacher. I studied 17 years.' Katarina wanted sufficient competence in English to secure her the kind of employment that would make life 'normal' again. However, Katarina did not want employment that was simply an extension of the work done in the home. She said that when she worked as a dishwasher and kitchen help she felt 'another'. Katarina wanted to do skilled work done by people who are highly educated and was eager to find employment that would give her a good income, an intellectual challenge and access to social networks of educated Canadians. She chose a computer course for upgrading purposes so that she could have contact with people who, as she said, think like her. Likewise, at another time she said, 'I choose computer course, not because I have to speak, but because I have to think.'

It was in her quest for skilled employment that Katarina felt marginalized in Canada, not by virtue of being Polish, but by virtue of being an immigrant. Because of her investment in the professional status she had acquired in Poland, Katarina bitterly resisted being positioned as unskilled and uneducated. Like Eva, when Katarina first arrived in Canada, the only employment she could find was in an 'ethnic' workplace, in Katarina's case, a German restaurant where she spoke predominantly German. In one meeting she said that the immigration officials think that 'immigrants must work as a dishwasher for the first ten years they are here: "You are immigrant" '. When Katarina found part-time employment as a homemaker for the Community Service, she saw this type of work as a temporary experience, a good job 'for the time being'. Ironically, however, this type of work gave her many opportunities to practice speaking English. It brought her into contact with lonely, elderly people who were always grateful for her assistance, assistance provided gratis by the Community Service. She worked on a one-to-one basis with her clients and did not need to seek entry into a social network in order to speak English. Her clients welcomed the opportunity to talk to her:

I work still at the same place in the Community Service. Yesterday I worked for an older married couple. They were more than 80 years old. How lonely people can be! I didn't think about it before. A lot of people don't think about it either. If people are young they are able to do all. Old people very often can't do nothing. They live by themselves and it is sad for them. There are only photographs of their children and their grandchildren in their homes.

It seems that Katarina was in a position of power relative to the older people she worked for, and never experienced feelings of alienation or inadequacy in her workplace. On the contrary, she felt sorry for these lonely people who were unable to fend for themselves. She gradually lost feelings of anxiety ('uptight') while speaking and did not take offence, for example, when an elderly person asked her why she came to Canada without knowing English.

> From September 1990 during my work I have contact with Canadian people. I see myself that each month I'm not so uptight when I speak. I have contact with big variety of speaking. There are people who I understand very good but there are people who I have to hear carefully. They speak quickly and unclearly. About a month ago I worked with one Canadian woman, who asked me why I came to Canada without knowing English. She was 84 years old. Other people with whom I work, try to explain me, when I don't understand something.

Katarina therefore had many opportunities to practice English. She attributes this to the fact that she has contact with a lot of people and indicated that her work helped her to improve her English: 'I have contact with Canadian people. I speak with them. I sometimes call to my supervisor. I have to listen what Canadian people tell me and I have to give answers.' She also commented that after the ESL course, her spoken English was very poor: 'I had understood all tenses, but their using were difficult.' On 17 February 1991, she remarked on the progress she had made in learning English by comparing two interviews she had had in the previous six months:

> On Wednesday I had interview in Ontario College in Newtown. I am going to take after [skills] course, Computer Programmer Course. I don't have to pass an examination of mathematics. I only have to pass an exam of English. I can compare this interview with another which I have had six months ago. The first interview took place in the Community Service. I wasn't able to tell a lot about myself after ESL course during that interview. On Wednesday I was able to ask and understand about my course, about another course and requirements for these courses.

In sum, although Katarina had an ambivalent attitude towards English because of the threat it posed to her relationship with her daughter, she was very eager to learn it so that she could become part of a social network of people who would value the professional status she had acquired in Poland – people who would think as she does. She wanted a normal life again, where she could enjoy respect from educated people. She went so far as to change her profession because of her need to find stimulation in her work, and to meet like-minded people. Unlike the subjects in Rockhill's study who wanted to move out of the factory and find 'clean work', Katarina already had a history of clean work and wanted to return to it. Katarina's story indicates that a language learner's investment in the target language must be understood with reference to class structures as well as gender and race. While Eva's data highlights the relationship between ethnocentrism and language learning, and Mai's data highlights the relationship between language learning and patriarchy, Katarina's draws attention to the relationship between language learning and class relations.

In Poland, Katarina and her husband had achieved status and respect as members of a professional class of people, who had high levels of responsibility in their work and relative autonomy. In this context, it was their education that had given them access to power and prestige. When Katarina and her family arrived in Canada, their primary concern was to regain a similar class position in Canada, and they turned to education to offer them this opportunity. Because of her lack of fluency in English, Katarina assumed that she would not be able to find employment as a teacher in Canada, and therefore sought out a profession, computer science, that would accommodate her second language skills. She was prepared to forgo full-time job opportunities in unskilled work, and use the family's resources to pay for her 18-month computer course, in the hope of achieving long-term job satisfaction. Both she and her husband shared these goals. English, for Katarina, was perceived as a resource that would secure for her the educational training that she sought, and ultimately a responsible job in which she could work autonomously. She was not interested, as she said, in learning '72 definitions for test'; she was not primarily interested in learning English so that she could speak. She was interested in learning English so that she could work in a stimulating job and form a set of relationships with people of her professional class.

I do not think it is coincidental that the person Katarina befriended in the ESL class was Felicia, a former teacher. Indeed, there were times when I perceived that Katarina had an ambivalent relationship to me – a fellow professional, a woman, and a mother, but someone who had come to Canada with the linguistic resources to secure professional work in the country. In one telephone call, for example, she said to me, 'Imagine you in Poland or Russia as a dishwasher, homemaker – You don't have problems with the language. You don't have to struggle with the language.' Nevertheless, Katarina was sufficiently comfortable to utilize the resources that I willingly offered. I helped both Katarina and her husband prepare résumés when they were looking for jobs, had a number of discussions with Katarina about appropriate schooling for her daughter, and tried to help her find employment in the computer industry. During the data collection period, I sensed that Katarina felt her life was on hold, and that everything she was doing in Canada was a temporary diversion in the trajectory of her life. Ironically, perhaps, one of the main reasons why Katarina's English improved is likely because of her regular contact with people who were not active professionals. While Katarina says that she feels uncomfortable talking to people who are teachers and doctors, she feels very comfortable talking to the people she tends in her homemaking job. This gives her many opportunities to practice English in the informal context of her workplace. In Chapter 7 I will discuss in some detail how Katarina's investment in her professional identity leads to disruption in her learning of English in the formal context of the school.

Martina

'If I want to learn, I must do it by myself.'

When Martina and her family arrived in Canada, neither Martina nor her husband Petr knew any English. Her children, however, had learnt some English in Austria while they were waiting for their Canadian visas. Initially, Martina was dependent on her children to perform the public/private tasks of settling into a new country. Unlike Katarina, Martina could not rely on her husband to perform these tasks because his English was as limited as hers was. When Martina went looking for a job, she took her eldest daughter with her, even though her daughter would cry because nobody wanted to employ her mother. When Martina wanted to help serve customers at Fast Foods, she asked her daughters to tell her what words to use. As Martina's English improved, she took on more and more of the public/private tasks in the home. Many of Martina's diary entries describe the way that she used English to perform a wide variety of tasks in the home and community. It was Martina rather than her husband Petr who did most of the organization in the family, such as finding accommodation, organizing telephones, buying appliances and finding schools for the children. She helped her children in many ways. She took over the paper rounds for her son Milos when he was ill, accompanied her daughter to her TOEFL exam and bought stationery for the children. Martina also helped her husband to perform public tasks in English. When Petr was laid off work, he relied on Martina to help him apply for unemployment insurance and he asked Martina to help him prepare for his plumber's certificate by translating the preparation book from English to Polish.

I suggest that Martina's investment in English was largely structured by an identity as primary caregiver in the family. She wanted to learn English so that she could take over the private/public tasks of the home from her children. The very reason why Martina and Petr came to Canada was to find a better life for their children. Martina was anxious not to jeopardize the children's future by having them take on more domestic and public tasks than were absolutely necessary. As well, because Martina had the responsibility for dealing with the public world, she was also anxious to understand the Canadian way of life – how things get done in Canadian society. Unlike Katarina, she could not rely on her husband to do this; indeed, her knowledge of English served as a resource for her husband. Like Katarina, Martina also wanted to learn English so that she could find a professional job for herself in Canada. However, as I will demonstrate, the conditions of possibility were more constrained in Martina's case than in Katarina's.

In the community in which Martina lived there were few anglophones with whom she could practice speaking English. As Martina said in an interview:

M.   I never heard English in this building.
B.   Really.
M.   Because in this door live some Chinese. They've been in Canada maybe nine years, but when they open door, they talk Chinese or Vietnamese, I don't know. And always if we open I heard the washer room Polish, or sometime Yugoslavish, or Portuguese or – I don't know what language. But it is not English. Maybe they are some English but I didn't see if it's one family or two –
B.   Really Martina. So there are a lot of immigrants here.
M.   Yes. I think because this building is quite a cheap. There are a lot of immigrants because a lot of people move in and move out.

Although there were few anglophone resources in her immediate community that Martina could draw on, Martina, like Mai, made use of her family's resources to help her to practice English. Her daughters taught her how to deal with customers, she would borrow her children's books from school and try to read them, her children would bring her books from the library and she would occasionally test her children on the work that she was doing in her skills course. Martina would also make superfluous phone calls to practice her English. For example, when her husband Petr wanted to sign up for an English course in Winchester, Martina decided to phone a number of schoolboards to practice her query. As she said,

About two weeks ago I called to the Separate School Board in Winchester and I asked for a booklet of the schools. I got it and then I tried to find some evening ESL course for Petr. They told me that I have to call on Wednesday about 6 o'clock. Then I tried to call some schools in Newtown for practise.

Because Martina was the primary caregiver in the home, she could not – would not – succumb to the nervousness and anxiety that she often felt when dealing with Canadians. She couldn't give up. Despite what might be considered to be a high affective filter, she refused to be silenced. Her identity as mother was more powerful than her identity as immigrant:

The first time I was very nervous and afraid to talk on the phone. When the phone rang, everybody in my family was busy, and my daughter had to answer it. After ESL course when we moved and our landlords tried to persuade me that we have to pay for whole year, I got upset and I talked with him on the phone over one hour and I didn't think about the tenses rules. I had known that I couldn't give up. My children were very surprised when they heard me.

Like Katarina, Martina wanted to be a good mother, but she did not define her motherhood in the same way that Katarina did. Unlike Katarina, she saw little threat that English would undermine her relationship with her children. She did not mind, for example, if her children did not learn Czech at school. 'My children say if we learn Czech at home it's enough.' An explanation for Martina's position may be that her children are older than Katarina's one child, and that their command of Czech is fully developed. Her children are young adults and have already undergone primary socialization by their parents. Furthermore, since Martina has taken over many of the public/private tasks in the home and is more organized and capable than her husband, Petr, she has an authority and esteem in the home that is not shared by Katarina or Mai's sister-in-law, Tan.

As the primary caregiver in the family, Martina was not only interested in practicing English, but in understanding how Canadians conduct themselves in the public world. Martina and her family had a number of unfortunate experiences in Canada as a result of unscrupulous landlords and appliance dealers. However, she did not passively accept the exploitation she had experienced, but actively sought a variety of methods to investigate the Canadian way of life. Since she had little contact with Canadians in general, she turned to television soap operas for guidance, writing as follows:

Why I chose 'One life to live' is a long story. When we came to Austria everybody told us that they didn't like the immigrants, but I met a lot of people who liked us. Not everybody is the same. The first month in Austria during the 'steel days'[1] we got the washer, the iron and other things. They weren't new, but we could use them. First month in Canada was very difficult, because we weren't able to communicate and understand. When we bought the refrigerator – it didn't work, it warmed up. Every second week a repairman came and after one week it stopped to work again. Then we decided to return it and we asked for a small freezer but they didn't have one. The manager told my daughter that she must wait and call every month. I was very disappointed and I wanted to know something about Canadians. First time we watch 'Who's the boss?' or 'The Cosby show' – it was funny, but I was looking for something else. After the ESL course when I had the interview, they asked me very different questions, the ones that we didn't study in school and I was very

surprised. Then I started to watch 'All my children' – not every day – and
'One life to live'. In both soap operas there are stories from actual people's
experiences and very few from work. There are different personalities.
The life is full of love, hate, danger and lies. When I told these stories to
my children I use some English phrases – leave me alone, what's going on,
etc. These phrases sound better in English.

Martina explained to me that she was fascinated by soap operas in Canada
because they were so different from the kind of soap operas she would watch
in Czechoslovakia. In her native country, all the television shows depicted
hard-working people devoted to the service of the state's economy. She
jokingly told me that Petr said his hands got sore just watching Czechoslovakian TV. Canadian soap operas, in contrast, only used work as a backdrop
to the domestic lives of the characters in the soap operas – lives that were
filled with love, hate, danger and lies. These soap operas, Martina said,
helped her to make sense of the experiences she had had in Canada. In
addition, they gave her much exposure to spoken English and were relatively
easy to understand.

Like Katarina, Martina was anxious to find employment in a job in which
she could practice her English on a regular basis and utilize the skills that
she had acquired in her native country. However, her search for employment
as a surveyor proved fruitless. She attributes her lack of success to ethnocentric practices in Canada. 'Because of my accent, some people treat me as if I
am less worthy than they are (especially when I was looking for a job)', she
wrote. As she understands it, an immigrant is someone who is less worthy
than Canadians. Although conscious of this marginalization, Martina does
not seem to resist it. In fact, she appears sympathetic to Canadians who are
'fed up' with people who can't speak English. She says that both her limited
command of English and her lack of Canadian experience are handicaps.
Significantly, Martina believes that one of the reasons why she was unable to
find a job in her profession was her lack of understanding of Canadian
cultural practices, noting as such in the following interview:

M.   I heard that in Canada you have to – sell yourself –.
B.   Exactly. Exactly.
M.   But I'm not the person. I never had problems with work because
     when I finish the school and I only fill the application at school and
     the school give us a company who had to keep us. And I work for one
     company for 16 years, and all the time only different branches.

Martina said she did not know how to market herself correctly. In this
regard, she explained that the knowledge that she has brought with her from
Czechoslovakia on how to conduct a job interview did not seem appropriate
in the Canadian context:

I was there, I had interview about two hours long. They want to know everything about me. They asked different questions. I never heard these questions. Some question was 'What I will do if the boss was shouting at me.' And I was very surprised. I thought 'My boss never, never shouted at me.' And I don't know, I said 'If I do something bad, I try to do better. And I will apologize.' But I don't know because never, never, I don't think about it.

Martina's limited knowledge of Canadian cultural practices mitigates against the possibility of getting a job in which she is competent, a job that will give her the opportunity to practice English with her co-workers. As Eva and Mai's experiences indicate, competence in a job gives a person a great deal of symbolic capital that carries with it the right to speak and converse in the workplace.

Because Martina was unable to get a job that does justice to her skills, she was prepared to take on unskilled work (kitchen help, cashier) while she attempted to improve her spoken English. She did not seem to have as much resistance as Katarina had to doing such work. It may be that she simply has fewer choices than Katarina – her husband Petr, a plumber, was constantly worried that he would become unemployed – and in fact, was laid off once the family moved to Winchester. In addition, Martina seemed to accept that her age made her less mobile than a younger person, and that getting a job in her profession would be difficult because of her second language skills and her lack of Canadian experience. Her major priority was not to join the Canadian professional classes, but to ensure the immediate survival of her family.

Although Martina sometimes despaired that she would 'clean all [her] life', she thought that this was preferable to remaining at home under depressing conditions. Although at home she had exposure to English through television and reading, these activities did not give her practice in speaking English. However, the kind of work that was available to Martina had given her little access to anglophone social networks. When she was working as a kitchen help at Fast Foods, the only people she came in contact with were her manager and the young part-time workers. While the manager and the part-time workers had a social relationship, Martina was excluded from interaction with them. Like Eva, she did not have the symbolic capital to enter the social network in the workplace, and she only had access to customers through her own initiative. It is important to note, however, that Martina did actively take initiative – she did not passively accept her marginalization, writing as follows:

My experiences with young Canadians were very bad, maybe I didn't have fortune. Usually I worked only with my manager, but when was P.A. day or some holidays for students, the manager stayed in his office and I worked with some students. Very often I worked with two sisters Jennifer (12 years) and Vicky (15 years) and the assistant manager who was on cash. These two girls loved talking but not with me. Even though I was very busy, they talked with young customers and laughed and sometimes looked at me. I didn't know if they laughed at me or not. When we didn't have any customers, they went to the manager office and tried to help the manager with 'wheel of fortune' on the computer. Later when some customers came in and I called these girls, they went but they made faces. I felt bad and I wanted to avoid this situation. In the evening I asked my daughter what I had to tell the customer. She answered me 'May I help you' then 'pardon' and 'something else'. When I tried first time to talk to two customers alone, they looked at me strangely, but I didn't give up. I gave them everything they wanted and then I went looking for the girls and I told them as usually only 'cash'. They were surprised but they didn't say anything. I tried doing that only a few times because I didn't have more chances.

Martina's marginalization, however, may have been exacerbated by the fact that she was a lot older than her co-workers. As she said:

In restaurant was working a lot of children but the children always thought that I am – I don't know – maybe some broom or something. They always said 'Go and clean the living room', and I was washing the dishes and they didn't do nothing. They talked to each other and they thought that I had to do everything. And I said 'No'. The girl is only 12 years old. She is younger than my son. I said 'No, you are doing nothing. You can go and clean the tables or something.'

This comment, I think, is highly significant. It depicts very clearly that a learner's identity is not only constituted by social interaction, but also constitutive of social interaction. Martina's identity as mother in the private sphere of her life leads her to situate the actions and comments of her younger co-workers in the public sphere within a domestic framework. She positions her co-workers as children, younger than her own, who have no right to give orders to her. The social meaning Martina attributed to the children's words and actions must therefore be understood with reference to the construction of Martina's identity across social space. This is an issue that will be discussed further in Chapter 6.

Despite the fact the Martina worked very diligently and conscientiously at Fast Foods for a period of eight months, she was nevertheless almost invisible there. When, for example, she needed to get a reference from Fast Foods so that she could get accommodation for her family, nobody at Fast Foods acknowledged her existence. She explained this in an interview with me:

> M.   When we moved they [the landlords] want some reference. Then I said, 'Can they [Fast Foods] give me reference?' because I was work-ing for 8 months. And if they tell me – I work from 6.30 to 2 or 3 o'clock – and if some student didn't come, they said, 'If I can stay for one or two hours?' I don't have any problem because when children come home – I always cook in the evening and when they come they only heat up little. I said 'It's OK.' Then I decided to put the Fast Foods on the application form, for this apartment. Then the manager called them. They said I never worked at the restaurant. Then the manager called me: 'I lie.' And I said 'No, it's true,' and I bring them three checks, and then he believes me. But it was so –
>
> B.   Terrible
>
> M.   – bad because I said 'oh, what am I supposed to do because –'
>
> B.   Why did they say that Martina?
>
> M.   Because they said that in Fast Foods they always telephone for some students, and maybe the students was working for short time, and when somebody asks 'No, no, she's not working. I never met her. Bye bye.' And we saw that we couldn't find any apartment because if we put – because they want know if we work, what we are for people.

One of the ways in which things get done in Canadian society is through the practice of providing personal references to help a person secure a job, accommodation, a bank loan. As a newcomer, however, Martina and her family did not have access to a network of social contacts who could verify what they were 'for people'. However, even though Martina had worked in a Canadian institution for eight months, she could not rely on her co-workers or management to respect this cultural practice. Such marginalization must be understood with reference to inequitable relations of power in Canada which sometimes render immigrants voiceless and invisible. Indeed, when one company asked Martina if she had a Canadian friend, the only person who came to Martina's mind was me. Martina believes that only time, hard work and courage will make a difference in their lives.

In sum, Martina's primary investment in English was to help her secure the survival of her family and a better life for her children. Her identity as mother and primary caregiver was one which structured her relationship to both the private and the public world and had a marked impact on the ways she created opportunities to practice English interact in the workplace. As primary caregiver in the family, Martina learnt very soon that in Canada 'you have to do things yourself'. Martina said, for example, that her children had never received English grammar lessons at school: 'They studied from books on their own. If I want to learn, I must do it by myself.' It was with great initiative that Martina took it upon herself to create opportunities to speak English and to learn about Canadian society. From attending ESL classes to making practice telephone calls and watching soap operas, Martina persevered in her efforts. Marginalization did not silence her. She knew she could not give up.

Despite the fact that Martina showed remarkable resourcefulness and progress in her second language learning, she frequently referred to herself as stupid and inferior because she could not speak English fluently. She said she was stupid for directing a telephone installer to the kitchen when he requested the use of the bathroom; she was stupid because she worked for four dollars an hour as a kitchen help; she was stupid because she took on extra tasks to help out her manager; she was inferior because she was not able to speak English fluently. Although marginalization did not silence Martina, she seemed to accept being positioned as an immigrant. Indeed, she appears sympathetic to anglophone Canadians, saying 'Some Canadians are fed up with people who are not able to communicate well English.' My understanding of Martina's position is that she believes that progress and success in life are a function of an individual's own capability and courage and not a function of larger, structural possibilities. Successful people are those who take initiative and 'do things yourself'. By extension, failure must be attributed to personal inadequacy or individual failure. It is for this reason, I think, that Martina had little resentment towards Canadians or Canadian social institutions, despite her marginalized status, and believed that Canada is a good country for immigrants. In order to succeed, an immigrant needs to work hard, be patient and have courage. Given this position, Martina was often bewildered when confronted with evidence that seemed to contradict her vision of Canada. She did not expect landlords to exploit her, appliance dealers to deceive her, employers and co-workers to ignore her and management to terminate her husband's employment. Despite her courage and her initiative in learning and practicing English, Martina felt that she has not found acceptance and respect in Canada. Indeed, she did feel some ambivalence about the family's decision to immigrate. Nevertheless, she has not given up. The last news of Martina was that she had taken a tax preparation course, graduating top of her class with 99 per cent. Her eldest daughter has been accepted to do a professional degree at a university, and her two younger children were doing well at school. Her courage may yet be vindicated.

Felicia

'I've never felt an immigrant in Canada, just as a foreigner person who lives here by accident.'

In Peru, Felicia had a relatively comfortable identity as the wife of a successful businessperson. They lived in the most exclusive part of town, owned a beach cottage, travelled and sent their children to private schools. However, because of the nature of her husband's work, her husband was subject to death threats and lived in fear for his life. It was for this reason that the family decided to leave Peru and settle in Canada, because 'the terrorism was increasing in Peru'. The transition from Peru to Canada was extremely difficult for Felicia, who was very unhappy that they immigrated. Felicia thinks she and her husband were duped by the local authorities in Peru who encouraged them to come to Canada. What has made the transition particularly difficult is the fact that Felicia's husband did not manage to get a good job in Canada, which led to a substantial change in the family's quality of life. As Felicia wrote:

> We downed our standard of living in Canada. We used to have a relaxed life in our country. My husband had a very good job. Canada doesn't give my husband the opportunity to work. I never will understand why the government gave him the professional visa.

Felicia has had to make many adjustments after the opulent lifestyle she led in Peru, saying life is very hard in Canada: 'It is just work, work, work.' In Peru the family would spend weekends at their beach cottage, but now they spend the weekends delivering flyers. How her changed class position affects Felicia's investment in English and practice of English is a highly complex issue and must be understood with reference to the construction of Felicia's identity. As indicated in Chapter 3, Felicia draws a distinction between different classes of immigrants: those who 'never had anything' in their countries of origin and those who were 'professional people and wealthy people'. She argues that people who never had anything are happy in Canada because they are not selective in their choice of work and can ultimately accumulate material goods. However, professional people lose rather than gain when immigrating to Canada because they are not as welcome here as they expected they would be. In Felicia's view, the Canadian government wants immigrants to spend a lot of money, but does not offer compensatory opportunities for them. Felicia bitterly resents the fact that the symbolic and material resources she and her family had enjoyed in Peru have little meaning in the Canadian context. As Connell *et al.* (1982) have argued, it is not who people are or what they own that is central to an understanding of class relationships. Rather, it is what people *do* with their resources that is significant. Felicia is resentful that, while the family does have symbolic resources in the form of skills and education, they have struggled to utilize these resources to maintain the class position that they had established in their home country. Felicia's husband submitted hundreds of résumés to prospective employers, contacted corporate headhunters and asked friends for assistance in his quest for employment. I, for example, was asked to review his résumé and introduce him to headhunters. I also helped Felicia find a childcare position at a local school. It is interesting that the only two women who used me as a resource (rather than simply a reference) were Katarina and Felicia, both of whom had vested interests in professional class relationships.

In Peru, Felicia's own status, self-esteem and material prosperity were associated with her husband's occupation and income. Since the birth of her children over 15 years prior to their immigration, Felicia had not worked in her profession as a teacher, and was a full-time homemaker. The only employment that Felicia was able to get in Canada was to deliver flyers and take care of children. When she arrived in Canada, and her husband could not find a job, there was little that Felicia could do to help either her husband or her family, organizationally or materially. At one time, Felicia ruefully declared that everybody in her family had some talents and achievements except her, 'whose English is poor'. Like Katarina's husband, Felicia's husband had developed good English skills before arriving in Canada. Her husband had gone to an English-medium school in Peru, and his work had brought him in contact with anglophones in the international arena. When Felicia was growing up in Peru, it was not deemed necessary for women to learn English, and Felicia had gone to a convent where Spanish was the medium of instruction. In English she learnt 'the verb "to be" and nothing else'. She said that in Peru English has become very important, given the influence of television, international communication and business, and her children had gone to a private English-medium school in Peru. Both her husband and children were therefore competent speakers of English before emigrating from Peru. Consequently, when Felicia arrived in Canada, her husband took on the responsibility of communicating with the public world. Unlike the situation in Martina's home, Felicia's family was not dependent on her English skills for a better life. English therefore did not have the same value for Felicia as it did for Martina, who was responsible for communicating with the public world in order to ensure the adequate functioning of the family. Further, unlike Katarina and like Martina, English did not represent a threat to her relationship with her daughter and two sons. In Felicia's home, Spanish was consistently used as the language of the home. Apart from the parents, the two older boys always used Spanish, as did the younger daughter. Felicia did not express any anxiety that her daughter would lose command over her mother tongue; she was confident that her daughter had enough support from all members of the family to pursue her knowledge of Spanish. As a result, like Martina, Felicia did not feel strongly that her children should learn their mother tongue at school or that English would threaten her relationship with her young daughter.

Felicia could not claim membership of the professional classes in Canada, nor was she comfortable with her lower standard of living, despite the fact that Canada provided a society in which 'there is not terrorism or many thiefs'. Felicia attributed their unfortunate circumstances to the fact that

Canada is not a friendly country. Indeed, Felicia gradually came to the conclusion that she was being positioned as an immigrant in Canada, a position, as indicated in the following extract, that she bitterly resented:

> Sometimes, I perceive that some Canadians look down at the immigrants, I don't know why, if ALL Canadians came from other countries too. Canada is formed from immigrants . . . Canadians think that here there isn't discrimination, but I don't think so. I hope that, in the future, I could change my mind.

Like Katarina, who also had great investment in the class position she had held in her home country, Felicia vehemently resisted being positioned as an immigrant in Canadian society. Katarina and Felicia both perceived that if they were positioned as immigrants they would be denied access to the social networks that they felt appropriate for their educational level and material status respectively. While Katarina resisted the immigrant label by pursuing educational goals, Felicia, who was ten years older than Katarina, felt less able to begin a new professional life. For this reason, Felicia retreated into an identity as a wealthy Peruvian, rejecting entirely any identification with her immigrant status. As she poignantly said, 'I've never felt an immigrant in Canada, just as a foreigner person who lives her by accident.' A 'foreigner person', like a tourist, is someone who is not subject to the social relations of power in the host country – she or he is a temporary sojourner, and has an independence and mobility that an immigrant does not have. Foreign people can thus relate to their hosts from a position of strength rather than a position of weakness. Felicia nurtures her Peruvian identity, has many Peruvian friends and likes to be known by her fellow workers as a friend from Peru.

How this identity impacts on Felicia's investment in English and opportunities to speak English is significant. To the extent that her Peruvian identity is validated, Felicia feels comfortable speaking English; if this identity is not validated, if she is positioned as an immigrant, Felicia is silenced. It is for this reason that Felicia feels most comfortable speaking to people she knows well. These are the people who have familiarity with her history and her Peruvian identity and would not dismiss her as an immigrant. The situation that she finds most comfortable is to meet regularly with another language learner on a one-to-one language exchange in her home. Felicia describes how, in their weekly meetings, they practice their mutual target languages.

> Like always we could speak very well. I feel very well talking with her, because she motivates my English and she is patient; she is interested in everything that I tell her. She has the same problem with her Spanish and it is good for both of us to feel comfortable.

With strangers, however, Felicia feels very uncomfortable. For example, she avoids speaking to the people in her apartment building. It seems she would rather be thought of as a timid or unfriendly person than an immigrant.

> In my building, live many senior people and when I meet them at the elevator always they tell me something about the weather or any other thing, but I answer with short answers because I can't talk fluently and fast. I think that maybe I look like a timid or unfriendly person.

Given her investment in her Peruvian identity, I think it is also highly significant that Felicia says 'I feel uncomfortable with new people and never can speak English in front of Peruvian people who speak English correctly.' Felicia would vehemently resist any unfavorable comparisons between herself and the class of Peruvians with whom she would like most to be associated – a phenomenon I will discuss more fully in the next chapter. As Connell *et al.* (1982) have argued, class is not a system of categories, but a system of relationships between people.

In her workplace at the Fair Lawns Recreational Centre, a centre that is located in an opulent part of town, Felicia has succeeded in projecting an identity of a wealthy Peruvian. Her co-workers, who live in the neighborhood of the recreational centre, know that she owns property in Peru, that she wants to buy a house in Newtown, and that she has three successful children and a professional (if unemployed) husband:

> I was talking with the ladies who work with me about a land that I'm selling in Peru. Last month there was a person interested to buy it. My sister-in-law was talking with her for many days, and called me by telephone collect, receiving my instructions to sell, but at last the lady didn't buy the land. And I have to pay about $600 for calls.

The women at this centre seem to have welcomed Felicia – a visitor rather than an immigrant – into their social network. They invite her home for dinner, discuss Peruvian news items with her, and are very patient with her English. Indeed, Felicia indicates that her progress in English can be attributed to the women she works with at this centre. It appears that Felicia's strategy of asserting her Peruvian identity has been vindicated, at least with respect to the opportunities available to her to practice English. However, although Felicia does interact with the women at work and has many opportunities to talk, it appears that her role is a relatively passive one. She tends to listen more than she talks: She does not want to appear an uninteresting person because of her lack of fluency in English. Thus, while she has overcome the hurdle of being considered an immigrant in the workplace, she feels that her lack of fluency in English makes her an uninteresting foreign person.

I listen to more English at my work than I have to talk. Sometimes the ladies ask me something about my country or my family, but I think that I'm not an interesting person because my English is limited and I have to think before talking. I feel confident with them because it is about 8 months that we worked together and I see them every day. They are very nice and patient with my English. I understand most that they talk, but I sometimes have to guess something.

Felicia does take the opportunity to talk to the toddlers in the childcare centre, although they tend to be very young and remain in the centre for only brief periods of time. However, Felicia is very reluctant to talk to the children's mothers: 'I avoid talking with the children's mothers because my English is too poor and I don't feel well talking with strangers. I would like to tell the mothers many things about their babies but I prefer to be silent. I only tell what is necessary.' Felicia prefers to be silent than to risk the possibility of being positioned as an immigrant in Canada: Strangers would have little knowledge of her Peruvian history and social class. Thus the opportunities open to Felicia to practice English are constrained by the risk of her being marginalized as an immigrant.

By way of comparison, when Felicia accepts another part-time job at an after-school childcare programme, she quits this job after only a few days because she feels both incompetent and marginalized at the school. Because she had to deal with older children, she needed fairly advanced English skills and struggled to maintain discipline in the programme. The children, furthermore, appeared to have little respect for her Spanish background and marginalized her as different. In addition, she was the only adult in the programme, and had no support from or communication with adults who might be more sympathetic than the children towards her Peruvian identity.

I started to work on Wednesday. Wednesday was okay, there were 19 children to look after and I could communicate with them and with the teacher who used to do this work before. Yesterday I went with Maria, she spoke to me in Spanish many times, there were different children than the day before, two of them were very active and the kind of children that don't like to obey. I had to call them the attention many times and I felt that my English was limited. One of the older children asked me, you have an accent, don't you? I answered yes, I do. He asked me if my language was French, and I answered not, but it is close to French. When his mother came to pick him up, I asked him his name, and he answered 'I don't know to tell my name in Spanish', and I answered him, 'You don't have to tell me your name in Spanish, you have to tell it in English.' Yesterday I didn't feel very well there.

Comment

In this chapter I have argued, with reference to the three older women in the study, that their investment in English and their opportunities to practice English must be understood in the context of their changing identities across historical time and social space. While recognizing the multiplicity and complexity of identity, an examination of their identities as mother offers a particularly interesting opportunity for comparative analysis. I have asked the question: 'To what extent is an immigrant woman's gendered identity as "mother" implicated in her investment in the target language and her interaction with target language speakers?' Perhaps the first and most important point to note is that the children of immigrant women are or will likely become target language speakers. Katarina, who had only one child, was acutely aware of this. Indeed, two concerns weighed heavily on her mind: Maria might grow up speaking a language that Katarina could not understand, and Maria might forget the only language that Katarina *could* understand. The solution to her dilemma was twofold: Maria had to become bilingual, and Katarina had to learn English as quickly and efficiently as possible, notwithstanding her ambivalence towards the language. Her investment in English was not, however, a one-to-one gender mapping: The data indicate convincingly that Katarina's desire to be recognized as a professional was also of great importance to her. Further, Katarina had none of the ambivalent feelings towards her native language, Polish, that Mai's sister had towards Vietnamese, or, for that matter, that Anzaldúa's mother, quoted at the beginning of this chapter, had towards Chicano Spanish. Why some minority languages have greater value than others is a topic that will receive greater attention in Chapter 6.

Although Martina and Felicia were both mothers of three children, all of whom were fluent speakers of their native language as well as English, their positions within their respective families were very different, which in turn influenced their investment in the English language and their relationship with target language speakers. Martina was not only the mother in the family but the primary caregiver, with an unemployed husband who had very limited proficiency in English. While her children initially took responsibility for interacting with the larger anglophone community, Martina wanted to learn English as quickly as possible so that she could take over such responsibilities from her children. To be a good mother in this context, then, extended not only to the private sphere of the home, but to all the public institutions outside of it. For this reason, Martina could not give up and, notwithstanding adverse experiences in the public world, would not be silenced. Unlike Martina, Felicia had a husband who was fully competent, not only in the English language, but in the cultural practices of Canadian society. And, unlike Katarina, she had a secure relationship with her children.

Thus, while her identity as mother in the private sphere of her home was secure, the only identity that had any public value for her was that of wealthy Peruvian. When she was able to assert her identity as a wealthy Peruvian to a sympathetic interlocutor, she would feel sufficiently comfortable to speak; conversely, she would rather not speak than be positioned as an immigrant. Given the particular circumstances of her private and public identity, her ambivalence towards English can be better understood. In the next chapter, I move from a predominantly descriptive presentation of the language learning experiences of the five women to a more analytical and interpretative discussion of the data.

Note

1. Martina explained that 'steel days' were days on which people leave second-hand steel appliances outside for other people to pick up if needed.

6

Second language acquisition theory revisited

No researcher today would dispute that language learning results from participation in communicative events. Despite any claims to the contrary, however, the nature of this learning remains undefined.

(SAVIGNON, 1991, p. 271)

Language is more than a mode of communication or a system composed of rules, vocabulary, and meaning; it is an active medium of social practice through which people construct, define, and struggle over meanings in dialogue with and in relation to others. And because language exists within a larger structural context, this practice is, in part, positioned and shaped by the ongoing relations of power that exist between and among individuals.

(WALSH, 1991, p. 32)

At the 1999 TESOL convention in New York, USA, Julian Edge and I (Edge and Norton, 1999) debated the extent to which it is productive to incorporate notions of power into theories of SLA. The point I made at the time is that, if we avoid naming and confronting questions of power in social interaction, we may struggle to understand the language learning experiences of our students. If we assume, for example, that all relationships between language learners and target language speakers are egalitarian ones, we might expect learners to enjoy the comfort and ease that Katarina experienced in her interactions with the elderly people in her Community Service job. However, this leaves unanswered questions about Eva's relationships to her co-workers at Munchies, Mai's at the Fabric Factory and Martina's at Fast Foods. Without incorporating theories of power in SLA (see Chapter 1), the nature of participation in communicative events may not only remain undefined, but unexplained. Such debates over power are not unique to SLA, however, and extend to the broader area of applied linguistics. As indicated in Chapter 5, Lakoff (1975) and Tannen (1990) have different interpretations of the speech production of women and men because they have divergent views on questions of power. While Lakoff argues that the speech patterns of women and men are best understood in the context of inequitable relations of power, Tannen understands such speech patterns as markers of difference rather than inequity. Such debates are not trivial ones. How we name and understand difference has a direct bearing on how we address it, at both a theoretical and practical level. If women and men are understood to be different but equal, there is little need for social change; if inequities exist, there is greater demand for social action.

Drawing on data presented in previous chapters, I take the position that some of the current models of SLA, in neglecting to address questions of power, do not do justice to the language learning experiences of immigrant language learners. It is important to note, further, that the data I present have striking similarities to the data presented in the larger, ESF project (Bremer *et al.*, 1996). I begin the chapter by revisiting theories of natural language learning, the acculturation model of SLA and the affective filter hypothesis, respectively. In the penultimate section, I argue that a post-structuralist conception of identity and Bourdieu's (1977) notion of legitimate discourse are theoretically useful in helping to explain the findings from my study and are a valuable contribution to SLA theory. In the final section, I extend these ideas to argue for a conception of language learning as a social practice.

Natural language learning

With reference to the learning of English as a second language, my research suggests that Spolsky's (1989) description of natural language learning, as outlined in Chapter 1, does not adequately reflect the experiences of the immigrant women in my study. Drawing on the data, I address each of the five characteristics of natural language learning that he outlines, with the caveat that Spolsky is reporting on current theory in the field rather than articulating a personal position.

The first claim that Spolsky makes is that, in natural language learning, the target language is used for authentic communication and not for contrived, classroom purposes. Under such conditions, there is a negotiation of meaning that is a valuable form of practice. What the data from my study indicate, however, is that target language speakers are frequently unwilling to engage in a negotiation of meaning with language learners. It was only on rare occasions that native English speakers would take the time to repair a breakdown in communication. More often than not, the native speakers would indicate through paralanguage their impatience with these foreign women: 'I could see by their face that they think this',·said Eva. Martina said that the expressions on the faces of the students she worked with at Fast Foods were sometimes worse than their comments.

The second claim is that in natural language learning, the learner is surrounded by fluent speakers of English. For three of the immigrant women in the study, Eva, Katarina and Martina, English was hardly ever spoken in their neighborhoods. All three lived in a community where accommodation was particularly inexpensive and tended to attract those people who had limited means of financial support, many of whom were ESL immigrants. English was spoken in Mai and Felicia's neighborhoods, but Felicia was afraid to speak for fear that she would be marginalized as an immigrant. Mai never once indicated that she spoke English to any of her affluent, predominantly anglophone neighbors. The only dependable exposure that the women had to spoken English was through television and radio, but these did not provide the women with opportunities to practice their speaking. A number of the women resorted to eavesdropping to increase their exposure to spoken English, whether on the bus, in stores or in shopping malls. As Martina indicates, however, when she sometimes tried to engage anglophones in social conversation in these public places, they would 'run away'. It was only in the workplace that some of the women were surrounded by fluent speakers of English. These fluent speakers of English, however, were organized in social networks to which the women struggled, and often failed, to gain access. Even in a supportive environment such as Felicia's, the tendency was for the learners to listen rather than speak. When the environment became hostile, as it did when workers were laid off at Mai's work, not only was Mai unable to speak, but the language medium of the workplace changed. Mai was then faced with the difficult decision of abandoning her social network at work or abandoning her attempts to speak English.

The third claim is that the outside world is open and stimulating, where there is a multitude of contextual clues for understanding language in use. For the women in the study, the outside world was not open and stimulating but one which, at best, 'went by without emotion' (Felicia), at worst was 'all storm and big windy' (Mai). All the women were intimidated by strangers – by people who did not know them, their personal histories, and the fact that they were not uneducated, illiterate, immigrants. The kind of contextual clues they would find in the outside world were those that dismissed them from the very open and stimulating environments they sought: 'They thought I was a broom or something', said Martina; 'They took advantage of me because they knew I wouldn't say anything', said Eva. The kinds of social contexts in which the women felt most comfortable to speak were familiar, friendly, intimate environments, where people were patient with their English. It is striking, in retrospect, to note that the place where the women spoke most comfortably and at length was in my car, when I used to drive them home from our diary study meetings. In the car we were all in close physical contact with one another; we were all removed from the stresses of the home, the workplace and the school; and we had all enjoyed an evening of intimate talk, in which experiences of marginalization were explored in the light of social relations of power rather than personal inadequacy. We were all in a mobile, insulated capsule, safe from the assaults of the 'open and stimulating' world. And we never stopped talking.

The fourth claim that is made is that, in natural language learning, the language used is free and normal, rather than carefully controlled and simplified. While the women were exposed to English spoken at a normal pace, they certainly did not feel free to use English as they would have liked to. Felicia, for example, frequently wished to tell the mothers of the children she tended stories of what had happened during the day, but refrained from doing so for fear of appearing incompetent. Eva wanted to tell her co-worker at Munchies to stop exploiting her, but only felt free, ultimately, to joke lightly when the co-worker was not doing her fair share of the work. Mai wanted to tell her brother that he could not control her life, but it was at times easier to be quiet and say nothing. Because most social interactions that the women encountered were marked by inequalities of gender and ethnicity, the language used was seldom free and normal but a mechanism of social control.

The final claim made is that in natural learning situations, where attention is on the meaning of the communication, 'the [native] speaker makes an effort to see that language is comprehensible' (Spolsky, 1989, p. 173). Martina's landlord never made it clear to Martina that she would be liable for a year's rent if she broke her lease; nor did the appliance dealer make it clear to her that she would have to wait for months to replace the refrigerator that kept warming up. The immigration officials never made it clear to Felicia that Canada was not always a land of milk and honey. The research suggests that the onus is on the learner to understand and be understood, and not on the native speaker to ensure that the learner understands. Whenever a breakdown in communication occurred, it is significant that the learner felt ashamed, while the target language speaker felt impatient or angry. It was for this reason that the women's desire to make themselves understood was even stronger than their desire to understand. One of Mai's co-workers from the first job that Mai had in Canada explained to Mai at a later date that she had stopped trying to talk to Mai because it had made her so tired. Martina said that Canadians are fed up with people who don't speak English. Eva said that her co-worker had indicated that he didn't like working with people who aren't Canadian. Felicia said that Canadians looked down on immigrants.

In sum, natural language learning does not necessarily offer language learners the opportunity to learn a second language in an open and stimulating environment, in which learners are surrounded by fluent speakers of the target language, who generously ensure that the learner understands the communication directed at the learner, and who are prepared to negotiate meaning in an egalitarian and supportive atmosphere. The research suggests that natural language learning is frequently marked by inequitable relations of power in which language learners struggle for access to social networks that will give them the opportunities to practice their English in safe and supportive environments. The reality for most of the women in the study was that the outside world was frequently hostile and uninviting. Native speakers of English were often impatient with their attempts at communication and more likely to avoid them than negotiate meaning with them. The multitude of contextual clues that they picked up were that native speakers did not like to talk or work with immigrants.

Bourdieu's (1977) notion of the legitimate speaker, introduced in Chapter 1, helps to explain the natural language learning experiences of these immigrant women. He argues that, when a person speaks, the speaker wishes not only to be understood, but to be 'believed, obeyed, respected, distinguished' (p. 648). However, Bourdieu takes the position that a speaker's ability to command the listener is unequally structured for different speakers because of the symbolic power relations between them. His position, he argues, is distinct from that of the linguist (as well, I have argued, from many SLA theorists) who has only an abstract notion of competence:

> The linguist regards the conditions for the establishment of communication as already secured, whereas, in real situations, that is the essential question. He takes for granted the crucial point, namely that people [who] talk to each other, are 'on speaking terms,' that those who speak regard those who listen as worthy to listen and that those who listen regard those who speak as worthy to speak.

> (p. 648)

Drawing on Bourdieu, I take the position that the women's experiences of natural language learning were generally alienating ones because they could not command the attention of their listeners; nor were they regarded as worthy to speak. It is for this reason, I suggest, that the women were more concerned that they be understood than that they understand: If they could not impose reception, if they had no right to speak, they were *ipso facto* unworthy people. Because the linguist's abstract notion of competence does not address real situations (or what SLA theorists call natural situations of social interaction), Bourdieu argues that the expanded definition of competence should include the 'right to speech' (1977, p. 648). This is an issue that will be addressed more fully in the final section of this chapter.

Alberto and the acculturation model of SLA

In 1973 a research project was undertaken at Harvard University by Cazden, Cancino, Rosansky and Schumann (1975) to conduct a 10-month longitudinal study of the untutored acquisition of English by six native speakers of Spanish – two children, two adolescents and two adults. The study focused on the subjects' acquisition of *wh*-questions, negatives and auxiliaries. Data collection involved the recording of both spontaneous and experimentally elicited speech. Schumann presents the findings on the 33-year-old, working-class Costa Rican subject, Alberto, in whom Schumann took a particular professional interest, to support his pidginization hypothesis (1976b, 1978a) and the acculturation model of SLA (1978b, 1986). There are a number of reasons why I would like to examine the acculturation model of SLA in some depth. The model was developed specifically with a view to explaining the language acquisition of adult immigrants. 'This model accounts for second-language acquisition under conditions of immigration', says Schumann (1978b, p. 47). As such, it is particularly germane for the purposes of my study. Further, the model is based on the premise that there is a causal link between acculturation and SLA: 'SLA is just one aspect of acculturation and the degree to which the learner acculturates to the TL (target language) group will control the degree to which he acquires the second language' (1978b, p. 34). In addition, Schumann (1978b, p. 48) states that the model 'argues for acculturation and against instruction'. In other words, if acculturation does not take place, instruction in the target language will be of limited benefit to the language learner – a theory which has important implications for the second language education of adult immigrants. Finally, the model has been highly influential in the field of SLA, featuring prominently in the established literature on SLA theory (see for example H.D. Brown, 1994; Ellis, 1997; Larsen-Freeman and Long, 1991; Spolsky, 1989).

In his study, Schumann noted that Alberto showed very little linguistic development during the 10-month research study, far less in fact, than the other five subjects. Alberto was characterized as using a reduced and simplified form of English, what Schumann calls a pidginized English. Schumann argues that three explanations are considered for the lack of development in Alberto's speech: ability, age and social and psychological distance from speakers of the target language. Schumann dismisses the first two reasons on the grounds of lack of evidence and concludes that it is the 'social and psychological distance' between Alberto and the target language community that accounts for Alberto's pidginized speech. In his later work, Schumann (1978b) refined his earlier theories into the acculturation model of SLA, the central premise of which is as follows:

I would like to argue that two groups of variables – social factors and affective factors – cluster into a single variable which is the major causal variable in SLA. I propose that we call this variable acculturation. By acculturation I mean the social and psychological integration of the individual with the target language group. I also propose that any learner can be placed on a continuum that ranges from social and psychological distance to social and psychological proximity with speakers of the TL, and that the learner will acquire the language only to the extent that he acculturates.

(p. 29)

While the details of acculturation model are accessible in the numerous publications listed above, what is of particular relevance to the focus of my study is the process whereby Schumann reached his conclusions and the theoretical adequacy of the model that he developed on the basis of his findings. I return then to the data on which Schumann bases his acculturation model of SLA: the pidginized speech of a 33-year-old working-class Costa Rican named Alberto.

In the original 1973 study conducted by Cazden *et al.* (1975) there were, as indicated above, six subjects: two children, two adolescents and two adults. While the first four subjects were the children of upper middle-class Latin American professional immigrants, Schumann describes Alberto as belonging to 'a social group designated as lower-class Latin American worker immigrants' (1976b, p. 400). During the course of the 10-month study, Alberto's incorrect usage of the English negative, interrogative and auxiliary did not improve, while that of the other subjects did. Schumann argues that since the Latin American worker immigrant group was at a greater social distance from Americans than are professionals, he would expect the worker's use of English to be functionally restricted and to pidginize. 'This is precisely what we found in Alberto', argues Schumann. In order to get some assessment of Alberto's psychological distance from Americans, Alberto was given a questionnaire to fill out on his attitude and motivation. Unexpectedly, the questionnaire indicated that Alberto 'seemed to have a positive attitude and good motivation, and hence little psychological distance' (Schumann, 1976b, p. 403) from the target language community. It is significant that Schumann dismisses this evidence on the grounds that Alberto may not have been entirely candid in his answers. Because Alberto was not responding as expected, Schumann assumed that Alberto was not telling the truth.

While Schumann accused Alberto of saying 'what he thought the experimenter wanted to hear' (1976b, p. 403), Schumann does not consider the possibility that the experimenter would only hear what he wanted to prove – namely that a learner whose language pidginizes must *ipso facto* be unmotivated and have negative attitudes towards the target language community. Schumann does not consider two alternative possibilities to explain his data: First, that a highly motivated Alberto *was* telling the truth and did indeed have positive attitudes towards Americans; second, that the reason why Alberto's language pidginized was very simply because the members of the dominant anglophone community had ambivalent attitudes towards Alberto, offering him limited opportunities to practice English, rather than the reverse situation. In essence, if Schumann found that Alberto's lack of progress in language learning was due to the social and psychological distance between Alberto and anglophones, it may be because the dominant power structures within society had relegated Alberto to a marginalized status and then blamed him for his inability to acculturate.

The strength of the acculturation model is that it highlights the sociocultural context of language learning without neglecting the role of individuals in the language learning process. It recognizes, furthermore, the importance that must be placed on regular contact between language learners and speakers of the target language for successful language learning to take place. However, I wish to call into question the theoretical adequacy of the model and argue for a different conception of the relationship between the adult immigrant language learner and the target language community than that presupposed by this model. In order to defend my position, I examine three assumptions of the acculturation model in some depth.

Assumption 1:   If a second language group is inferior or subordinate to the target language group, it will resist learning the second language.

The first point to note here is that the acculturation model does not theorize inferiority and superiority with reference to inequitable relations of power, in which second language groups are socially structured as inferior to the dominant group. The data from my study indicate that the participants did not arrive in Canada feeling inferior or what Martina called less worthy than Canadians; they were constructed as such by the signifying practices of the dominant society. The social meaning of immigrant is one that was constructed within and by the everyday experiences of the women in the study in the multiple domains of their lives. For example, as a result of her interaction with immigration officials, Katarina concluded that immigration officials think that immigrants 'must work for first ten years as dishwasher'. Thus, one of the social meanings of immigrant, for Katarina, is that it connotes a working-class position. This view is corroborated by other participants, who noted that an immigrant is someone who is considered to work in unskilled jobs, someone who, as Eva put it, has very little education and is too stupid to do skilled work. An immigrant is also a person who, as Felicia said, people look down on. Mai had to struggle against being positioned as an immigrant on the grounds of her language and her race while Martina said that her lack of fluency in English made her feel inferior. For all the women, the social meaning of immigrant was not newcomer with initiative and courage, but uneducated, unskilled minority. The only woman who would speak under such conditions of marginalization was Martina, and she did so only because she could not give up if her family were to thrive in Canada.

The second point to note, in relation to Assumption 1, is that, even though the women felt marginalized in Canadian society, they did not resist learning English. On the contrary, they strongly believed that command of the English language would rid them of the immigrant label and help them obtain the opportunities for which they had come to Canada. Indeed, the data indicate that the people who resist interaction are more likely to be members of the dominant language group rather than immigrant language learners. It is quite possible that Alberto, like the women in the study, may have simultaneously chafed against his inferior status while still seeking opportunities to speak to anglophones. He did, after all, devote ten months of his time with anglophone researchers practicing the negative construction in English.

Assumption 2:   If members of the second language learning group give up their lifestyles and values and adopt those of the target language group, they will maximize their contact with the target language group and enhance SLA.

Assumption 3:   Positive attitudes between the target language group and the second language group will enhance SLA.

Assumption 2 given above is described in the acculturation model as the integration strategy of assimilation (Schumann, 1978b). The model states that, while it is not essential for a language learning group to give up its lifestyles and values in order to enhance SLA, the group must minimally adapt to the lifestyle and values of the target language group for acquisition to take place; it can still maintain its own lifestyles and values for intragroup use. Positive attitudes (Assumption 3) between the two groups will facilitate assimilation and thus enhance the SLA of the language learner group. The problem with Assumptions 2 and 3 is that they take for granted that members of the target language group are happy to accommodate attempts by the second language group to assimilate and that they will reciprocate the positive attitudes of the language learner group. The model does not consider the possibility that inequitable power relations may prevent members of the language learner group from maximizing their contact with target language speakers, notwithstanding the positive attitudes of the language learner group. More significantly, however, the model does not consider the possibility that SLA may, in contradistinction to the model's predictions, be impeded if language learners give up their lifestyle and values in favour of those of the target language group. As a particularly striking – and tragic – example of this, I wish to focus on the data obtained on Mai's language learning experiences in her brother's home.

I noted in Chapter 4 that Mai had many opportunities to practice speaking English in her place of residence because her nephews were monolingual speakers of English, and could not converse in Vietnamese, their mother tongue. Furthermore, Mai took on the position of a language broker in her brother's home, interpreting between her nephews and her parents, and occasionally between her nephews and their mother. The nephews were surprised that, although Mai had only been in Canada a short time, she was a better speaker of English than their mother, who had lived in Canada for over ten years. A central concern here is the fact that Mai's nephews had undergone a process of what Lambert (1975) calls subtractive bilingualism, in which a second language was learnt at the cost of losing the mother tongue, and that Mai's sister-in-law was unable to interact successfully with her own children – in either her mother tongue or the target language. What is equally disturbing, given Assumptions 2 and 3, is that Mai's brother and sister-in-law had actively sought to assimilate into the anglophone Canadian world and had highly positive attitudes towards Canadians. Something had gone terribly wrong.

I suggest that the reason why Mai's extended family was populated by monolingual speakers, when a process of rich bilingualism might have taken place, is partly because Mai's extended family was caught up in a discourse of racism in Canadian society and perhaps in other countries in which her brother had lived, travelled and worked. As I have indicated in Chapter 4, Mai learnt very soon after arriving in Canada that her brother thought Canadians were superior ('high'), while Vietnamese and Chinese people were inferior ('low'). Mai was shocked at how much her brother had changed: He had little regard for his own history and way of life; he had little respect for his own parents, he thought Vietnamese and Chinese people were bad people, and he (and his wife) had not actively encouraged their children to maintain their mother tongue. Given Mai's brother's experience of overt or covert racism, it is not difficult to see how his sons could have grown to despise their appearance, reject their histories and lose their command of Vietnamese, their mother tongue. Mai, who believed that a person cannot just discard everything that one values (and who, significantly, had made great progress in learning the target language) was aware of this tragedy, and vowed the following: 'I think I won't let it happen to my children if I have in my future.'

The acculturation model does not acknowledge that situations of additive[1] and subtractive bilingualism must be understood with reference to larger social structures in which (in the Canadian context) language learners of European descent do not experience the racism that is experienced by people of Vietnamese descent. Consider Katarina, for example, who compared her experiences of living in Austria, where she said Polish people are considered 'second category' people with her experiences in Canada, where she said Canadians accept Polish people. In contrast to Mai's sister-in-law who did not encourage her sons to learn Vietnamese, Katarina actively sought to ensure that her daughter Maria maintained her mother tongue while learning English. Furthermore, the acculturation model does not address the point that immigrant language learners are generally more invested in relationships with target language speakers than the reverse situation. The immigrants are the ones who need to make contact with members of the target language community if their language learning is to improve, and they are far more vulnerable to the attitudes of the dominant group than the dominant group is vulnerable to them. Despite the marginalization experienced by the women in my study, the only one who expressed negative attitudes towards Canadians as a group was Felicia, who indicated that she thought Canadians are not friendly people. Even this attitude, however, did not deter Felicia from seeking opportunities to practice English with a fellow learner in the non-threatening environment of her home. The remaining four women frequently indicated their desire to have more contact with Canadians.

In sum, the acculturation model draws sharp distinctions between the social (group differences between the language learner group and the target language group) and the individual, who may be motivated or unmotivated. The model places the onus on the adult immigrant to make the appropriate adjustments to the target language community in order to increase contact with target language speakers, thereby enhancing the SLA process. To the extent that progress is not made in language learning, the model holds the language learner responsible for resisting acculturation. Differences between language learners and target language speakers are not theorized in terms of unequal relations of power, which compromise efforts by language learners to interact with target language speakers and promote SLA. Indeed, it is a tragic irony that in the only case where a family rejected its own values and lifestyle in favour of the perceived values of anglophone Canadians, the social fabric of the family was destroyed, together with any hope of bilingual language development.

The affective filter

As indicated in Chapter 1, most current models of SLA note the importance of affective factors in the second language learning process. Krashen (1981, 1982) has in fact hypothesized that comprehensible input in the presence of a low affective filter is the major causal variable in SLA. In Krashen's view, this affective filter comprises the learner's motivation, self-confidence and anxiety state and these are variables that pertain to the individual rather than the social context. I have indicated, however, that many second language theorists are not in complete agreement with Krashen's conception of the affective filter or his understanding of how affective variables interact with the larger social context. By reexamining the notions of motivation, self-confidence and anxiety with reference to my data, I will argue that a language learner's affective filter cannot be understood apart from his or her relationship to larger, and frequently inequitable social structures.

Motivation

All the participants in the study were highly motivated to learn English. They all took extra courses to learn English, they all participated in the diary study, they all wished to have more social contact with anglophone Canadians and all of them, except Martina, indicated that they felt comfortable speaking to friends. It is significant, however, that all the women felt uncomfortable talking to people *in whom they had a particular symbolic or material investment*. Eva, who came to Canada for economic advantage, and was eager to work with anglophones, practice her English and get better jobs, was silenced when the very customers she depended on made comments about her accent. Mai, who came to Canada for her life in the future and depended on the wishes of management for her job security and financial independence, was most uncomfortable speaking to her boss. Katarina, who came to Canada to escape a communist and atheistic system, and had a great investment in her status as a professional, felt most uncomfortable talking to her teacher, the doctor and other anglophone professionals. Martina, who had given up a surveyor's job to come to Canada for the children, was frustrated and uncomfortable when she could not defend her children's rights in the public world. Felicia, who had come to Canada to escape terrorism, and had great investment in her Peruvian identity, felt most uncomfortable speaking English in front of Peruvians who speak English fluently.

Despite being highly motivated, there were particular conditions under which the women were most uncomfortable and unlikely to speak. As argued in Chapter 1, the concept of motivation as currently taken up in the SLA literature conceives of the language learner as having a unified, coherent identity which organizes the type and intensity of a language learner's motivation. My data indicate that motivation is a much more complex matter than hitherto conceived. A learner's motivation to speak is mediated by other investments that may conflict with the desire to speak – investments that are intimately connected to the ongoing production of the learners' identities and their desires for the future. In order to capture the complex interaction of different forces on the women's desire to speak and practice English, I have talked about the women's investment in English, rather than their motivation to speak. By exploring the women's investment in English, it is possible to understand how and to what extent they created and responded to opportunities to practice English. I will consider each of the women in turn.

For Eva, English represented a means towards economic independence in the public world, and access to higher education. Her investment in English must be understood with reference to her gendered identity as a young, single woman, her reasons for immigrating to Canada – for economic advantage, and her plans for the future – to study at college. Unfettered by heavy domestic duties and childcare responsibilities, she was able to seek and obtain full-time employment in workplaces that would give her increased exposure to English and opportunities to practice English. As she gradually assumed the identity of a valued co-worker and multicultural citizen, she began to speak more.

English for Mai represented a means towards gender emancipation in the home as well as economic independence in the private and public world. Mai's gendered identity as a single woman was one that was constantly undermined, initially in her home, and ultimately in the workplace. It was command of English that gave her an identity as a language broker in her home and the prospect of an attractive career in the public world. Her investment in English must be understood with reference to the constraints of her domestic life, her reasons for coming to Canada 'for my life in the future', and her plans for the future – 'to take some higher course at college'. She was extremely diligent in her attempts to practice English, and drew constantly on resources in the home, workplace and community to do so. Her new position as a wife in a patriarchal marriage, however, may ultimately undermine her opportunities to speak and practice English.

For Katarina, English was not an unqualified boon as it represented a threat to her gendered identity as a mother. It also represented a challenge to her authority in the private world because her husband, who was more competent in English than she was, took charge of the private/public communicative tasks when they first moved to Canada. However, English was also her means towards entry into a professional world where life would be normal again, as it had been in Poland. A normal life for Katarina was one in which fellow professionals would validate her symbolic resources, and one in which she could have regular social contact with Canadians who shared her values and educated status. As will be examined more fully in Chapter 7, Katarina withdrew from social interaction and resisted opportunities to learn English when her symbolic resources were not validated.

For Martina, English represented a means towards a better future for her children, which was her reason for coming to Canada. Her desire to learn English to get a better job was secondary to the needs of her family, particularly because her husband was unable to help perform the private/public communicative tasks necessary to preserve the continuity of family life. Although she was a highly educated woman, Martina did not demand respect for her educated status in the same way that Katarina had, and she did not react as strongly as Katarina had towards being positioned as an immigrant. Because her investment in English had less to do with her own life chances than with the life chances of her children, marginalization did not silence Martina: In the interests of her children, she knew she could not give up. She took every opportunity to practice English, even if it meant phoning strangers on vague pretexts, and she did not withdraw when people treated her with disrespect.

For Felicia, English represented the means towards her acceptance as an interesting person who could actively participate in social interactions with Canadians rather than passively observing them. Because she had three children, two of whom were adolescents, she was not concerned, as Katarina was, that English would threaten her gendered identity as a mother. However, because all her family were more competent in English than she was, she was not required to deal with the public anglophone world in the same way that Martina had. Felicia knew that she had to 'practice, practice, practice' in order to improve her English, but, unlike Martina, did not make use of every opportunity to speak. Her fear of being marginalized as an immigrant was greater than her desire to practice English in the public world. For this reason, she retreated into the safety of her home to practice English with another language learner who validated her Peruvian identity. As will be discussed more fully in Chapter 7, Felicia totally withdrew from social interaction when her Peruvian identity was negated.

Anxiety and self-confidence

The confusion in the literature about the role of motivation in SLA is paralleled by debate over the role of anxiety and self-confidence in SLA.[2] Spolsky (1989, p. 115), for example, has argued that 'there is a specific kind of anxiety that in the case of many learners interferes with second language learning'. He argues that this anxiety is most often focused on listening and speaking skills. Bailey (1983), on the other hand, distinguishes between facilitating and debilitating anxiety, suggesting that anxiety is not a permanent predisposition of a learner, but is context-dependent. In Krashen's affective filter hypothesis, anxiety and poor self-confidence (along with low motivation) are considered individual characteristics of a poor language learner. My data suggest that there is a variety of ways in which anxiety and self-confidence influence the extent to which learners create and respond to opportunities to practice the target language. The data indicate that in the natural language learning situation, a learner's anxiety is, as Spolsky argues, associated with the learner's oral skills rather than literacy skills. Felicia made the point that it is 'easier for me yet, understand when I read, than when I listen (or hear)'. Martina, for example, says 'if I wrote I can correct by myself and I can think about it. The problem with speaking, I don't have time to think about it. But if I write something, it's not big problem'. Eva points to a related problem when she says that, unlike the Canadians at her work who are fluent in English, she cannot take her customers' orders and speak to them at the same time: 'They don't understand sometimes what it is and then I have to explain everything. And it's hard for me, because for another person who can speak English fluently, it's not as hard, and I cannot do this all the time – write and speak'. The problem, Eva says, is one of time: 'I wouldn't speak to the customers because I wouldn't feel confident to speak to the customers. Because I do not have enough time to speak to them.'

The effect of what Norton Peirce, Swain and Hart (1993) refer to as the locus of control in a communicative event helps to explain the women's lack of confidence in their oral skills. On the basis of their findings on self-assessment among French immersion students, Norton Peirce *et al.* argue that, if learners control the rate of flow of information in a communicative event, the locus of control will be in their favour and they will be relatively more confident about their language skills than in communicative events in which the locus of control is not in their favour. The important issue here is whether or not a particular communicative event is time-dependent. In activities that take place in real time, that is when the learner has little time to process information, the learner will have limited time to activate the schemata necessary to help decode the utterance. If the utterance does not take place in real time, the learner will take as much time as is necessary to activate such schemata. Since oral activities take place in real time, learners have little control over the rate of flow of information in these communicative events, which in turn increases their levels of anxiety.

While the locus of control is a useful construct to explain the anxiety that learners experience when called upon to exercise their oral skills in social interaction, it does not address the extent to which feelings of anxiety and lack of confidence are socially constructed in and by the lived experiences of learners. Like the women in Rockhill's study, instead of feeling a sense of accomplishment at the great progress they had all made in learning English, the participants in my study tended to feel ashamed, inferior and uninteresting because of their second language abilities. Such feelings of inadequacy and poor self-confidence must be linked to the power relations that the women had to negotiate in their social interactions in the wider community and their marginalized positions as immigrants. In this regard, Eva's response to the question, 'When do you feel most comfortable speaking English?' is significant: 'It much depends on the speaker I talk to. If one doesn't constantly show his or her superiority my English is more fluent and relaxed. I become tense and tend to forget even simple grammar rules if one does make comments about my accent.' Such data indicate very clearly that anxiety is not an inherent trait of a language learner, but one that is socially constructed within and by the lived experiences of language learners.

The data indicate further that anxiety is not only constructed within social interaction but also with reference to the learner's preoccupation with stressful day-to-day living conditions. Mai, for example, made the following comment: 'I feel comfortable using English most of the time except when I have some problems because by that time the problems always in my mind it makes me feel uncomfortable to using English.' Of all the women in the study, Mai had arguably the most stressful life in Canada, given that both her home and ultimately her work environments offered her little comfort or refuge from the 'stormy and windy' immigrant experience. With problems 'always on my mind' Mai felt at times uncomfortable using English, irrespective of the particular social interaction she was engaged in. In contrast, Mai said in an interview that if she feels 'comfortable or happy, so I can think very easy'. Felicia made a similar point when she wrote that learning English is hard 'because I live here with many tensions'.

In the Levi Strauss study, Norton Peirce, Harper and Burnaby (1993) found that some women dropped out of the EWP program because they felt nervous and anxious during the ESL class. Such anxiety was partly socially constructed by the conditions of their work. Because job security was determined by the worker's ability to achieve what is called their 100 per cent – the minimum productivity level required to maintain their positions at the company – some workers were distracted during the ESL class: They were thinking of work that needed to be done and sewing mistakes that needed to be corrected. As one worker said (Norton Peirce, Harper and Burnaby, 1993, p. 19), 'The thing is, sometimes I make a lot of mistakes at my work, and I'm think about it. I want the class finish fast so I can go back to work to look at the work.' Their anxiety could not be considered an invariant personality trait but a condition constructed by poor economic conditions and limited life chances.

Reconceptualizing identity

In suggesting that the relationship between the individual and the social in the context of second language learning should be reconceptualized, I am drawing particularly on feminist poststructuralism as represented in the work of Weedon (1997). Feminist poststructuralism, like much postmodern educational theory (Cherryholmes, 1988; Giroux, 1988; Simon, 1992), explores how prevailing power relations between individuals, groups and communities impact on the life chances of individuals at a given time and place. The work of feminist poststructuralists, however, is distinguished from that of other postmodern theorists in the centrality it accords to women's experience, and the rigorous and comprehensive way it links individual experience and social power in a theory of subjectivity. Subjectivity is defined as 'the conscious and unconscious thoughts and emotions of the individual, her sense of herself and her ways of understanding her relation to the world' (Weedon, 1997,

p. 32). Thus, while feminist poststructuralism is not an orthodoxy, but 'a field of critical practices that cannot be totalized' (Butler and Scott, 1992, xiii), it seeks to harness social theory and make it accountable to women's interests. Having noted the limitations of theories of natural language learning, the acculturation model and the affective filter hypothesis for explaining my data, I have found feminist poststructuralism compelling in its explanatory potential. The theory of subjectivity, in particular, has helped me to formulate a concept of identity that is useful in understanding the women's stories, a concept which promises to be theoretically productive in SLA theory. In this regard, three defining characteristics of subjectivity are central: the multiple, nonunitary nature of the subject, subjectivity as a site of struggle and subjectivity as changing over time.

Identity and the nonunitary subject

Weedon (1997) argues that the terms subject and subjectivity signify a different conception of the individual than that associated with humanist conceptions of the individual dominant in Western philosophy. While humanist conceptions of the individual – and many definitions of the individual in SLA research – presuppose that every person has an essential, unique, fixed and coherent core (introvert/extrovert; motivated/unmotivated), poststructuralism depicts the individual – the subject – as diverse, contradictory, dynamic and changing over historical time and social space. Subjectivity is conceived of as multiple rather than unitary, decentered rather than centered. The concept of identity as non-unitary and contradictory helps to explain the following data. Eva wanted to be regarded as an equal in the workplace, but she wanted her co-workers to recognize and respect her difference. As she said, 'When I started to work there, they couldn't understand that it might be difficult for me to understand everything and know about everything what it's normal for them.' Mai wanted to resist the patriarchal forces in her family and lead a life independent of her brother, but she did not want to be marginalized as someone who had no man; she wanted to be accepted by the Italian women at work, but she did not want to learn Italian at the expense of learning English. Katarina wanted her daughter to learn English, but she didn't want her daughter's knowledge of English to undermine their relationship; she wanted to take English courses, but she also wanted to take computer courses that would give her the opportunity to think. Martina was uncomfortable speaking English but, in the interests of her children, refused to be silent; she felt stupid because of her English skills, but graduated at the top of her tax preparation course. Felicia wanted to 'practice, practice, practice' speaking English, but she didn't want to speak in public; she wanted her husband to find a job, but she didn't want him to deliver pizza.

The position that identity is nonunitary and contradictory has important implications for understanding how the women responded to and created opportunities to speak English. To illustrate this point, consider some of the multiple sites of Martina's identity formation: She was an immigrant, a mother, a language learner, a worker, a wife. As a socially constructed immigrant woman, Martina never felt comfortable speaking. As she said, 'I feel uncomfortable using English in the group of people whose English language is their mother tongue because they speak fluently without any problems and I feel inferior.' Significantly, however, despite feelings of inferiority and shame, Martina refused to be silenced. I suggest that the reasons why Martina refused to be silenced were because her identity as a mother and primary caregiver in the home led her to violate the appropriate rules of use governing interactions between legitimate speakers of English (anglophone Canadians) and imposters (Bourdieu, 1977). The multiple sites of identity formation explain the surprises in Martina's data. Two examples come to mind which are described below.

Martina surprised her children (and no doubt her landlord and herself) by entering into a long conversation with her landlord on the phone in which she insisted that her family had not broken their lease agreement. As she wrote:

> The first time I was very nervous and afraid to talk on the phone. When the phone rang, everybody in my family was busy, and my daughter had to answer it. After ESL course when we moved and our landlords tried to persuade me that we have to pay for whole year, I got upset and I talked with him on the phone over one hour and I didn't think about the tenses rules. I had known that I couldn't give up. My children were very surprised when they heard me.

Further, Martina surprised customers at Fast Foods (who looked at her strangely) and co-workers (who were surprised, but said nothing) by taking the initiative to serve the customers while the other workers were playing a video game in the manager's office.

> When I tried first time to talk to two customers alone, they looked at me strangely, but I didn't give up. I gave them everything they wanted and then I went looking for the girls and I told them as usually only 'cash'. They were surprised but they didn't say anything.

I suggest that Martina's perseverance ('I couldn't give up', 'I didn't give up') and her courage to challenge linguistic rules of use that limited possibilities for herself and her family intersect with her identity as a mother: As a primary caregiver, she could not rely on her husband to deal with the public world and defend the family's rights against unscrupulous social practices. Martina had to do this herself, regardless of her command of the English tense system, regardless of the strange looks she received from her interlocutors, regardless of her feelings of inferiority. As well, Martina drew on her symbolic resources as a mother to *reframe* the power relations between herself and her co-workers. Thus, instead of conceding to their power as legitimate speakers of English who had the power to demand obedience of imposters of the language, she reframed their relationship as a domestic one in which, as children, they had no authority over her, as a parent. I repeat the relevant extract from Martina, quoted in Chapter 5:

> In restaurant was working a lot of children but the children always thought that I am – I don't know – maybe some broom or something. They always said 'Go and clean the living room', and I was washing the dishes and they didn't do nothing. They talked to each other and they thought that I had to do everything. And I said 'No'. The girl is only 12 years old. She is younger than my son. I said 'No, you are doing nothing. You can go and clean the tables or something.'

Identity as a site of struggle

In feminist poststructuralist theory, subjectivity is theorized as produced by and producing the meaning-making practices of the home, the workplace, the school, the community. Subjectivity is produced in a variety of social sites, all of which are structured by relations of power in which the person takes up different subject positions as teacher, child, feminist, manager, critic. The subject, in turn, is not conceived of as passive; he or she is conceived of as both subject of and subject to relations of power within a particular site, community and society: the subject has human agency. Thus the subject positions that a person takes up within a particular discourse are open to contestation: While a person may be positioned in a particular way within a given discourse, the person might resist the subject position, or even set up a counter-discourse which positions the person in a powerful rather than marginalized subject position. The concept of identity as a site of struggle is a logical extension of the position that identity is multiple and contradictory. If identity were unitary, fixed and immutable, it could not be subject to change over time and space, nor subject to contestation.

The conception that identity is a site of struggle helps to explain how the participants in the study created and responded to opportunities to speak English. As described above, witness how Martina set up a counter-discourse in her workplace by resisting the subject position immigrant woman in favour of the subject position mother. This not only gave her the right to speak, but, in effect, silenced the co-workers who had been exploiting her. Eva was positioned as ignorant by her co-workers, so she surprised them by teaching them to use some of her languages. By subverting their respective knowledge/power subject positions, she slowly gained access to the social network in the workplace, which in turn gave her increased opportunities to speak English. Mai was positioned as a helpless girl by her brother, so she became a language broker in the home: She did not overtly challenge her brother's authority, but was able to set up a counter-discourse to the patri-archal relationship between them. Chapter 7 will examine in greater detail Katarina and Felicia's struggle over identity in the formal context of the school.

Identity as changing over time

In taking the position that subjectivity is multiple, contradictory and a site of struggle, feminist poststructuralism highlights the changing quality of a person's identity. As Weedon (1997) argues, 'the political significance of decentring the subject and abandoning the belief in essential subjectivity is that it opens up subjectivity to change' (p. 32). It is partly for this reason that I have critiqued the notions of a language learner's attitudes and motivation in SLA theory. Not only are such characteristics socially constructed, but they change over historical time and social space. This is a crucial point for second language educators in that it opens up possibilities for educational intervention, an issue that will be taken up more comprehensively in the next chapter. The conception of identity as subject to change has important implications for the way the women in the study responded to and created opportunities to practice English. The data that I will use to illustrate this point is taken from Eva's experiences in the workplace. The central point I wish to make here is that it was only over time that Eva's conception of herself as an immigrant with no right to speak changed to a conception of herself as a multicultural citizen with the power to impose reception (Bourdieu, 1977).

When Eva first started working at Munchies, she did not think it was appropriate for her to approach her co-workers, and attempt to engage them in conversation.

> When I see that I have to do everything and nobody cares about me because – then how can I talk to them? I hear they doesn't care about me and I don't feel to go and smile and talk to them.

Note that Eva does not complete a crucial part of her sentence. 'Nobody cares about me because –' Because why? I suggest that nobody acknowledged Eva because she had the subject position of immigrant in the workplace: She was someone who was not fluent in English; she was not Canadian; she was stupid; she had the worst type of work in the store. To speak under such conditions would have constituted what Bourdieu calls 'heretical usage' (1977, p. 672). Eva accepted the subject position immigrant; she accepted that she was not a legitimate speaker of English and that she could not command reception of her interlocutors. As she herself said, when she first arrived in

Canada, she assumed that, if people treated her with disrespect, it was be-cause of her own limitations. She conceded to the appropriate rules of use in her workplace, rules that Eva herself accepted as normal: 'I think because when I didn't talk to them, and they didn't ask me, maybe they think I'm just like – because I had to do the worst type of work there. It's normal.'

As Eva's sense of who she was, and how she related to the social world began to change, she started to challenge her subject position in the workplace as an illegitimate speaker. It is significant that her co-workers were surprised by her actions, supporting the view that the linguistic rules of use that Eva initially observed in the workplace were indeed an integral part of the power relations at her workplace. As Eva continued to develop what I have called an identity as a multicultural citizen, she developed with it a sense of her right to speak. If people treated her with disrespect, it was their problem and not her problem. Thus when the male customer asked her if she puts on this accent so that she could get more tips, Eva had been angry rather than ashamed; she had spoken out, rather than been silenced. When she said to him, 'I wish I did not have this accent because then I would not have to listen to such comments', she was claiming the right to speak as a multicultural citizen of Canada. Nevertheless, even though Eva, at one diary study meet-ing, had expressed the view that she no longer felt like an immigrant in Canada, she said, less than a year later, that she still felt like an immigrant because she was *positioned* as one: 'Because of my distinguishable pronuncia-tion I am viewed as an immigrant by others and therefore I still feel like one.' Thus, although Eva's identity had changed over time, it remained a site of struggle.

Language learning as a social practice

In this section I will take the position that Bourdieu's notion of legitimate discourse and poststructuralist theories of identity, as articulated above, are highly productive for conceptualizing language learning as a complex social practice, rather than an abstract, internalized skill. By social practice I refer in particular to its formulation by Lave and Wenger (1991, pp. 49–50):

> In contrast with learning as internalization, learning as increasing participa-tion in communities of practice concerns the whole person acting in the world. Conceiving of learning in terms of participation focuses attention on ways in which it is an evolving, continuously renewed set of relations . . . Insistence on the historical nature of motivation, desire and the very relations by which social and culturally mediated experience is available to persons-in-practice is one key to the goals to be met in developing a theory of practice.

In seeking to ground these theories, I will focus in some detail on an extract from Eva's diary:

> Everybody working with me is Canadian. When I started to work there, they couldn't understand that it might be difficult for me to understand everthing and know about everthing what it's normal for them. To explain it more clearly I can write an example, which happened few days ago.
> The girl which is working with me pointed at the man and said:
> 'Do you see him?' I said
> 'Yes, Why?'
> 'Don't you know him?'
> 'No. I don't know him.'
> 'How come you don't know him. Don't you watch TV. That's Bart Simpson.'
> It made me feel so bad and I didn't answer her nothing. Until now I don't know why this person was important.

The extract illustrates that a breakdown in communication has occurred in Eva's workplace.[3] Eva's co-worker, Gail, has initiated a conversation with Eva, the topic of which is Bart Simpson, an icon of popular culture in North America. When Eva admits that she has no knowledge of this television character, Gail's response is accusing: 'How come you don't know him.' Eva is silenced by Gail's response. Although Eva is eager to interact with anglophones, practice her English and enhance her language learning she resists the opportunity to speak. In a follow-up interview, when I asked Eva why she had not responded to Gail, she explained that she had felt humiliated at the time. As she said, '"You don't watch TV?" And I felt "What are you doing?" I was thinking like "This strange woman".' These data provide a powerful illustration of the relationship between language, identity and language learning. Language is not just a neutral form of communication, but a practice that is socially constructed in the hegemonic events, activities and processes that constitute daily life – the practices that are considered normal by the dominant society. When Eva admits her ignorance of Bart Simpson, she is positioned as someone who is strange, someone who does not have the cultural knowledge that is commonsense in the workplace. Gail's subject position is that of knower, and it is that knowledge that gives her power. Significantly, because Eva does not have access to that knowledge, she is silenced.

Bourdieu's (1977) notion of legitimate discourse, as described in Chapter 4, helps to explain why this breakdown in communication occurred. Because Eva did not have the knowledge that Gail assumed she should have, Eva was positioned as an illegitimate receiver of Gail's utterance, an imposter. Significantly, as soon as Gail recognized that Eva was an imposter, she brought closure to the conversation. Note that Gail's question to Eva was rhetorical – she did not expect, or possibly even desire a response from Eva. 'How come you don't know him. Don't you watch TV. That's Bart Simpson.' I suggest that what made Eva feel bad was being exposed as an imposter, a person strange to legitimate discourse. Because Eva accepted the subject position of imposter, she could not claim the right to speak. Thus, while Eva had been offered the opportunity to engage in social interaction, to practice her English, her subject position within the larger discourse of which she and Gail were a part undermined this opportunity: 'It made me feel so bad and I didn't answer her nothing.' Such discourse must be understood not only in relation to the words that were said, but in relationship to larger, inequitable structures within the workplace, and the larger society, in which immigrant language learners are often considered illegitimate speakers of English. Note how Eva was sent off to do the menial jobs in the restaurant so that the other workers could continue their conversations without her, further denying her the opportunity to engage in social interaction in English. As Eva wrote, 'They take advantage of me, because they know that I wouldn't say anything. I tried talk to them few times, but for them it's better to send me somewhere, to do something.' Bourdieu (1977, p. 648) makes the point that the 'most radical, surest, and best hidden censorships are those which exclude certain individuals from communication'.

Given this larger social context, it comes as little surprise that Eva 'didn't answer her nothing' when Gail positioned Eva as ignorant in the Bart Simpson exchange. Because of the construction of Eva's identity as immigrant, the social meaning of Gail's words to her were understood by Eva in this context. Had Eva been, for example, an anglophone Canadian who endorsed public rather than commercial television, or perhaps no television at all, she could have set up a counter-discourse to Gail's utterance, resisting being positioned as a potentially legitimate receiver of Gail's utterance. However, because of the unequal relations of power between Gail and Eva, it was Gail who could determine the grounds on which legitimate discourse was to be determined. Like her fictional compatriot, Saliha, in the neighboring province of Quebec, it would be a long time before her interlocutor would let her answer in longer sentences.

Comment

In this chapter I have noted the tendency in the field of SLA to avoid questions of power, arguing that the refusal to name and address power relations limits our ability to do justice to the complex experiences of language learners across historical time and social space. The data suggest, in particular, that current conceptions of natural language learning, acculturation and the affective filter should be called into question. Drawing on feminist poststructuralist theories of subjectivity, as well Bourdieu's notion of legitimate discourse, I have argued that the learning of a second language is not simply a skill that is acquired with hard work and dedication, but a complex social practice that engages the identities of language learners in ways that have received little attention in the field of SLA. Poststructuralist theories of identity and Bourdieu's (1977) conception of the right to speech are important contributions to SLA theory, as is Lave and Wenger's (1991) insistence on the need to conceptualize learning as situated within particular communities of practice in which learners, to a greater or lesser extent, participate. In Chapter 7, I examine the implications of my data for classroom practice, elaborating on what the right to speak might mean for language learning and teaching.

Notes

1. A process whereby a person learns a second language without losing the mother tongue (Lambert, 1975).
2. Like Gardner and MacIntyre (1993), I address these issues simultaneously since they have an inverse relationship to each other.
3. Eva explained later that there was a customer with a Bart Simpson T-shirt on.

7

Claiming the right to speak in classrooms and communities

In spite of trendy jargon in textbooks and teacher's manuals, very little is actually communicated in the L2 classroom. The way it is structured does not seem to stimulate the wish of learners to say something, nor does it tap what they might have to say.

(LEGUTKE AND THOMAS, 1991, pp. 8, 9)

After ESL course when we moved and our landlords tried to persuade me that we have to pay for whole year, I got upset and I talked with him on the phone over one hour and I didn't think about the tenses rules. I had known that I couldn't give up.

(MARTINA, A LANGUAGE LEARNER)

'Culture gap. Chinese teachers don't think the way most Westerners think', said a Chinese teacher in explaining why communicative language teaching methods don't work in China (Burnaby and Sun, 1989, p. 229). In their research in China in the late 1980s, Burnaby and Sun found that traditional teacher–student relationships in China presuppose certain behaviors and teaching methods and that, if teachers used communicative language teaching methods, they might expect students to complain. Resistance from students is not unique to the Chinese context, and this chapter will explore acts of resistance in two language classrooms in Canada. I begin the chapter by examining the expectations that Eva, Mai, Katarina, Martina and Felicia had of formal language classes. Then, drawing on the stories of classroom resistance by Katarina and Felicia, I argue that language teachers need to develop an understanding of their students' investments in the target language and their changing identities. With reference to a story by Mai, however, I note that incorporating student experience into classroom pedagogy is not unproblematic, given the dangers of essentializing student identity.

After examining the diary study as a pedagogical practice, I conclude that classroom-based social research might help to integrate formal and natural sites of language learning. This approach encourages students to adopt the identity of ethnographer rather than language learner in relation to the target language community. By reframing the relationship between language learners and target language speakers, I argue, learners can claim the right to speak outside the classroom. Furthermore, in response to Legutke and Thomas (1991, p. 8), it is hoped that classroom-based social research may 'stimulate the wish of learners to say something' *in* the classroom. This approach is inspired by Martina, quoted above, who is a language learner of great courage and insight.

Formal language learning and adult immigrants

In Chapter 6, I have drawn on my data and poststructuralist theory to argue that identity is a site of struggle and change. Immigrants who attend a language class bring not only their local experiences into the classroom, but also their memories of experiences in their native country and their own visions of the future they desire in their new country. Furthermore, they bring their own desires of what a language course should provide to help them settle into a new country and their own expectations of how formal language training can enhance the process of second language learning. To investigate the expectations that the participants had of formal ESL courses, and how these expectations intersected with their experiences of language learning outside the classroom, I closely examined the women's responses to the question, 'What has helped you the most to learn English?' This question was asked in the first questionnaire in December 1990 as well as the second questionnaire a year later. I also used data collected in the first questionnaire which sought to determine what kinds of ESL courses the students considered best for adult immigrants and how courses could be modified to meet their needs.

In answer to the question, 'What has helped you the most to learn English?', there are quite striking differences between the women's responses in December 1990 and their responses in December 1991. In December 1990, three of the five women (Eva, Katarina and Martina) stressed the fact that it was the six-month ESL course that had helped them most in learning English. Furthermore, in the first questionnaire, all the women except Felicia indicated the importance of instruction in English grammar, pronunciation and vocabulary.[1] Katarina summed up the impressions of the group when she wrote in December 1990:

If sombody wants to live for good in Canada, should be spoken the English language. In [a preferred course] people will spend most of the time learning English grammar, pronunciation and vocabulary because it is base English.

By December 1991, however, only one woman, Martina, indicated that teachers were the most important influence on her language learning progress. Four of the five women stressed the importance of speaking regularly to anglophones, echoing Felicia's comment on the need for 'practice, practice, practice'. The comment made by Eva is representative of the perceptions of the group as a whole: 'The English as a Second Language course helped me to learn the basics of English. Later, practicing English in everyday conversations helped me to be more fluent.' All of the women indicated that they would like to meet more Canadians socially and to have more opportunity to practice speaking English outside the classroom.

The data that I have examined on natural language learning indicate, however, that, while the women can have exposure to English through television, radio and newspapers, the opportunity to practice speaking English outside the classroom is dependent largely on their access to anglophone social networks. Access to such networks was difficult to achieve for these immigrant women. In Eva's case, she had to struggle to gain entry into the social networks in the workplace. Even then, her access to these networks might have had less to do with her hard work than the social outings that the management organized on a regular basis. While Mai had no difficulty gaining access to the social network in her workplace (perhaps because all her co-workers were immigrants), this solidarity was soon lost when workers started to lose their jobs. Katarina had the unique opportunity to speak to the elderly and patient Canadians that she tended on a regular basis; she indicates, however, that she has little social contact with other Canadians. Despite eight months of conscientious work at Fast Foods, Martina never managed to penetrate the social network at work; however, she took the opportunity to practice English whenever she could create an opportunity to do so. Felicia had the opportunity to practice speaking English at work, although she said she was more likely to listen than to speak.

What are the implications of these findings on natural language learning for second language pedagogy? In essence, all the women wanted more practice using English in the classroom so that they could transfer their skills to learning contexts outside the classroom. While all the women indicated that they had learnt a lot in the six-month ESL course subsidized by Employment and Immigration Canada, a number indicated that the course did not give them sufficient opportunity to practice what they had learnt in class. Felicia, for example, called the course passive: 'It might be less theory and more practice', she said. Eva said that the lack of opportunity to practice

English in the classroom meant that she felt scared when she had to use the language outside the classroom:

> Practice is the best thing to learn. When we were by the school we were in a lot of contact with English, but when I had to go out to work and speak the language, I was so scared. You don't have the practice, just the structures.

Although all the women agreed they needed the opportunity to practice English in the classroom, they did not agree on what kind of curriculum the language teacher should follow. The women had different expectations of formal language classes because of their unique experiences of natural language learning outside the classroom. They looked to the formal language classroom to *complement* the kind of learning that took place in other sites. Thus Mai, for example, who had the opportunity to speak English in the workplace, wanted the opportunity to *write* in the ESL class: 'Speaking I can learn every way – outside, in the bus, on the bus, or on the train. Everywhere. But for reading and writing I have to go to school.' Martina, on the other hand, who had a great deal of writing practice in her upgrading courses, wanted the opportunity to talk in the ESL class: 'If I wrote, I can correct by myself and I can think about it. The problem with speaking – I don't have time to think about it. But if I write something, it's not big problem.'

As a result of their experiences of natural language learning, the women also indicated that they would like an ESL course to familiarize them with the cultural practices of Canadian society. As Eva said of the ESL course, 'We were talking about different things I didn't know and I didn't hear about it. In home I stay in the Polish community and don't hear about it.' The women suggested that the ESL course had given them a rather idealized picture of the kinds of communicative contexts in which they would be required to use English outside the classroom. Martina gave a graphic example of this with reference to the job interview process: 'After the ESL course when I had the interview, they asked me very different questions, the ones that we didn't study in school and I was very surprised.' Such a comment was an echo of a previous statement she had made on another occasion:

> Ya, I was there. I had interview about two hours long. They want to know everything about me. They asked different questions. I never heard these question. Some question was 'What I will do if the boss was shouting at me.' And I was very surprised. I thought 'My boss never, never shouted at me.' And I don't know, I said 'If I do something bad, I try to do better. And I will apologize.' But I don't know because never, never, I don't think about it.

On the basis of these data, it is possible to conclude that the women had the following expectations and desires of a formal ESL course: It should help students to learn the basics of English grammar, pronunciation and vocabulary, it should create opportunities for students to speak and write English so that they will not be scared to interact with target language speakers outside the classroom, and it should help students to become familiar with the cultural practices of their new society, without resorting to idealization. The study indicates, however, that language learning is not an abstract skill that can be easily transferred from one context to another. It is a social practice that engages the identities of learners in complex and sometimes contradictory ways. For example, the anxiety the women experienced when they attempted to speak outside the classroom was not an invariant characteristic of their ability in the target language. Their anxiety was differently constructed in diverse encounters with target language speakers and must be understood with reference to their investment in particular kinds of social relationships. As demonstrated in Chapter 3, while the women could all speak in the company of friends, they were intimidated in different ways by different kinds of strangers. Eva could speak to strangers, but she was always self-conscious about her accent. Mai could speak to her co-workers but not to her boss. Katarina could speak to elderly people, but not to anglophone professionals. Martina could speak to anybody, but felt constantly inferior. Felicia could speak to her co-workers, but not in front of Peruvians who speak English fluently.

The implications of these findings for second language teaching are as follows. First, unsurprisingly, the language teacher needs to help prepare learners to speak the target language outside the classroom. This is particularly important in the context of second, as opposed to foreign language classrooms. Burnaby and Sun (1989) found that the academic study of grammar, literature and literary texts, as opposed to a focus on spoken English, was appropriate for the uses of English as a foreign language in China. In second language contexts such as Canada, however, it is not enough for the learner to know the 'theory' and the 'tenses system'; it is not enough for learners to have 'the structures, but not the practise'. Language learners need regular practice in speaking and writing in the language classroom so that they can feel more confident in interaction with target language speakers outside the classroom. Second, the study indicates that it is equally important for the language teacher to understand what opportunities are available for the learner to interact with target language speakers outside the classroom and how these opportunities are socially structured. Unless the language teacher understands what possibilities are available for the language learner to speak outside the classroom, practice in the classroom may not facilitate practice outside the classroom. As a corollary of the second point, my study suggests that the language teacher needs to understand how learners respond to these opportunities to practice and the extent to which learners create or resist opportunities to interact with target language speakers. In other words, the teacher needs to develop an understanding of the learners' investments in the target language and their changing identities.

Beyond communicative language teaching

The findings from the study will not come as any surprise to the language teacher who has been trained in the principles of communicative language teaching. As Savignon (1991) notes, communicative language teaching has become a term that in fact frames competence in terms of social interaction, and views the learner as a partner in the learning process:

> Drawing on current understanding of language use as social behavior, purposeful, and always in context, proponents of communicative language teaching offer a view of the language learner as a partner in learning; they encourage learner participation in communicative events and self-assessment of progress.

(p. 273)

Notwithstanding the more critical European focus in communicative language teaching, going back to the 1970s (see Candlin, 1989), most theories of communicative language teaching do not address relations of power between language learners and target language speakers. In the North American context, a communicative approach to language teaching is associated most often with the Canale and Swain (1980) framework, while in England and Europe, the 'notional–functional' approach has preceded communicative language teaching (see Breen and Candlin, 1980). While these approaches have had a profound effect on language teaching internationally, it is interesting that their limitations have achieved greatest attention in countries outside of the North American/European context. Thus I have noted, in the South African context, that innovations in language teaching have called into question dominant curriculum frameworks (Norton Peirce, 1989). As the South African scholar, Gardiner (1987) has argued:

> People's English cannot construct itself upon the implementation of the English as a Second/Foreign Language principles generated so industriously and marketed so assiduously by British universities, publishers and agents of its Foreign Office. That would be tantamount to changing the names of the actors but retaining the same old play. Not only should future syllabi be reconceptualized; they must proceed from a different set of principles.

(p. 60)

The different set of principles that Gardiner refers to include the recognition of the political nature of language and a reconceptualization of the meaning of language competence. The spirit of Gardiner's words is clearly evident in the work of such scholars as Janks (1997), Ndebele (1987) and Stein (1998), whose work has a more critical edge than that associated with dominant conceptions of communicative language teaching.

In other parts of the world, such as China, critiques of communicative language teaching stem from a different source than that of the South African critiques. The research of Burnaby and Sun (1989), for example, indicates that Chinese teachers have mixed reactions to communicative language teaching methods because of the purposes for which English, in particular, is used in the country. While they believe communicative methods are appropriate for students who plan to study in an English-speaking country, they are not appropriate for students living in China, who use the language primarily for reading and translation. Further, such teachers claim that communicative methods call for resources that are not readily available in China, and that some teachers lack confidence in their ability to teach communicatively. As one teacher said, 'I can only teach English to some extent. If I am asked to give more explanations on the language and cultural differences, it's impossible for me' (Burnaby and Sun, 1989, p. 228).

Another limitation of communicative language teaching methods is that many do not actively seek to engage the identities of language learners in the language teaching process. Even in dialogue journal writing, which is arguably a classic communicative teaching method, students are discouraged from writing about issues that directly engage their sense of who they are and how they relate to the social world. Thus Peyton and Reed's (1990) handbook, *Dialogue Journal Writing with Nonnative English Speakers*, while claiming to 'individualize language and content learning' (p. 18), simultaneously offers advice on how the teacher can prevent writing from becoming too personal:

> Some teachers are afraid that leaving the choice of topics entirely open to students encourages them to write about very personal topics or family matters that the teacher is not prepared to deal with, and that the writing can turn into a counseling session. This does occur at times. However, it need not continue. Teachers can gently point out that they are not comfortable discussing that topic and introduce another one.

(p. 67)

Savignon (1991) notes, however, that communicative language teaching is an approach that looks to further language acquisition research to inform its development. While my study suggests that immigrant learners welcome some communicative language teaching in the classroom, it also suggests that communicative language teaching should take seriously the lived experiences of language learners. The study makes problematic the very notions of communicative competence, social interaction and social behavior. I have argued that the linguistic rules of use, while being appropriate to a given situation, may not be desirable if language teachers wish to address the silencing that language learners may experience in their communities. I have taken the position that any given social interaction must be understood with reference to relations of power between interlocutors as well as the ongoing production of a language learner's identity. It is for this reason that Eva felt bad in the Bart Simpson episode, and did not continue her interaction with Gail; it is for this reason that Felicia felt uninteresting when she struggled to interact with her co-workers at Fair Lawns Recreation Centre, and chose to listen to her co-workers rather than speak to them.

But how does the teacher take seriously the lived experiences of language learners? How can the lives of language learners become an integral part of the second language curriculum when a teacher may have thirty students in the classroom, all with different histories, experiences and expectations? My position is that the identities and lived experiences of language learners are already part of the language learning/language teaching experience, whether or not this is formally recognized in the second language curriculum. What the language teacher needs to understand is *how* the identities of learners are engaged in the formal language classroom, and how this knowledge can help teachers facilitate the language learner's interaction with target language speakers in the wider community. To illustrate and extend this argument, I draw attention to two stories of classroom resistance by Katarina and Felicia.

Katarina's story[2]

Once the women had completed the six-month ESL course, two of the women, Katarina and Martina, were given the opportunity to take a nine-month subsidized English skills upgrading course. Katarina and Martina were in the same class and had the same teacher. After four months in this course, Katarina dropped out in anger and indignation. At a diary study meeting, Katarina explained why she did not want to attend the class, saying that she had come into conflict with her teacher because her teacher had said that Katarina's English was not good enough to take a computer course. Katarina said that her teacher intimated that Katarina spoke 'immigrant English'. Katarina was angry and never returned to the class.

At the meeting, Katarina suggested that the instructor did not take her teaching job seriously because the students were immigrants. Katarina said she was made to feel stupid in class. Katarina liked her first ESL class, where she learnt new vocabulary, read the newspaper and learnt grammar, but with the second ESL teacher, she felt like a student in first grade. She objected to having to learn '72 definitions for test' and listen to the teacher all day. At the meeting she asked Martina how she felt about the teacher, saying 'Immigrants, immigrants – Martina, maybe you think this is normal?' Martina, however, did not take exception to the instructor and remained in the course until she was awarded a certificate. Katarina, on the other hand, entered the computer course that was considered too advanced for her and successfully completed the 18-month program. Why did one woman feel angry and marginalized by the teacher's pedagogy and ultimately drop out of the course, while the other remained indifferent and continued till the end?

Felicia's story

At another diary study meeting, Felicia described her unhappy experiences in a Grade 12 ESL course that she was taking with a group of adult immigrants in a local school in Newtown. The teacher had asked each of the students to bring in information about their home country to share with the class. After the session, the teacher summarized the main points that had been raised, but neglected to mention the points that Felicia had made about Peru. Felicia was angry and asked the teacher why she had not included Peru in her summary. The teacher explained that Peru was not a major country under consideration. Felicia never returned to the class.

In seeking to understand why Katarina and Felicia resisted attending their ESL classes, it is necessary to address the relationship between identity and formal language learning. As indicated in Chapter 5, Katarina had been a teacher in Poland and had taught for 17 years. In this position, she had accumulated valued symbolic capital. When she came to Canada, she could not find employment as a teacher, and enjoyed little status or respect as a part-time homemaker for the Community Service, a job that was only good 'for now'. She eagerly sought recognition from people who were fellow professionals and wished to have a profession in which she could meet like-minded people. Thus Katarina had a great investment in her teachers, not only because in the learning of a second language 'very important is a teacher', but because she sought affirmation of her symbolic capital from her teachers.[3] When Katarina felt that her English teacher in the skills course failed to acknowledge her professional history, positioning her as an immigrant, she was angry. When, indeed, the teacher appeared to discourage Katarina from taking a computer course that would give her access to the very professional social networks she sought, she dropped out of the course. Katarina refused to take up the subject position of the uneducated, unskilled immigrant in her language class. And since the teacher appeared not to acknowledge her as a fellow professional, there was no subject position available to Katarina in this social site. It was an act of resistance on her part to remove herself from the scene of conflict. Martina, in contrast, understood her teacher's behavior as normal and did not resist being positioned as an immigrant – a recurring theme in the data. Although a highly educated person herself, she did not seek access to professional social networks and she did not expect her teachers to validate her history or personal experience. She successfully completed the upgrading course.

With reference to Felicia's response to her ESL teacher's omission of Peru in a summing-up exercise, I thought at the time that Felicia had overreacted to this event. However, when I understand the event within the context of Peru as symbolic of Felicia's own identity, the teacher's marginalization of Peru takes on added significance. Felicia's friends at work validated her Peruvian identity, but it appeared that her ESL teacher did not. Indeed, the very reason why Felicia may have been accepted by her friends at work was because she took up the subject position of a wealthy Peruvian rather than a recent immigrant in the workplace. Felicia therefore had great investment in her identity as a Peruvian and it was important to her that this identity be validated. Dropping out of the Grade 12 ESL class was not only an act of resistance on Felicia's part, but also a desperate attempt to hold onto her belief in the efficacy of her Peruvian identity, an identity which enabled her to claim the right to speak.

In sum, I suggest that these stories demonstrate convincingly that the historically and socially constructed identity of learners influences the subject position they take up in the language classroom and the relationship they establish with the language teacher. Whether or not the identities of a learner are recognized as part of the formal language curriculum, the pedagogy that a teacher adopts in the classroom will nevertheless engage the identities of learners in diverse and sometimes contradictory ways. It is only by understanding the histories and lived experiences of language learners that the language teacher can create conditions that will facilitate social interaction both in the classroom and in the wider community, and help learners claim the right to speak. Likewise, unless learners believe that their investments in the target language are an integral and important part of the language curriculum, they may resist the teacher's pedagogy, or possibly even remove themselves from the class entirely.

Rethinking multiculturalism

Having argued that the language teacher needs to incorporate the lived experiences of language learners into the formal language curriculum and take cognizance of their multiple and changing investments in the target language, I need to address the persistent question of how to do this. How can the language teacher make the identities and lived experiences of the language learner an integral part of classroom practice? To begin an exploration of this question, I will draw on data from Mai's classroom experience in which the teacher attempted to incorporate the learners' histories into the classroom context.

Mai's story

After the completion of the Employment and Immigration Canada course, Mai continued taking ESL courses at night in order to improve her spoken and written English. She had to make great sacrifices to attend these courses. After a long day at work, she rushed home, made dinner and rushed out again to take public transportation to her class. At night, she would come home, exhausted and with some dread that potential assailants were chasing after her while she was walking from her bus stop to her home at 10.30 pm. Given the sacrifices that Mai made to attend these courses, she expressed great frustration that she was not learning anything in one particular course she was attending. In an interview with Mai, I questioned her more closely about the way the teacher taught the course. Mai explained that it was centred around student presentations of life in their home countries. She described how frustrating it was to sit for a whole lesson and listen to one student speak (emphasis added):

> I was hoping that the course would help me the same as we learnt [in the six-month ESL course], but some night we only spend time on one man. He came from Europe. He talked about his country: what's happening and what was happening. *And all the time we didn't learn at all*. And tomorrow the other Indian man speak something for there. Maybe all week I didn't write any more on my book.

After struggling through this course for a number of weeks, after feeling that she didn't learn at all, Mai never went back to the class.

It could be argued that the Mai's ESL teacher was attempting to incorporate the lived histories of the students into the classroom by inviting them to make public presentations about their native countries. The teacher was giving the students the opportunity to practice speaking in the classroom, and inviting them to share their heritage with the rest of the class. This approach, however, clearly backfired, at least as far as Mai was concerned. Mai was convinced that she did not learn at all when she sat mute, listening to a fellow classmate discuss his native country. Her classroom learning did not warrant the many sacrifices she had to make to attend the ESL class.

I wish to argue that that there are at least three reasons why the teacher's methods silenced Mai rather than encouraged her active participation. First, the method presupposed that student experience is uni-dimensional. I have demonstrated in this book that identity is not a fixed category, but one that is multiple and changing. While an immigrant learner's experiences in his or her native country may be an important part of a learner's identity, these experiences are constantly being mediated by the learner's experiences in the new country, across multiple sites in the home, workplace and community.

What Mai's teacher did was to validate only one aspect of the learners' histories. The teacher did not provide the learners with the opportunity to critically examine their experiences in their native country in the light of more recent experiences in Canada, or to critically examine their experiences in Canada in light of experiences in their native countries. The teacher's approach is one which exoticizes multiculturalism, rather than critically engages it. As Schenke (1991, p. 48) has noted,

> The question of how histories, stories, and memories are made to be true in relation to the persuasions of discourse is fundamental to an understanding of how speaking and silence get shaped and regulated within ESL practice. Taking multiculturalism as a case in point, what comes to count as students' speaking is often little more that an atomized and disconnected 'exchange' of cultural exoticisms and curiosities. Divested of the lived histories and relations of power through which they come to be told, such stories populate classroom knowledge with racial, religious, gendered, and culinary eccentricities (the list goes on) that defy any engagement other than that of a 'friendly and respectful' acknowledgment of cultural pluralisms.

Second, the method did not take into account that the learners may have little investment in one another's presentations. While the teacher might have considered her teaching methods student-centred and the students partners in learning, the approach could be regarded as little more than transmission teaching in a multicultural guise. Such disconnected exchanges in the classroom give listeners few entry points for discussion and critique. Mai had no investment in her fellow student's description of his home country in Europe; she had no stake in learning about life in India. As she said to her co-workers in The Fabric Factory, who wanted her to learn Italian, 'The thing I need now is English language.' Mai wanted the opportunity to practice English in the ESL classroom; she did not want to be a passive recipient of another student's exotic stories. In Bourdieu's terms as described in preceding chapters, the ESL classroom was not a legitimate context for such stories. It was for this reason that Mai felt she didn't learn at all in her ESL class and that a potentially rich opportunity for language learning and teaching had been forfeited. Mai's story illustrates that incorporating student experiences into the classroom should be a more complicated process than commodifying multicultural histories in the form of student presentations. Indeed, it problematizes the very notion of multicultural education, a theme that is receiving increasingly critical attention in the field of second language education. Kubota (1999), for example, argues persuasively that applied linguistics literature on the teaching of writing creates a cultural dichotomy between the East and the West, constructing essentialist representations of Japanese culture. She argues for a critical multiculturalism in which language teachers need to go beyond simply affirming and respecting the culture of the Other and romanticizing its authentic voices' (Kubota, 1999, p. 27). She suggests, instead, that such teachers need to explore how cultural differences as a form of knowledge are produced and perpetuated, and how teachers can work towards social transformaton.

Third, the method was tantamount to an abdication of the teacher's authority. This is a theme discussed insightfully by Giroux (1988), who uses the notion of the teacher's 'emancipatory authority' (1988, p. 90) to argue that teachers are intellectuals who need to play an active and critical role in the classroom:

The concept of emancipatory authority suggests that teachers are bearers of critical knowledge, rules, and values through which they consciously articulate and problematize their relationship to each other, to students, to the subject matter, and to the wider community. Such a view of authority challenges the dominant view of teachers as primarily technicians or public servants, whose role is primarily to implement rather than conceptualize pedagogical practice. The category of emancipatory authority dignifies teachers' work by viewing it as a form of intellectual practice.

In this view, student-centred learning does not presuppose that the teacher is invisible in the classroom, who simply affirms student experience but has little authority or expertise to provide direction and critique of such experience. The challenge for the teacher is to develop a practice which, as Simon (1992) argues, acknowledges student experience as legitimate curricular content while simultaneously challenging both the substance and the form of such experience. With this caveat in mind, I turn now to an analysis of the diary study as a particular kind of practice that offered possibilities for the engagement of student experience and student identity, but which ultimately did not fully realize its transformative potential.

The diary study as a pedagogy of possibility

With reference to data from the study and the stories of Katarina, Felicia and Mai in particular, I have argued that the language teacher needs to help language learners bridge the gap between their learning of the target language in the language classroom and their opportunities to practice it in the wider community. In order to bridge this gap, I have suggested that the lived experiences and identities of language learners need to be incorporated into the formal curriculum. I have noted, however, that essentializing student experience will compromise the conditions necessary for reflection and critique of personal experience in the classroom. I now wish to address what type of pedagogy might be productive in the teaching of a second language to immigrant language learners. Drawing on Simon (1992, p. 56), I am using the term *pedagogy* to distinguish it from the term *teaching*:

> In staff rooms and classrooms, teaching manuals and curriculum guidelines, teaching is most commonly referred to as the strategies and techniques used in order to meet a set of predefined (often given) set of objectives. Not unsurprisingly, talk and writing about teaching are primarily carried out in the language of method for the purpose of proposing viable class-room suggestions . . . But in my view, something is missing from such discussion of teaching. When we teach, we are always implicated in the construction of a horizon of possibility for ourselves, our students, and our communities . . . To propose a pedagogy is to propose a political vision.

Like Simon, and countless other second language educators, my teaching is centrally concerned with the enhancement of human possibility. In attempting to bridge the gap between language learning in classrooms and communities, I would like to suggest that the diary study itself represented what Simon would call a pedagogy of possibility for the immigrant women in my study. In this section, I examine the purposes, strengths and limitations of the diary study as a form of pedagogy before turning to a consideration of how insights from the diary study might inform practice in second language classrooms.

The diary study was framed as a project about the learning of English as a second language in Canada. The way that it proceeded, however, was a project about the complexities of living as a woman in a new and sometimes threatening society, coping with the daily demands of family, work, schooling, housing, unemployment – much of which was conducted in a language that was only just beginning to make sense. It took place at a time when the women were beginning to question the usefulness of formal ESL classes and were confronting the lack of congruence between their understanding of the world and their experience of it in Canada. It was a time when they saw the need for practice in the target language, but also a time when they were beginning to understand that their access to anglophone social networks was compromised by their position as immigrants in Canadian society. It was a time when they had a lot to ask, much to say and a great deal to resist.

Though scarcely articulated at the time, the model of the diary study that was used in the research had its origins in the consciousness-raising groups associated with the second wave of feminism that Weiler (1991) describes in her work. Through the collective exploration of personal experiences of language learning and social interaction with members of the target language group, I hoped that the participants would uncover, in the words of Haug (1987, p. 41), 'the points at which change is possible, the points where our chains chafe most, the point where accommodations have been made'.

While my role within the group remained that of teacher/researcher, my authority was not derived from hierarchical educational structures, but rather from my command of the target language and my history as the former teacher of the participants in the study. It may also have been derived from my position as a professional, white, middle-class member of the dominant anglophone community, a woman with access to desirable symbolic and material resources. However, partly because I had come to know and understand some aspects of the respective histories of each of the women – the talent and resources they had brought with them to Canada – I believe the women felt comfortable in my presence. Certainly, whatever authority I may have had did not appear to silence them.

It is possible that the very architecture of the diary study meetings helped to reduce the power differentials associated with the more formal ESL classroom. We were all located in the private sphere of a home, where the domestic position of a woman as homemaker is more foregrounded than her professional position as teacher/researcher. We sat in a circle, the configuration of which changed each week. The only blackboard was a child's blackboard which was used on rare occasions. Such a setting, I believe, not only reduced the power differentials between me as a teacher and them as students, but also reframed the women's expectations of whose knowledge was considered more legitimate and valid. Further, not only was my status as teacher reframed, but so was the status of the students. In this context, I was not the gatekeeper of a finite body of knowledge, nor were the women students who vied with each other for access to my closely guarded resources. This had, I believe, a significant impact on the comfort levels in the group. Given the non-stop discussion that characterized our meetings, I think that the setting was a relatively egalitarian one. However, though the relationships between the women were equitable, their experiences as immigrant women were differently constructed across time and space. A fundamental premise of the diary study, reinforced by the architecture of the setting, was that each woman was an expert on her own life. Through the use of the weekly charts, the diary entries and the feedback to the women, I tried to help each woman explore and articulate in English her personal experiences of language learning in the home, the workplace, the school and the community. This approach was a radical departure from the pedagogy that had been used in the ESL course, where writing was primarily confined to filling in blanks and writing decontextualized sentences. Indeed, my purpose was to create conditions to promote what Cameron *et al.* (1992) have referred to as 'empowering research'.

In reflecting on why it was that the diary study was a particularly important source of data on identity and language learning, I have found the work of Clark and Ivanic (1997) helpful. Drawing on their research on the teaching of writing, they demonstrate that acts of writing depend on the multiple identities that writers bring to such acts and propose four interrelated factors that contribute to the notion of the writer identity: The autobiographical self is one that has been shaped by a writer's life-history up to the moment of writing, the discoursal self addresses the on-going construction of identity implicated in each act of writing, and the self as author addresses the question of ownership and voice in the writing process. These three writer identities, in turn, are understood in the context of a larger, more abstract notion of writer identity which addresses the subject positions that are available to writers within particular communities, at particular points in time. It is possible that the diary study provided subject positions for these women that had hitherto not been available in their experience as immigrant language learners, and that they were able to explore, to a greater or lesser extent, their autobiographical, discoursal and authorial identities in the act of constructing each diary entry.

At the risk of idealizing the outcomes of the diary study, I think that the quality and quantity of writing that the women produced and the range of issues that we discussed in the meetings were remarkable.[4] Topics included children's schooling, workplace conflict, popular TV programs, stories from the women's native countries, the weather, the recession and the Gulf War. After scarcely a year and a half in Canada, the women were able to make themselves clearly understood in both spoken and written form in the target language. This is not to say that their grammar was excellent, their pronunciation clear and their vocabulary extensive – rather, they were able to give voice to the complexity of their experience. Furthermore, it was at least of symbolic importance that, as the diary study progressed, the women began relating stories of how they had stood up for their rights in the workplace. At one diary study meeting, for example, Mai, Felicia and Eva described how they had resisted exploitative actions in their respective jobs. The stories which follow illustrate how central language was in this process.

In Mai's workplace, one of the workers had asked her to turn some very heavy drapes inside out, a job normally reserved for another stronger worker at the factory. Although on a previous occasion, Mai had reluctantly agreed to do this, she had felt frustrated and angry at having acquiesced. This time, when asked to do the task again, Mai had told the worker that, if she wanted Mai to do the job, the worker had to check it out with the supervisor first. The worker had been surprised and never asked Mai to perform this task again. After Mai had spoken up, Felicia then relayed a story about how she had spoken up for her rights at a school where she was doing after-school childcare. One teacher had apparently told Felicia, in front of a parent, not to record the children's names in a particular format. Felicia felt angry and humiliated, but refused to remain silent. She turned to the teacher and said, 'Either I am the teacher or you are. If you are, I am going home.' Eva then relayed a story about how the manager tried to send her home early one day when work was slow but had still retained the part-time workers. Eva had felt angry and had said that it was not fair that she – a full-time worker – should have to go home while the part-time workers were allowed to remain on-site. (Eva would not get paid for the hours she went home early.) The next day, Eva had felt sick and had decided to stay home. She simply told the management that she was not coming in to work. Eva said she thought this worried the management and, the next day when she returned to work, Eva had been given more responsible work to do. She felt happy that she had spoken up.

Notwithstanding these stories, however, I think the focus of our meetings was more on the expression of experience than the analysis of experience. While there was much discussion on how being positioned as an immigrant constrained the opportunities for the women to interact with anglophones, there was little reflection on the ways in which gender, class and race were implicated in larger, inequitable social structures. Three examples will illustrate this point. First, at one diary study meeting, Felicia was expressing concern at her husband's unemployed status, saying she pitied him. Katarina expressed her sympathy for Felicia's plight by saying: 'Women can always clean the house, but men must do something.' There was general agreement with the sexist assumptions underlying this statement: in other words, that the work women do in the home is not classified as doing something[5]; and that employment is a right for men and by extension only a privilege for women. Second, in an interview I had with Eva just before our first diary study meeting, Eva was explaining why her co-workers at Munchies did not talk to her: 'I think because when I didn't talk to them, and they didn't ask me, maybe they think I'm just like – because I had to do the worst type of work there. It's normal.' Eva said that it was understandable – 'normal' – that a person who had a job with little status should be marginalized by co-workers. Eva never challenged the classist assumptions underlying this statement. Third, when I was taking Mai home from a diary study meeting, Mai was describing the alienation that her nephews experienced as Chinese/Vietnamese people in Canada. The eldest child, Trong, for example, had chosen to change his name from a Vietnamese one to an anglicized one. Mai told me that she had encouraged her nephews not to reject their heritage, explaining 'With your hair, your nose, your skin, you will never be perfect Canadians'. Mai did not problematize the racist belief that perfect Canadians exist and that perfect Canadians are white.

I did not take up these issues with the women, but let them pass. During the course of the diary study I did not know how and to what extent I should disorganize and challenge the commonsense understandings of gender, class and race that the women expressed. My position as researcher and my desire to maintain solidarity with the women, to create a comfortable space where they could express their confusion, their anger and their joy, kept me silent. I could affirm, but not negate. The danger of remaining silent on such issues, however, became apparent to me in a telephone call I had with Katarina in January 1993, long after the diary study was over. She was telling me that she had moved from her old apartment block to a new one. It was with pride that she said, 'There are very few immigrants here. It's mainly old people.' It became immediately apparent to me that she was implicated in reinforcing and reproducing the marginalizing discourse on immigrants. Furthermore, as the diary study progressed, it also became apparent to me that Mai could not or chose not to discuss with the group the racism that her extended family had experienced in Canada. The only times when she expressed concern about her brother's attitudes towards Vietnamese people, about the fact that her nephews hated their appearance, were in moments when the two of us were alone together. Such times arose when I was driving her to or from her home, or when we were both waiting for other members of the group to arrive for the start of a meeting. Mai used her diary to express feelings of anxiety and alienation, but often chose not to read particularly troublesome experiences to the group.

Harper, Norton Peirce and Burnaby (1996) make the point that attempts to incorporate women's experience in the second language classroom paradoxically may serve to maintain the present status and conditions that women face at work and in society at large. Accommodating women's experience rather than problematizing it ultimately may not work in the best interests of women. They stress the importance of identifying and intensifying the moments where an opening is created for critical reflection on issues of gender and race. This theme is addressed insightfully by Schenke (1996, p. 156) who draws on her feminist/anti-racist work to argue for a practice of what she calls historical engagement in the ESL classroom.

> By *historical*, I refer to the ways in which we live our personal and collect-
> ive histories in the present and how acts of remembering can fashion new
> stories out of the familiar refrains of the old. By *engagement*, I refer to the
> willingness to involve ourselves (students and teachers) strategically in crit-
> ical analyses of the cultural/racial/gendered production of our everyday lives.

Such memory work, she argues, is not just a way of sharing personal experiences, but a way of investigating how and what we choose to remember, how such choices are socially and historically constructed, and how we can remember differently. The focus of such memory work is the recognition that language learners come to classrooms already knowing and that the struggle to understand new cultural practices proceeds from memories and experiences of past cultural practices.

Such insights are shared by Stein (1998) who, working in a South African context, describes the way in which a teacher can use performance and autobiographical narrative to interpret, rename and validate students' histories and experiences of literacy. Drawing on the work of Simon (1992), she describes how her students have been doing a pedagogy of remembrance in which the past is re-discovered by the present in a way that gives hope for the future. Collaboration is central to her pedagogy, in that students work together to help one another interrogate the frame in which memories are constructed. She cautions, however, that 'the process of remembering is not merely an act of repetition of the past but an act of re-membering or collecting one's "members" – one's prior selves and the figures and events that belong to one's life story – in a purposeful and conscious way' (1998, p. 523).

The relevance of such insights for my study is profound, helping me to understand Katarina's resistance to the teacher who did not validate her identity as a fellow professional, or Felicia's anger at the teacher who knew little of her memories and experiences of Peru. There is another dimension to the analysis, however. In this book I have noted that it is not only engagement with historical memory that is important in understanding identity and language learning, but also engagement with alternative identities that are site, and not time, specific. Thus Martina, for example, in claiming the right to speak in her workplace, drew on her memories as a mother, memories constructed in the private domain of her life, to *reframe* her relationship with her co-workers, who populated the public domain of her life: 'The girl is only 12 years old. She is younger than my son. And I said, "No, you are doing nothing. You can go and clean the tables or something."' By claiming a new identity within the discourses of the workplace, Martina could claim the right to speak. How teachers might help language learners claim new identities, reframe their relationships with target language speakers and claim the right to speak, is addressed in the next section.

Transforming Monday morning

In his paper on the concept of method, Pennycook (1989) argues persuasively that language teachers need to understand our practice, not in terms of totalizing or universal discourses on methods, but in terms of local complexities and possibilities. In different parts of the globe, this challenge has been taken up by teachers in elementary and secondary classrooms, colleges and communities. While Canagarajah (1993) in Sri Lanka and Lin (1996) in Hong Kong, for example, address the ambivalent responses of students to the dominance of English in their societies, Kalantzis, Cope and Slade (1989) in Australia address the response of the education system to the increasing linguistic diversity of the student population. The central point here, as Morgan (1998) notes, is that teachers need to respond to the particular challenges and possibilities of their own communities. 'If theoretical knowledge is to be relevant', he suggests, 'it must begin by negotiation and a considerable amount of local autonomy' (1998, p. 131).

It is in this spirit that I have drawn on insights from the diary study, the literature I have read and my own classroom experience to offer some suggestions as to how the identities and investments of language learners can be integrated into the language classroom. In providing a framework for what I have called classroom-based social research I do not, however, wish to advocate a new method of language teaching. I offer this framework as a contribution to conversations on language teaching that have begun long before this study was conducted and will no doubt continue for years to come. Without neglecting a focus on grammar, pronunciation and vocabulary (the basics), I will argue that classroom-based social research might help the learner understand how opportunities to speak are socially structured, how the learner might create possibilities for social interaction with target language speakers, and how the teacher might gain insight into the learners' identities and investments. In this regard, it is a response to an observation by Bremer *et al.* (1996, p. 236) that 'Classroom learning needs to be complemented by structured opportunities outside the classroom for minority workers to interact with speakers of the dominant language'. It is inspired by observations of Martina, who, in constructing for herself alternative identities from which to speak, has simultaneously opened up such possibilities for other learners.

I define classroom-based social research as collaborative research that is carried out by language learners in their local communities with the active guidance and support of the language teacher. The goals of such research are for learners to investigate systematically, with the use of observation charts and log books, what opportunities they have to interact with target language speakers, whether in the home, the workplace or the community. Through social research, the learners will become increasingly aware of the opportunities available to them to use the target language in the wider community and how they might transform such possibilities in keeping with their desires for the future. As well, learners are encouraged to reflect critically on their engagement with target language speakers. That is, learners are encouraged to investigate the conditions under which they interact with target language speakers, how and why such interactions take place and what results follow from such interaction. In this way, learners will develop insight into the way in which opportunities to speak are socially structured, and how social relations of power are implicated in the process of social interaction. As learners develop an understanding of how power acts on and through social interaction, they might learn to challenge social practices of marginalization. Learners are encouraged to pay particular attention to those moments when an occurrence, action or event, surprises them or strikes them as unusual. By recording their surprises in the data collection process, learners become more aware of differences between cultural practices in their native countries and cultural practices in their new society. Given the identity of student researcher/ethnographer rather than adult immigrant, they may be able to critically engage their histories and their memories from a position of strength rather than a position of weakness. With this enhanced awareness, the learner can use the language teacher as an important resource for further learning.

Learners may reflect on their observations in diaries or journals. This creates opportunities for them to write about issues in which they have a particular investment. Learners can use their diaries to critically examine any communication breakdowns that may have occurred with target language speakers. These diaries can be written in the target language and collected regularly by the teacher for comment and feedback. The diaries give the language teacher access to information about the learners' opportunities to practice the target language in the wider community, their investments in the target language and their changing identities. The teacher can help the learner critically reflect on findings from the research and make suggestions for further research and reflection where necessary. Finally, learners can use the data they have collected as material for their language classrooms, to be compared and contrasted with the findings of their fellow ethnographers. In comparing and contrasting their data with other learners, the learners will have an investment in the presentations that their fellow students make, and a meaningful exchange of information may ensue. Learners may begin to see one another as part of a social network in which symbolic resources can be produced, validated and exchanged. The teacher can also use this information to structure classroom activities and develop classroom materials that will help learners claim the right to speak in the wider community. Furthermore, the teacher will be able to guide classroom discussion from a description of the findings of the research to a consideration of what the research might indicate about broader social processes in society. In this way, the teacher can help learners interrogate their relationship to these larger social processes, and find spaces for the enhancement of human possibility.

Concluding comment

I would like to conclude this book with a reflection on the following comment by Luke (in press):

> While recognising that a significant majority of migrants continue to be positioned in lower socioeconomic classes and localities in the countries of the EEC, North America, Japan, Australia and other Asia-Pacific economies – much as their postwar predecessors were – there is also the need to develop narrative descriptions of minority identity that are not victim-oriented, that begin to describe the complexity, the play and the power of new identities of difference within white-dominated cultures, and that supplant the liberal condescension that continues, to cite Bob Dylan's 1960s song, to 'pity the poor immigrant'.

This, I believe, is a timely reminder that in an era of increasing globalization, language teachers need to rethink our conceptions of the immigrant students we encounter in our classrooms, whether young or old, female or male, rich or poor, Asian or English. Equally important, we need to re-examine our own identities as teachers, researchers, community members and global citizens. In this book I have argued that essentialist notions of language learners are untenable, and that it is only by acknowledging the complexity of identity that we can gain greater insight into the myriad challenges and possibilities of language learning and language teaching in the new millennium.

Notes

1. Felicia had already received instruction in English grammar in Peru, where she had learnt 'the verb "to be" and nothing else'.
2. As a foil to Katarina's story, I have included an account from Martina, who was in the same upgrading course as Katarina was.
3. It is instructive to note, by way of comparison, that Katarina never took offense when the elderly people she worked for asked her questions that could potentially have been offensive, such as why she had come to Canada without knowing English.
4. Auerbach (1989) notes similar writing progress in what she calls a social–contextual approach to ESL literacy for adult immigrants.
5. See Rossiter (1986) for an insightful analysis of the social construction of homemaking.

References

Acton, W. and de Felix, J. W. (1986). Acculturation and mind. In J.M. Valdes (ed.) *Culture Bound: Bridging the Culture Gap in Language Teaching*. Cambridge: Cambridge University Press.

Anderson, G. (1989). Critical ethnography in education: Origins, current status, and new directions. *Review of Educational Research*, 59 (3), 249–70.

Angelil-Carter, S. (1997). Second language acquisition of spoken and written English: Acquiring the skeptron. *TESOL Quarterly*, 31, 2, 263–87.

Anzaldúa, G. (1990). How to tame a wild tongue. In R. Ferguson, M. Gever, T. Minh-ha and C. West (eds) *Out there: Marginalization in contemporary cultures*. Cambridge, MA: MIT Press, pp. 203–11.

Auerbach, E. R. (1989). Toward a social–contextual approach to family literacy. *Harvard Educational Review*, 59, 165–81.

Auerbach, E. R. (1997). Family literacy. In V. Edwards and D. Corson (eds) *Literacy*. Vol. 2, *Encyclopedia of Language and Education*. Dordrecht: Kluwer Academic Publishers.

Bailey, K. M. (1980). An introspective analysis of an individual's language learning experience. In R. Scarcella and S. Krashen (eds) *Research in Second Language Acquisition*. Rowley, MA: Newbury House.

Bailey, K. M. (1983). Competitiveness and anxiety in adult second language learning: Looking at and through the diary studies. In H. D. Seliger and M. H. Long (eds) *Classroom oriented research in second language acquisition*. Rowley, MA: Newbury House.

Bakhtin, M. (1981). *The Dialogic Imagination*. Austin: University of Texas Press.

Barton, D. and Hamilton, M. (1998). *Local literacies: Reading and writing in one community*. London: Routledge.

Bell, J. (1991). *Becoming Aware of Literacy*. Unpublished PhD thesis, University of Toronto, Canada.

Benesch, S. (1996). Needs analysis and curriculum development in EAP: An example of a critical approach. *TESOL Quarterly*, 30, 723–38.

Beretta, A. and Crookes, G. (1993). Cognitive and social determinants of discovery in SLA. *Applied Linguistics*, 14: 250–75.

Bourdieu, P. (1977). The economics of linguistic exchanges. *Social Science Information*, 16 (6), 645–68.

Bourdieu, P. and Passeron, J. (1977). *Reproduction in Education, Society, and Culture*. London/Beverly Hills, CA: Sage Publications.

Bourne, J. (1988). 'Natural acquisition' and a 'masked pedagogy'. *Applied Linguistics*, 9 (1), 83–99.

Boyd, M. (1992). Immigrant women: Language, socio–economic inequalities, and policy issues. In B. Burnaby and A. Cumming (eds) *Socio–political Aspects of ESL in Canada*. Toronto: Ontario Institute for Studies in Education.

Breen, M. and Candlin, C. (1980). The essentials of a communicative curriculum in language teaching. *Applied Linguistics*, 1, 2, 89–112.

Bremer, K., Broeder, P., Roberts, C., Simonot, M. and Vasseur, M.-T. (1993). Ways of achieving understanding. In C. Perdue (ed.) *Adult language acquisition: Cross-linguistic perspectives*, vol. II: *The Results*. Cambridge: Cambridge University Press, pp. 153–95.

Bremer, K., Roberts, C., Vasseur, M.-T., Simonot, M. and Broeder, P. (1996). *Achieving Understanding: Discourse in Intercultural Encounters*. London: Longman.

Briskin, L. and Coulter, R. C. (1992). Feminist pedagogy: Challenging the normative. *Canadian Journal of Education*, 17 (3), 247–63.

Britzman, D. (October 1990). Could this be your story? Guilty readings and other ethnographic dramas. Paper presented at the Bergamo Conference, Dayton, Ohio.

Brodkey, L. (1987). Writing critical ethnographic narratives. *Anthropology and Education Quarterly*, 18, 67–76.

Brown, C. (1984). Two Windows on the classroom world: Diary studies and participant observation differences. In P. Larson, E. Judd, and D. Messerschmitt (eds) *On TESOL '84*. Washington, DC: TESOL.

Brown, H. D. (1994). *Principles of Language Learning and Teaching*. Englewood Cliffs, NJ: Prentice Hall.

Burnaby, B. (1997). Second language teaching approaches for adults. In G. R. Tucker and D. Corson (eds) *Second Language Education*. Vol. 4, *Encyclopedia of Language and Education*. Dordrecht: Kluwer Academic Publishers.

Burnaby, B., Harper, H. and Norton Peirce, B. (1992). English in the workplace: An employer's concerns. In B. Burnaby and A. Cumming (eds) *Socio–political aspects of ESL education in Canada*. Toronto: OISE Press.

Burnaby, B. and Sun, Y. (1989). Chinese teachers' views of western language teaching: Context informs paradigms. *TESOL Quarterly*, 23, 2, 219–36.

Butler, J. and Scott, J. W. (eds) (1992). *Feminists Theorize the Political*. New York: Routledge.

Cameron, D., Frazer, E., Harvey, P., Rampton, B. and Richardson, K. (1992). *Researching Language: Issues of Power and Method*. London: Routledge.

Canagarajah, A. S. (1993). Critical ethnography of a Sri Lankan classroom: Ambiguities in student opposition to reproduction through ESOL. *TESOL Quarterly*, 27, 4, 601–26.

Canale, M. and Swain, M. (1980). Theoretical bases of communicative approaches to second language teaching and testing. *Applied Linguistics*, 1, 1–47.

Canale, M. (1983). On some dimensions of language proficiency. In J. Oller (ed.) *Issues in language testing research*. Rowley, MA: Newbury House.

Candlin, C. (1989). Language, culture, and curriculum. In C. Candlin and T. F. McNamara (eds) *Language, learning and community*. Sydney: National Centre for English Language Teaching and Research, pp. 1–24.

Cazden, C., Cancino, H., Rosansky, E. and Schumann, J. (1975). *Second Language Acquisition Sequences in Children, Adolescents, and Adults*. Research report, Cambridge, MA.

Cherryholmes, C. (1988). *Power and Criticism: Poststructuralist Investigations in Education*. New York: Teachers College Press.

Clark, R. and Ivanic, R. (1997). *The Politics of Writing*. London: Routledge.

Clarke, M. (1976). Second language acquisition as a clash of consciousness. *Language Learning*, 26, 377–90.

Clyne, M. (1991). *Community Languages: The Australian Experience*. Cambridge: Cambridge University Press.

Connell, R. W., Ashendon, D. J., Kessler, S. and Dowsett, G. W. (1982). *Making the Difference. Schools, Families, and Social Division*. Sydney: George Allen & Unwin.

Cooke, D. (1986). Learning the language of your students. *TESL Talk*, 16 (1), 5–13.

Corson, D. (1993). Language, minority education and gender. Cleveland: *Multilingual Matters*.

Crookes, G. and Schmidt, R. (1991). Motivation: Reopening the Research Agenda. *Language Learning*, 41, 4, 469–512.

Cumming, A. and Gill, J. (1991). Learning ESL Literacy among Indo-Canadian women. *Language, Culture, and Curriculum*, 4 (3), 181–98.

Cumming, A. and Gill, J. (1992). Motivation or accessibility? Factors permitting Indo-Canadian women to pursue ESL literacy instruction. In B. Burnaby and A. Cumming (eds) *Socio–political Aspects of ESL education in Canada*. Toronto: OISE Press.

Cummins, J. (1996). *Negotiating identities: Education for empowerment in a diverse society*. Ontario, CA: California Association for Bilingual Education.

Cummins, J. and Corson, D. (eds) (1997). *Bilingual Education*. Vol. 5, *Encyclopedia of Language and Education*. Dordrecht: Kluwer Academic Publishers.

Dörnyei, Z. (1994). Motivation and motivating in the foreign language classroom. *Modern Language Journal*, 78 (3), 273–84.

Dörnyei, Z. (1997). Psychological processes in cooperative language learning: group dynamics and motivation. *Modern Language Journal*, 81, 4, 482–93.

Duff, P. and Uchida, Y. (1997). The negotiation of teachers' sociocultural identities and practices in postsecondary EFL classrooms. *TESOL Quarterly*, 31, 3, 451–86.

Edge, J. and Norton, B. (1999). Culture, power, and possibility in teacher education. Paper presented at the annual TESOL convention, New York, NY, March 1999.

Edwards, D. and Potter, J. (1992). *Discursive Psychology*. Newbury Park, CA: Sage.

Ellis, R. (1985). *Understanding Second Language Acquisition*. London: Oxford University Press.

Ellis, R. (1997). *Second Language Acquisition*. Oxford: Oxford University Press.

Fairclough, N. (1992). *Discourse and Social Change*. Cambridge: Polity Press.

Faltis, C. (1997). Case study methods in researching language and education. In N. Hornberger and D. Corson (eds) *Research Methods in Language and Education*. Vol. 8, *Encyclopedia of Language and Education*. Dordrecht: Kluwer Academic Publishers.

Foucault, M. (1980). Power/Knowledge: Selected Interviews and Other Writings 1972–1977, C. Gordon (trans.). New York: Pantheon Books.

Freedman, R. (1997). Researching gender in language use. In N. Hornberger and D. Corson (eds) *Research Methods in Language and Education*. Vol. 8, *Encyclopedia of Language and Education*. Dordrecht: Kluwer Academic Publishers, pp. 47–56.

Freire, P. (1970). *Pedagogy of the Oppressed*. New York: Seabury Press.

Freire, P. (1985). *The Politics of Education*. South Hadley, MA: Bergin-Garvey.

Gardiner, M. (1987). Liberating language: People's English for the future. In *People's Education: A collection of articles*. Bellville, South Africa: University of the Western Cape, Centre for Adult and Continuing Education, pp. 56–62.

Gardner, R. C. (1985). *Social Psychology and Second Language Learning. The Role of Attitudes and Motivation*. London: Edward Arnold.

Gardner, R. C. (1989). *Attitudes and Motivation. Annual Review of Applied Linguistics*, 1988, 9, 135–48.

Gardner, R. C. and Lambert, W. E. (1972). *Attitudes and Motivation in Second Language Learning*. Rowley, MA: Newbury House.

Gardner, R. C. and MacIntyre, P. D. (1992). A student's contributions to second-language learning. Part I: Cognitive Variables. *Language Teaching*, 25 (4), 211–20.

Gardner, R. C. and MacIntyre, P. D. (1993). A student's contributions to second-language learning. Part II: Affective Variables. *Language Teaching*, 26 (1), 1–11.

Gee, J. P. (1990). *Social Linguistics and Literacies: Ideology in Discourses*. Basingstoke: Falmer Press.

Giles, H. and Coupland, N. (1991). *Language: Contexts and consequences*. Buckingham, England: Open University Press.

Giroux, H. A. (1988). *Schooling and the Struggle for Public Life: Critical Pedagogy in the Modern Age*. Minneapolis: University of Minnesota Press.

Giroux, H. (1992). *Border Crossings: Cultural Workers and the Politics of Education*. New York: Routledge.

Goldstein, T. (1996). *Two Languages at Work: Bilingual Life on the Production Floor*. Berlin and New York: Mouton de Gruyter.

Goldstein, T. (1997). Language research methods and critical pedagogy. In N. Hornberger and D. Corson (eds) (1997) *Research Methods in Language and Education*. Vol. 8, *Encyclopedia of Language and Education*. Dordrecht: Kluwer Academic Publishers.

Gregg, K. (1993). Taking explanation seriously; or let a couple of flowers bloom. *Applied Linguistics*, 14, 276–93.

Hall, J. K. (1993). The Role of Oral Practices in the Accomplishment of Our Everyday Lives: The Sociocultural Dimension of Interaction with Implications for the Learning of Another Language. *Applied Linguistics*, 14, 2, 145–66.

Hall, J. K. (1995). (Re)creating our worlds with words: A sociohistorical perspective of face-to-face interaction. *Applied Linguistics*, 16 (2), 206–32.

Hall, J. K. (1997). A Consideration of SLA as a Theory of Practice: A Response to Firth and Wagner. *Modern Language Journal*, 81, 3, 301–6.

Hansen, J. G. and Liu, J. (1997). Social identity and language: Theoretical and methodological issues. *TESOL Quarterly*, 31, 3, 567–76.

Harper, H., Norton Peirce, B. and Burnaby, B. (1996). English-in-the-workplace for garment workers: A feminist project? *Gender and Education*, 8, 1, 5–19.

Haug, F. (ed.) (1987). *Female Sexualization: a Collective Work of Memory*, Erica Carter (trans.). London: Verso.

Heath, S. B. (1983). *Ways with Words: Language, Life, and Work in Communities and Classrooms*. Cambridge: Cambridge University Press.

Heller, M. (1987). The role of language in the formation of ethnic identity. In J. Phinney and M. Rotheram (eds) *Children's Ethnic Socialization* Newbury Park, CA: Sage, pp. 180–200.

Heller, M. (1992). The politics of codeswitching and language choice. *Journal of Multilingual and Multicultural Development*, 13, (1 & 2), 123–42.

Heller, M. (1999). *Linguistic Minorities and Modernity: A Sociolinguistic Ethnography*. London: Longman.

Heller, M. and Barker, G. (1988). Conversational strategies and contexts for talk: Learning activities for Franco-Ontarian minority schools. *Anthropology and Education Quarterly*, 19 (1), 20–46.

Henriques, J., Hollway, W., Urwin, C., Venn, C. and Walkerdine, V. (1984). *Changing the Subject: Psychology, Social Regulation, and Subjectivity*. London and New York: Methuen.

hooks, b. (1990). Talking Back. In R. Ferguson, M. Gever, T. Minh-ha and C. West (eds) *Out There: Marginalization in Contemporary Cultures*. Cambridge, Mass, MA: MIT Press.

Hornberger, N. and Corson, D. (eds) (1997). *Research Methods in Language and Education*. Vol. 8, *Encyclopedia of Language and Education*. Dordrecht: Kluwer Academic Publishers.

Hymes, D. (1979). On communicative competence. In C. J. Brumfit and K. Johnson (eds) *The communicative approach to language teaching*. Oxford: Oxford University Press, pp. 5–26.

Janks, H. (1997). Teaching language and power. In R. Wodak and D. Corson (eds) *Language Policy and Political Issues in Education*. Vol. 8, *Encyclopedia of Language and Education*. Dordrecht: Kluwer Academic Publishers, pp. 241–52.

Johnson, D. (1992). *Approaches to Research in Second Language Learning*. New York: Longman.

Kalantzis, M., Cope, B. and Slade, D. (1989). *Minority Languages and Dominant Culture: Issues of Education, Assessment and Social Equity*. London: Falmer.

Kanno, Y. (1996). *There's no place like home: Japanese returnees' identities in transition*. Unpublished doctoral dissertation, University of Toronto, Canada.

Klein, W. (1986). *Second Language Acquisition*. Cambridge: Cambridge University Press.

Kramsch, C. (1993). *Context and Culture in Language Teaching*. Oxford: Oxford University Press.

Krashen, S. (1981). *Second Language Acquisition and Second Language Learning*. Oxford: Pergamon.

Krashen, S. (1982). *Principles and Practice in Second Language Acquisition*. Oxford: Pergamon.

Kress, G. (1989). *Linguistic Processes in Sociocultural Practice*. Oxford: Oxford University Press.

Kubota, R. (1999). Japanese culture constructed by discourses: Implications for applied linguistics research and ELT. *TESOL Quarterly*, 33, 1, 9–35.

Lakoff, R. (1975). *Language and Woman's Place*. New York: Harper and Row.

Lambert, W. E. (1975). Culture and language as factors in learning and education. In A. Wolfgang (ed.) *Education of Immigrant Students*. Toronto: Ontario Institute for Studies in Education.

Lantolf, J. (1996). SLA Theory Building: 'Letting All the Flowers Bloom!' *Language Learning*, 46, 4, 713–49.

Larsen-Freeman, D. and Long, M. (1991). *An Introduction to Second Language Acquisition Research*. New York: Longman.

Lave, J. and Wenger, E. (1991). *Situated Learning: Legitimate Peripheral Participation*. New York: Cambridge University Press.

Legutke, M., and Thomas, H. (1991). *Process and Experience in the Language Classroom*. London: Longman.

Lemke, J. (1995). *Textual Politics: Discourse and Social Dynamics*. Bristol, PA: Taylor & Francis.

Leung, C., Harris, R. and Rampton, B. (1997). The idealised native speaker, reified ethnicities and classroom realities. *TESOL Quarterly*, 31, 3, 543–60.

Lewis, M. and Simon, R. (1986). A discourse not intended for her: Learning and teaching within patriarchy. *Harvard Educational Review*, 56 (4), 457–72.

Lin, A. (1996). Bilingualism or linguistic segregation? Symbolic domination, resistance and code-switching in Hong Kong schools. *Linguistics and Education*, 8, 1, 49–84.

Long, M. (1993). Assessment strategies for second language acquisition theories. *Applied Linguistics*, 14, 225–49.

Lorde, A. (1990). Age, race, class, and sex: Women redefining difference. In R. Ferguson, M. Gever, T. Minh-ha and C. West (eds) *Out There: Marginalization in Contemporary Cultures*. Cambridge, MA: MIT Press, pp. 281–7.

Luke, A. (1988). *Literacy, Textbooks and Ideology*, Basingstoke: Falmer Press.

Luke, A. (in press). Producing new Asian masculinities. In N. Bruce and C. Barron (eds) *Knowledge and Discourse*. London: Longman.

Luke, C. and Gore, J. (eds) (1992). *Feminisms and Critical Pedagogy*. New York: Routledge.

McKay, S. L. and Wong, S. C. (1996). Multiple discourses, multiple identities: Investment and agency in second language learning among Chinese adolescent immigrant students. *Harvard Educational Review*, 3, 577–608.

McNamara, T. (1997). What do we mean by social identity? Competing frameworks, competing discourses. *TESOL Quarterly*, 31, 3, 561–6.

Martin-Jones, M. and Heller, M. (1996). Introduction to the special issues on Education in multilingual settings: Discourse, identities, and power. *Linguistics and Education*, 8, 3–16.

Martin-Jones, M. (1997). Bilingual classroom discourse: Changing research approaches and diversification of research sites. In N. Hornberger and D. Corson (eds) (1997) *Research Methods in Language and Education*. Vol. 8, *Encyclopedia of Language and Education*. Dordrecht: Kluwer Academic Publishers.

May, S. (1997). Critical ethnography. In N. Hornberger and D. Corson (eds) (1997) *Research Methods in Language and Education*. Vol. 8, *Encyclopedia of Language and Education*. Dordrecht: Kluwer Academic Publishers.

Miller, J. (1999). *Speaking English and Social Identity: Migrant students in Queensland high schools*. Unpublished doctoral dissertation, University of Queensland, Australia.

Mitchell, C. and Weiler, K. (1991). *Rewriting Literacy: Culture and the Discourse of the Other*. Toronto: OISE Press.

Morgan, B. (1997). Identity and intonation: Linking dynamic processes in the ESL classroom. *TESOL Quarterly*, 31, 3, 431–50.

Morgan, B. (1998). *The ESL classroom: Teaching, Critical Practice, and Community Development*. Toronto: University of Toronto Press.

Morris, M. and Patton, P. (eds) (1979). *Michel Foucault: Power, Truth, Strategy*. Sydney: Feral Publications.

Naiman, N., Frohlich, M., Stern, H. H. and Todesco, A. (1978). *The Good Language Learner*. A Research in Education Series No. 7. Toronto: The Ontario Institute for Studies in Education.

Ndebele, N. (1987). The English language and social change in South Africa. *The English Academy Review*, 4, 1–16.

New London Group (1996). A pedagogy of multiliteracies: Designing social futures. *Harvard Educational Review*, 66, 60–92.

Ng, R. (1981). Constituting ethnic phenomenon: An account from the perspective of immigrant women. *Canadian Ethnic Studies*, 13, 97–108.

Ng, R. (1987). Immigrant women in Canada: A socially constructed category. *Resources for Feminist Research/Documentation sur la recherche féministe*, 16, 13–15.

Norton Peirce, B. (1989). Toward a pedagogy of possibility in the teaching of English internationally: People's English in South Africa. *TESOL Quarterly*, 23 (3), 401–20.

Norton Peirce, B. (1993). *Language Learning, Social Identity, and Immigrant Women*. Unpublished PhD dissertation. Ontario Institute for Studies in Education/ University of Toronto.

Norton Peirce, B. (1995). Social identity, investment, and language learning. *TESOL Quarterly*, 29 (1), 9–31.

Norton, B. (1997a). Language, identity, and the ownership of English. *TESOL Quarterly*.

Norton, B. (1997b). Critical discourse research. In N. Hornberger and D. Corson (eds) *Research Methods in Language and Education*. Vol. 8, *Encyclopedia of Language and Education*. Dordrecht: Kluwer Academic Publishers.

Norton, B. (forthcoming). Non-participation, imagined communities, and the language classroom. In M. Breen (ed.) *Thought and Action in Second Language Learning*. London: Longman.

Norton Peirce, B., Harper, H. and Burnaby, B. (1993). Workplace ESL at Levi Strauss: 'Dropouts' speak out. *TESL Canada Journal*, 10 (2), 9–30.

Norton Peirce, B. and Stein, P. (1995). Why the 'monkeys passage' bombed: Tests, genres, and teaching. *Harvard Educational Review*, 65 (1), 50–65.

Norton Peirce, B., Swain, M. and Hart, D. (1993). Self-assessment, French immersion, and locus of control. *Applied Linguistics*, 14 (1), 25–42.

Norton, B. and Toohey, K. (1999). Reconceptualizing 'the good language learner': SLA at the turn of the century. Paper presented at the annual conference of the American Association of Applied Linguistics, Stamford, Connecticut, USA.

Ochs, E. (1992). Indexing gender. In A. Duranti and C. Goodwin (eds) *Rethinking context*. Cambridge: Cambridge University Press, pp. 335–58.

Oxford, R. and Shearin, J. (1994). Language Learning Motivation: Expanding the Theoretical Framework. *Modern Language Journal*, 78, 1, 12–28.

Pennycook, A. (1989). The concept of method, interested knowledge, and the politics of language teaching. *TESOL Quarterly*, 23 (4), 589–618.

Pennycook, A. (1994). *The Cultural Politics of English as an International Language*. London: Longman.

Pennycook, A. (1998). *English and the Discourses of Colonialism*. London: Routledge.

Perdue, C. (ed.) (1984). *Second Language Acquisition by Adult Immigrants*. Rowley, MA: Newbury House.

Perdue, C. (ed.) (1993a). *Adult Language Acquisition: Cross-linguistic Perspectives*. Vol. I, *Field Methods*. Cambridge: Cambridge University Press.

Perdue, C. (ed.) (1993b). *Adult Language Acquisition: Cross-linguistic Perspectives*. Vol. II, *The Results*. Cambridge: Cambridge University Press.

Peyton, J. K. and Reed, L. (1990). *Dialogue Journal Writing with Nonnative English Speakers: A Handbook for Teachers*. Alexandria, VA: TESOL.

Rampton, B. (1995). *Crossing: Language and Ethnicity Among Adolescents*. London: Longman.

Rist, R. (1980). Blitzkrieg ethnography: On the transformation of a method into a movement. *Educational Researcher*, 9 (2), 8–10.

Roberts, C., Davies, E. and Jupp, T. (1992). *Language and Discrimination: A Study of Communication in Multi-ethnic Workplaces*. London: Longman.

Rockhill, K. (1987a). Literacy as threat/desire: Longing to be SOMEBODY. In J. Gaskill and A. McLaren (eds) *Women and Education: A Canadian Perspective*. Calgary, Alberta: Detselig Enterprises Ltd, pp. 315–31.

Rockhill, K. (1987b). Gender, language and the politics of literacy. *British Journal of Sociology of Education*, 18 (2), 153–67.

Rossiter, A. B. (1986). *From Private to Public: A Feminist Exploration of Early Mothering*. Toronto: Women's Press.

Rubin, J. (1975). What the 'good language learner' can teach us. *TESOL Quarterly*, 9, 41–51.

Sarangi, S. and Baynham, M. (1996). Discursive construction of educational identities: affirmative readings. *Language and Education*, 10, 2 & 3, 77–81.

Saussure, F. de. (1966). *Course in General Linguistics*. W. Baskin (trans.). New York: McGraw-Hill.

Savignon, S. (1991). Communicative language teaching: State of the art. *TESOL Quarterly*, 25 (2), 261–78.

Schecter, S. and Bayley, R. (1997). Language socialization practices and cultural identity: Case studies of Mexican descent families in California and Texas. *TESOL Quarterly*, 31, 3, 513–42.

Schenke, A. (1991). The 'will to reciprocity' and the work of memory: Fictioning speaking out of silence in ESL and feminist pedagogy. *Resources for Feminist Research/Documentation sur la recherche féministe*, 20 (3/4), 47–55.

Schenke, A. (1996). Not just a 'social issue': teaching feminist in ESL. *TESOL Quarterly*, 30, 1, 155–9.

Schumann, F. (1980). Diary of a language learner: a further analysis. In R. Scarcella and S. Krashen (eds) *Research in Second Language Acquisition*. Rowley, MA: Newbury House.

Schumann, J. (1976a). Social distance as a factor in second language acquisition. *Language Learning*, 26 (1), 135–43.

Schumann, J. (1976b). Second language acquisition: The pidginization hypothesis. *Language Learning*, 26 (2), 391–408.

Schumann, J. (1978a). *The Pidginization Process: A Model for Second Language Acquisition*. Rowley, MA: Newbury House.

Schumann, J. (1978b). The acculturation model for second-language acquisition. In R. C. Gringas (ed.) *Second Language Acquisition and Foreign Language Teaching*. Washington, DC: Center for Applied Linguistics.

Schumann, J. (1986). Research on the acculturation model for second language acquisition. *Journal of Multilingual and Multicultural Development*, 7 (5), 379–92.

Schumann, J. (1993). Some problems with falsification: An illustration from SLA research. *Applied Linguistics*, 14, 295–306.

Schumann, J. H. and Schumann, F. (1977). Diary of a language learner: An introspective study of second language learning. In H. D. Brown, C. Yorio, and R. Crymes (eds) *On TESOL '77: Teaching and learning English as a second language: Trends and Practice. Washington*, DC: TESOL.

Scovel, T. (1978). The effect of affect on foreign language learning: A review of the anxiety research. *Language Learning*, 28, 129–42.

Simon, R. (1987). Empowerment as a pedagogy of possibility. *Language Arts*, 64, 370–83.

Simon, R. (1992). *Teaching Against the Grain: Texts for a Pedagogy of Possibility*. New York: Bergin & Garvey.

Simon, R. I. and Dippo, D. (1986). On critical ethnographic work. *Anthropology and Education Quarterly*, 17, 198–201.

Simon, R. I., Dippo, D. and Schenke, A. (1991). *Learning work: a critical pedagogy of work education*. Toronto: OISE Press.

Smith, D. E. (1987a). *The Everyday World as Problematic: A Feminist Sociology*. Boston, MA: Northeastern University Press.

Smith, D. E. (1987b). Institutional Ethnography: A Feminist Method. *Resources for Feminist Research/Documentation sur la recherche féministe*, 15, 6–13.

Smith, D. E. (1987c). An analysis of ideological structures and how women are excluded. In J. S. Gaskell and A. T. McLaren (eds) *Women and Education: A Canadian Perspective*. Calgary, Alberta: Detselig Enterprises Ltd.

Smoke, T. (ed.) (1998). *Adult ESL: Politics, Pedagogy, and Participation in Classroom and Community Programs*. Mahwah, NJ: Lawrence Erlbaum Associates.

Solsken, J. (1993). *Literacy, Gender, and Work: in Families and in School*. Norwood, NJ: Ablex Pub. Co.

Spender, D. (1980). *Man Made Language*. London: Routledge & Kegan Paul.

Spolsky, B. (1989). *Conditions for Second Language Learning*. Oxford: Oxford University Press.

Stein, P. (1998). Reconfiguring the past and the present: Performing literacy histories in a Johannesburg classroom. *TESOL Quarterly*, 32, 3, 517–28.

Stern, H. H. (1983). *Fundamental Concepts of Language Teaching*. Oxford: Oxford University Press.

Tajfel, H. (ed.) (1982). *Social Identity and Intergroup Relations*. New York: Cambridge University Press.

Tannen, D. (1990). *You Just Don't Understand: Men and Women in Conversation*. New York: William Morrow.

Terdiman, R. (1985). *Discourse/counter-discourse: The Theory and Practice of Symbolic Resistance in Nineteenth-century France*. Ithaca: Cornell University Press.

Ternar, Y. (1990). Ajax là-bas. In L. Hutcheon and M. Richmond (eds) *Other Solitudes: Canadian Multicultural Fictions*. Toronto: Oxford University Press.

Thesen, L. (1997). Voices, discourse, and transition: In search of new categories in EAP. *TESOL Quarterly*, 31, 3, 487–512.

Toohey, K. (1996). Learning English as a second language in kindergarten: A community of practice perspective. *Canadian Modern Language Review*, 52, 4, 549–76.

Toohey, K. (1998). 'Breaking them up, taking them away': ESL students in Grade 1. *TESOL Quarterly*, 32, 1, 61–84.

Toohey, K. (2000). *Learning English in Schools: Identity, Social Relations, and Classroom Practice*. Clevedon: Multilingual Matters.

Tucker, R. and Corson, D. (1997). *Second Language Education*. Vol. 2, *Encyclopedia of Language and Education*. Dordrecht: Kluwer Academic Publishers.

van Daele, C. (1990). *Making Words Count: The Experience and Meaning of the Diary in Women's Lives*. Unpublished Doctor of Education thesis. University of Toronto, Canada.

van Lier, L. (1994). Forks and hope: pursuing understanding in different ways. *Applied Linguistics*, 15, 3, 328–46.

Wallerstein, N. (1983). *Language and Culture in Conflict: Problem-Posing in the ESL Classroom*. Reading, MA: Addison-Wesley.

Walsh, C. A. (1987). Language, meaning, and voice: Puerto Rican students' struggle for a speaking consciousness, *Language Arts*, 64, 196–206.

Walsh, C. A. (1991). *Pedagogy and the Struggle for Voice: Issues of Language, Power, and Schooling for Puerto Ricans*. Toronto: OISE Press.

Watson Gegeo, K. (1988). Ethnography in ESL: defining the essentials. *TESOL Quarterly*, 22 (4), 575–92.

Weedon, C. (1997). *Feminist Practice and Poststructuralist Theory*. Second Edition. London: Blackwell.

Weiler, K. (1988). *Women Teaching for Change: Gender, Class, and Power*. New York: Bergin & Garvey Publishers.

Weiler, K. (1991). Freire and a feminist pedagogy of difference. *Harvard Education Review*, 61 (4), 449–74.

Wenger, E. (1998). *Communities of Practice: Learning, Meaning, and Identity*. Cambridge: Cambridge University Press.

West, C. (1992). A matter of life and death. *October*, 61 (summer), 20–3.

Willis, P. E. (1977). *Learning to Labour: How Working Class Kids Get Working Class Jobs*. Farnborough: Saxon House.

Wodak, R. (1996). *Disorders of Discourse*. London and New York: Longman.

Wolcott, H. F. (1994). *Transforming Qualitative Data: Description, Analysis, and Interpretation*. Thousand Oaks, CA: Sage.

Wong Fillmore, L. (1991). When learning a second language means losing the first. *Early Childhood Research Quarterly*, 6, 323–46.

Yee, M. (1993). Finding the way home through issues of gender, race and class. In H. Bannerji (ed.) *Returning the Gaze: Essays on racism, feminism and politics*. Toronto: Sister Vision Press, pp. 3–44.

Yu, L. (1990). The comprehensible output hypothesis and self-directed learning: A learner's perspective. *TESL Canada Journal*, 8 (1), 9–26.

Zamel, V. (1987). Recent research on writing pedagogy. *TESOL Quarterly*, 21 (4), 697–715.

Index

teacher's authority 145
using lived experiences 139–44, 145,
    149–51
see also diary study; language
    teaching; natural language learning
Foucault, M. 7, 15
Frazer, E. 23–4, 147
Freedman, R. 87
Freire, P. 7
Frolich, M. 18 n3

Gardiner, M. 138
Gardner, R. C. 4, 5, 10, 18 n2, 132 n2
Gee, J. P. 13, 19 n9
gender
    and employment 28, 149
    and ethnicity 12, 35
    and identity 84–5
    and language learning 27–8, 87–8,
        150
    and language use 87, 110
    and power 110
    in the public world 12–13
Giles, H. 6
Gill, J. 44–5
Giroux, H. 7, 124, 145
Goldstein, T. 19 n6, 45–6, 72, 81
Gore, J. 20, 21
Gregg, K. 19 n10

Hall, J. K. 6, 18 n4
Hamilton, M. 36–7
Hansen, J. G. 5
Harper, H. 46–7, 58 n3, 124, 150
Harris, R. 6
Hart, D. 65, 123
Harvey, P. 23–4, 147
Haug, F. 146
Heller, M. 5, 6, 12, 19 n7, n9, 72
Henriques, J. 5–6
Hollway, W. 5–6
hooks, b. 27, 19 n8
Hornberger, N. 19 n6
Hymes, D. 15

identity
    changing over time 128–9
    class 102–3, 105

concepts of 6, 124–5
cultural 6, 19 n5
and desires 8
as foreigner 102–6
gendered 84–5
immigrant 50, 51, 85, 141, 143–4,
    153–4
and language 5–6
and language learning 6
and literacy 36–7
as mother 89–90, 95–6, 99, 107–8
nonunitary and contradictory 125–7,
    154
and power 7–10, 47
recognition 140–2, 151
as site of struggle 127–8, 129
social 6, 19 n5, 66–7, 85, 91
social interactions 99
and subject position 140–2
writers 147–8
see also ethnicity
immigrant language learners
    Canadian studies 43–7, 124
    class relations 92–3
    communication with native
        speakers 40–1, 44–5, 49–50, 64,
        95, 152–3 (*see also* workplace)
    discrimination 40, 54, 55, 70, 97,
        149–50
    European Science Foundation
        Project 35–6, 38, 40–1, 71, 110
    identities 139–42, 153–4
    international context 38–9
    language and family 75–80, 89–90,
        107–8
    as language brokers 79–80, 94–5
    performance 65
    pronunciation 50, 51
    as social researchers 152–3
    status 116–17
    USA 11, 41–2
    world view 58
    see also acculturation model of SLA;
        immigrant women in Canada;
        Ontario study
immigrant women in Canada 43
    action research study 47
    bilingual workplace study 45–6